Learning Adobe FrameMaker

IMPORTANT NOTICE

Printed in the United States of America by Shepard Poorman Communications Corporation, Indianapolis, Indiana.

Published simultaneously in Canada.

Adobe Press books are published and distributed by Macmillan Computer Publishing USA. For individual, educational, corporate, or retail sales accounts call 1-800-428-5331, or 317-581-3500. For information address Macmillan Computer Publishing USA, 201 West 103rd Street, Indianapolis, IN 46290. Macmillan's World Wide Web page URL is www.mcp.com.

Part Number: 9000-3152 (3/96)

Contents

Part I   **Introduction to FrameMaker**

Part II   Character and Paragraph Formats

Part III   **Graphics, Frames, and Page Types**

Part IV   **Tables, Variables, and Conditional Text**

Getting Started

Welcome to *Learning Adobe FrameMaker*® self-paced training from Adobe® Systems Incorporated. This workbook will teach you the basics of using FrameMaker document publishing software.

The exercises in this workbook take you through FrameMaker concepts step by step. The workbook is intended to complement other sources of information about FrameMaker, not substitute for them. If you're brand new to FrameMaker, you may want to start by using FrameMaker's online tutorial, a computer-based tour of FrameMaker basics. If you need more detailed information on specific topics, you can use online Help or refer to your printed manual, *Using FrameMaker*.

About the Screen Images in This Book

The FrameMaker user interface is very similar across platforms, so you can use this workbook on the Macintosh®, Windows™, or UNIX platforms. Notice that in the example below, the Paragraph Catalog looks much the same, even though the interface details of each platform are slightly different.

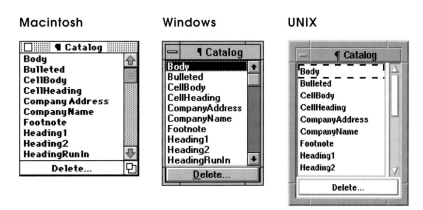

Most of the screen images in a given chapter are from a single platform, but the platform used changes from chapter to chapter. Where the differences in the user interface are significant, images from all three platforms are displayed.

Note: Windows screen images in this workbook were captured using Windows 3.1. Alert messages and dialog boxes may look slightly different in Windows 95.

Prerequisites

Before beginning the exercises in this workbook, you should have a working knowledge of your computer and its operating conventions. At a minimum, you should know how to use the mouse and pull-down menus, and how to open and close files. If you need to review these techniques, please see the documentation that comes with your system, or ask your system administrator for help.

Requirements

To complete the exercises in this workbook, you must have FrameMaker installed on your computer. No additional data disks are required. Your installation must include the following files, which come with FrameMaker. The FrameMaker files that must be installed for this tutorial are:

- Online manuals and online help
- Dictionaries
- Clip art
- Templates
- Sample files
- Tutorial files

If you discover that you are missing any of these files, either use your original FrameMaker installation disks or CD-ROM to install them, or ask your system administrator for help.

Before You Begin

Create a directory for practice files

All the files you create in this tutorial will be stored in a directory (a folder on the Macintosh) named "Class." This directory should be created either at the root level of your hard disk (Macintosh and Windows) or in your home directory (UNIX). You should create the directory before beginning the exercises. If you're not sure how to create a directory on your system, see Appendix A, "Creating a Directory."

Start FrameMaker

The FrameMaker application should be running before you begin the exercises. If you're not sure how to start FrameMaker on your system, see Appendix B, "Starting FrameMaker."

Technical Support

If you are a registered FrameMaker user in the United States or Canada and require technical support during this training, call (408) 975-6466 between 6:00 AM and 5:00 PM Pacific time.

PART I

....

Introduction to

FrameMaker

Overview of FrameMaker

Approximate time to complete: 15 minutes

Introduction

In this module, you'll be introduced to FrameMaker®, Release 5. FrameMaker is a powerful and efficient tool for creating, writing, and distributing documents, whether you print on paper, publish on the Internet, or distribute online.

Module Objectives

In this module, you'll

- Understand the basics of the FrameMaker conceptual model

- Become familiar with the capabilities of FrameMaker 5

How to Think about FrameMaker

FrameMaker can create BOOKS from multiple DOCUMENTS that have PAGES that contain OBJECTS that may hold TEXT. Each document also includes FORMATS to provide a consistent look and layout.

The FrameMaker conceptual model is shown in the following illustration:

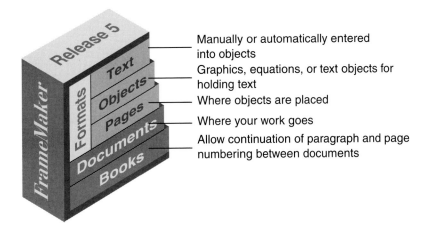

The model will appear at the beginning of each module to provide you with a conceptual framework on which to build your FrameMaker knowledge.

Specific parts of the model will be highlighted, as shown in the following examples, to indicate which portion applies to the current module.

A brief description of how the conceptual model applies to the current topic will appear beside the model.

Features

FrameMaker is a complete publishing system that you can use to produce documents ranging from simple one-page memos to complex multichapter books with imported graphics. It provides:

- Full word processing power
- Flexible page design
- Graphics tools, with color
- Book building and revision management
- Professional color control
- Stylized tables for organizing information
- Conditional text for multiple versions of a document
- Information links within and between documents
- Templates for standardized documents
- Typesetting and evaluation of mathematical equations
- Online Help system

Word Processing Capabilities

FrameMaker includes a wide range of powerful features for creating complex documents, but you can use it just as effectively to write a letter or prepare a simple flyer. FrameMaker provides you with:

- Text editing capabilities

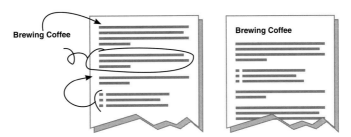

- Spell-checking
- Search capabilities
- Thesaurus

Special Copying Capabilities

You can copy a format to the FrameMaker Clipboard and paste it anywhere in the document or in another document.

Along with standard copy and paste commands...

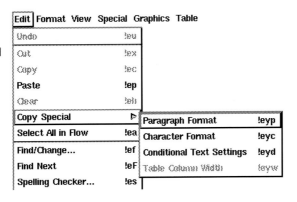

...there are commands to copy a selected paragraph format, character format, conditional text settings, or table column width.

Text Formatting

Every FrameMaker document comes with a set of formats, or styles. Using formats to change the appearance of the text helps give your document a consistent, professional look.

- Paragraph formats

  Determine how the titles, headings, lists, and paragraphs of text look on the page—their font, size, placement in the text column, space above and below, autonumbering, tabs, and so on.

- Character formats

  Allow you to select text within a paragraph and override its format. For example, you can make glossary terms within a manual bold or use italics to emphasize a word or phrase.

Each paragraph has a set of properties that determines its appearance and position on the page.

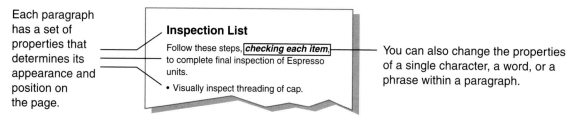

Inspection List

Follow these steps, checking each item, to complete final inspection of Espresso units.

• Visually inspect threading of cap.

You can also change the properties of a single character, a word, or a phrase within a paragraph.

- Table formats

  Determine what a table looks like, its placement in the text column, and so on.

Flexible Page Design

You can use FrameMaker in a number of ways to design pages in your document.

- Use FrameMaker templates.

- Use specially designed templates, created by you or someone else in your organization, to meet your day-to-day needs for simple documents such as letters, memos, and fax covers, or for more complex documents such as newsletters, technical manuals, reports, and product descriptions.

- Create master (background) pages that contain the design elements you want to appear on all body (foreground) pages.

A master page provides the background...

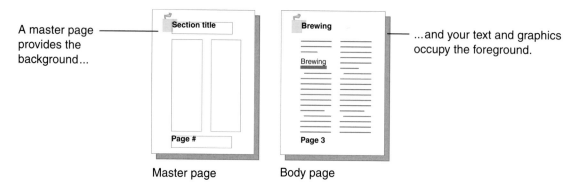

...and your text and graphics occupy the foreground.

Master page   Body page

You specify the number and position of text columns and the appearance of background text and graphics.

Portrait (vertical orientation) and landscape (horizontal orientation) pages can be mixed and can contain any combination of columns.

Graphic Tools

To add visual interest to a document, you can use FrameMaker drawing tools to draw and edit objects. You can put graphics directly on the page or anchor them to text, and prepare color separations for spot color and four-color process printing.

A graphic anchored to text...

...moves as text is edited.

On the UNIX platform, you can capture an image on your screen and then import the image into a document.

Book Building

FrameMaker provides a book-building feature that lets you manage multiple files as a single book. You can create a book, add chapters, and then automatically generate a table of contents, a list of figures, and an index for the entire book.

Create a book with multiple files, and then generate a table of contents, index, and so on.

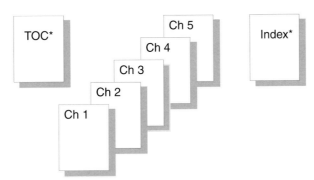

Stylized Tables for Organizing Information

For presenting information in a tabular format, you can use a FrameMaker table with any combination of lines and shading. You can straddle cells so that they extend across several rows or columns. For a professional look, you can rotate headings to create table categories that stand out.

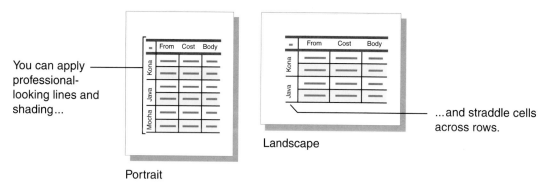

You can apply professional-looking lines and shading...

...and straddle cells across rows.

Portrait

Landscape

Multiple Versions of a Document

FrameMaker conditional text (and graphics) allows you to create and maintain one base document with variations you hide or display for printing.

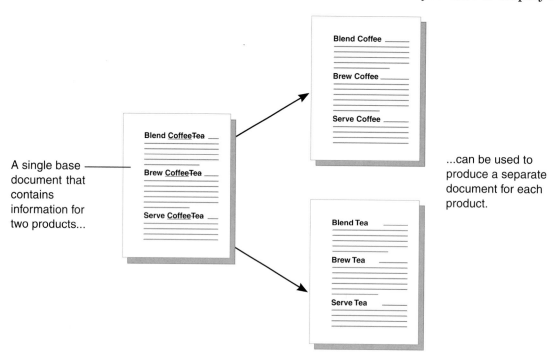

A single base document that contains information for two products...

...can be used to produce a separate document for each product.

Use conditional text to produce separate documents for similar products, for example, or to include comments you want to hide before you send the final copy to the printer.

Information Links

You can use FrameMaker hypertext commands to set up links between locations in the same or in different documents. Users viewing the document online need only click an active area to jump to related information.

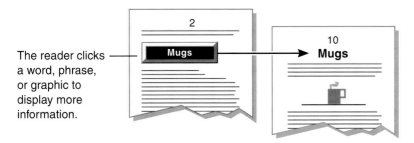

The reader clicks a word, phrase, or graphic to display more information.

Automatic Hypertext Links

When you generate a table of contents or an index for a manual, for example, you can create hypertext links to the information in the source document simply by turning on an option in a dialog box. FrameMaker creates a clickable hypertext link from each entry in the generated file to the page in the source document where the entry is located.

Templates for Standardized Documents

When you create a document from a template, you use the template's page layouts, predefined formats, and other properties. Each document you create from the template has a consistent look and can be easily updated when your design needs change.

FrameMaker comes with a variety of templates.

- Blank paper
- Business card and envelope
- Letter, memo, and fax cover
- Outline
- Newsletter
- Chapter, table of contents, and index for a book

You can open any template and begin preparing your document. To better suit your needs, you can modify an existing template, or even create your own template from scratch.

Typeset Mathematical Equations

FrameMaker provides a full palette of math elements to streamline creation of typeset equations. You create an equation by inserting an equation object of a particular font size in a document and then inserting the math elements—numbers, symbols, operators, and so on—in the object.

After you create equations, you can change their format—their fonts, alignment, exact positioning of math elements, and amount of white space around them. And you can use commands on the Equations palette to evaluate the equation mathematically.

Online Help System

FrameMaker's online help system is a reference guide to FrameMaker commands and dialog boxes; it explains what each command and dialog box does. If you can't find what you need by browsing the Main Menu, go to the Index.

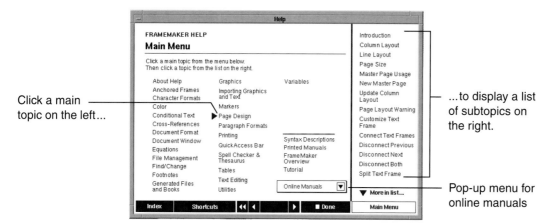

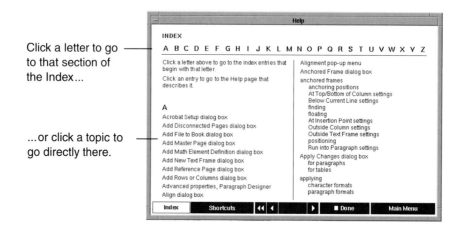

Working with Documents

2

Introduction

In this module, you'll become familiar with FrameMaker basics. You'll open a FrameMaker document, explore the document window, change your view of the document, and save and print it.

Module Objectives

In this module, you'll learn how to

- Start FrameMaker
- Open a file
- Identify the main features of the document window
- Use the Save As and Save command
- Set backup and save preferences
- Use View menu commands
- Page through a document
- Use zoom options
- Print a document
- Delete a document

FrameMaker Model

In this module, you'll interact with the *FrameMaker application* by using user interface commands. FrameMaker has many commands that increase productivity and work at all levels of the model.

Opening Files and Touring the Document Window

Exercise 1

Guided Tour

Opening sample files

The FrameMaker application includes a number of templates and sample files from which you'll create documents. In this exercise, you'll open a sample report.

> **Note:** In order to successfully complete this exercise, you should have followed the instructions in the "Getting Started" chapter of this workbook titled "Before You Begin."

1. Make the FrameMaker samples window appear (see steps below):

On the Macintosh, from the [?] menu, choose **Samples & Clip Art**.

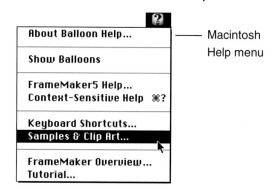

— Macintosh Help menu

In Windows, from the Help menu, choose **Samples & Clip Art**.

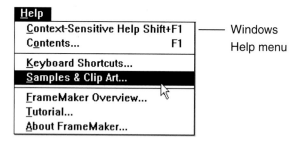

— Windows Help menu

In UNIX, you need to create a new blank document, then use the document's Help menu (not the Help button in the main FrameMaker window) to open the FrameMaker samples window (see the following steps).

a. In the main FrameMaker window, click **NEW**.

b. Click **Portrait** to create a blank vertically oriented document.

c. From the Help menu, choose **Samples & Clip Art**.

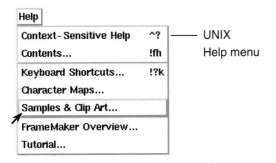

The FrameMaker samples window appears.

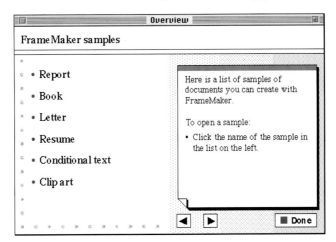

2. Click **Report**.

The sample report appears on your screen (see the pictures on pages 2-4 to 2-6). This may take a moment to completely display.

> **Note:** On some Macintosh and Windows monitors, the entire page as shown on the following pages may not be visible.

Touring the Document Window

The FrameMaker document window provides you with information in various locations around the window. That information includes the pathname and filename of the document, the dimensions of the document, the current formatting of text, the current page number, the magnification at which the document is displayed, and other information.

Other features of the document window—menu bars, buttons, and pop-up menus—are used to issue commands to the FrameMaker application.

Macintosh

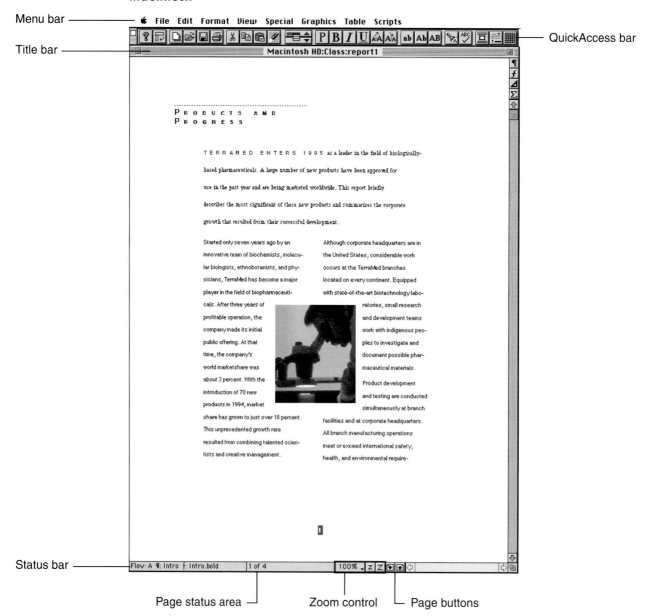

Menu bar ——

Title bar ——

QuickAccess bar ——

Status bar ——

Page status area ——   Zoom control ——   Page buttons ——

Windows

Menu bar ——

Formatting bar ——

—— QuickAccess bar

—— Title bar

Status bar ——

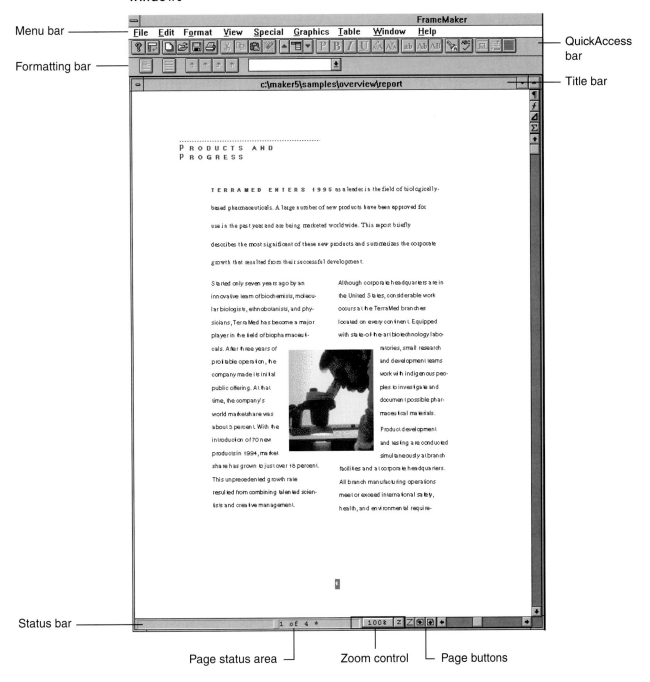

Page status area ⌐

Zoom control

⌐ Page buttons

UNIX

Title bar ————

Menu bar ————

Status bar ————

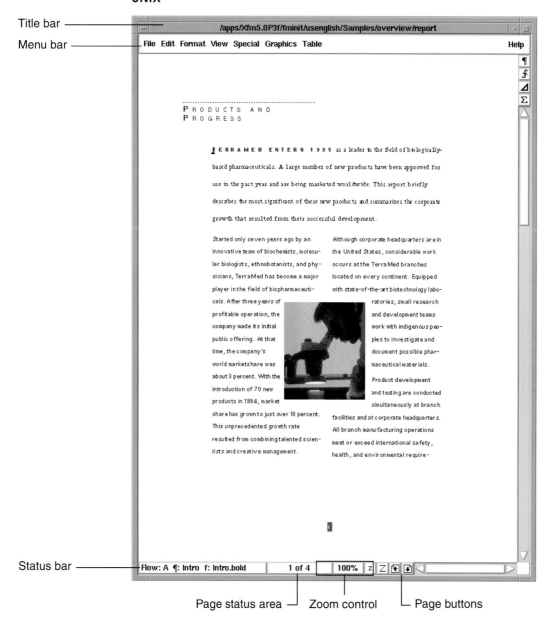

Page status area ——— Zoom control ——— Page buttons

Exercise 2

Guided Tour

Viewing title and menu bars

In this exercise, you'll take a look at the title and menu bars in a FrameMaker document window.

1. Look at the information displayed in the title bar of the document window.

   The pathname and filename are always displayed in the title bar of a document window.

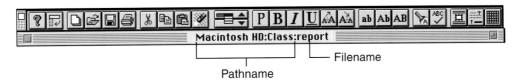

2. Press **View** to display the View menu.

   The menu bar is one of several ways to work with commands in FrameMaker.

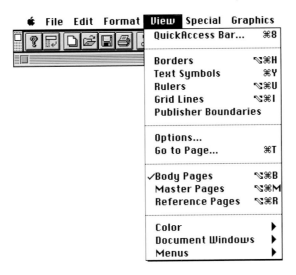

Exercise 3

Guided Tour

Viewing the formatting bar

When the formatting bar is displayed, it appears at the top of the document window just above the horizontal ruler. The formatting bar contains pop-up menus for changing the alignment and spacing of text, tab wells for adding tabs, and the paragraph format pop-up menu for quickly applying paragraph formats.

Using the formatting bar is generally the simplest way to format text. You may also use commands on the Format menu.

1. Display the **formatting bar** and **rulers** if they do not appear in your document window (see the following steps):

   a. If the rulers are not already visible, from the View menu, choose **Rulers**.

   b. If the formatting bar is not already visible, display the **formatting bar**.

Macintosh	Click the **formatting bar toggle**.
Windows	From the View menu, choose **Formatting Bar**.
UNIX	Click the **formatting bar toggle**.

Macintosh

Formatting bar toggle

UNIX

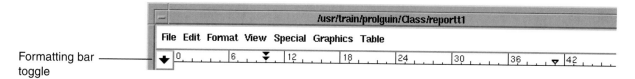

Formatting bar toggle

2. On the formatting bar, locate the Alignment pop-up menu, the Spacing pop-up menu, the Tab wells, and the Paragraph Format pop-up menu.

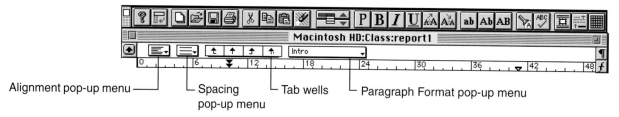

Alignment pop-up menu — Spacing pop-up menu — Tab wells — Paragraph Format pop-up menu

These features will be explored in detail in a later module in this workbook.

Exercise 4

Guided Tour

Using the status bar

The status bar is located at the bottom of the document window. The information displayed there changes depending on where the insertion point is located in the document.

1. Click anywhere in the first paragraph on the first page of the document. You now have an insertion point in the paragraph.

Insertion point —

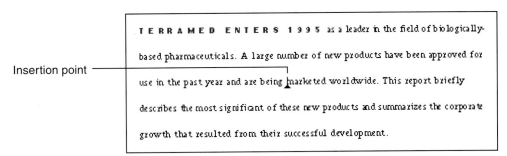

2. Look in the lower-left corner of the status bar to see that this text is assigned the paragraph format named Intro.

Name of current paragraph format

3. Put the insertion point in the paragraph in the left column of text, to the left of the picture.

The information changes to show that this text is assigned the Body paragraph format.

Name of current paragraph format

Exercise 5

Guided Tour

Viewing the QuickAccess bar

The QuickAccess bar provides buttons for frequently used FrameMaker commands. The buttons on the left side remain constant, but on the right you can choose from four "pages" of buttons designed for helping with specific tasks.

In this exercise, you'll view the different pages of buttons in the QuickAccess bar and change the orientation of the QuickAccess bar.

1. If the QuickAccess bar is *not* already visible on your screen, from the View menu, choose **QuickAccess Bar**.

2. If the QuickAccess bar is displayed vertically, click the [img] button to display it horizontally.

> **Note:** The buttons displayed on the right half of the QuickAccess bar may be different from those pictured below.

Macintosh

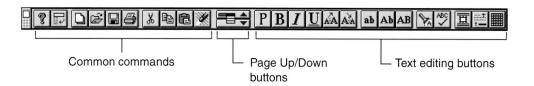

     Common commands   Page Up/Down   Text editing buttons
                                       buttons

Windows

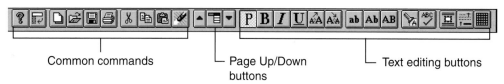

     Common commands   Page Up/Down   Text editing buttons
                                       buttons

UNIX

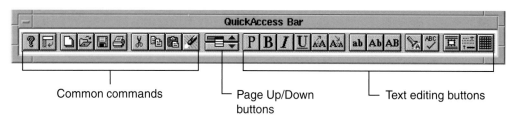

     Common commands   Page Up/Down   Text editing buttons
                                       buttons

3. Click the **Page Down** button to display the other pages of buttons.

Graphics buttons —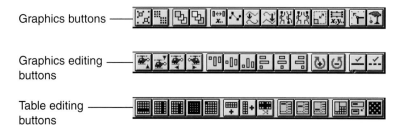

Graphics editing buttons

Table editing buttons

4. Click the **Flip** button.

└─── Flip button

The QuickAccess bar is "flipped" so it is displayed vertically.

Macintosh **Windows** **UNIX**

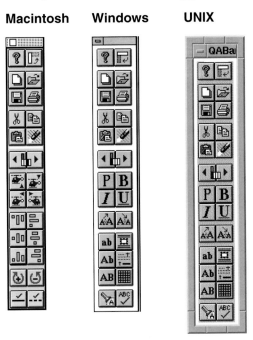

5. Drag the QuickAccess bar (by dragging the shaded or colored area at the top) to the right side of your screen.

6. If you'd like the QuickAccess bar to be hidden or displayed in a different position or orientation while you work, make that change now.

Saving Documents

Every time you open a sample file, you must *rename* it so as not to affect the original. To do this you use the Save As command.

Exercise 6   **Using Save As**

Guided Tour

1. Use the Save As dialog box to save the document in the Class directory or folder with the new filename report1:

   a. From the File menu, choose **Save As**.

   Macintosh

   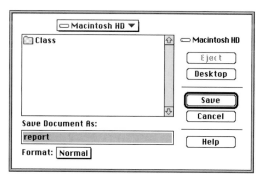

   Windows   **UNIX**

   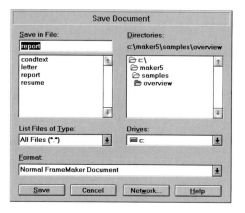   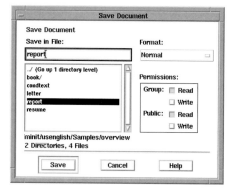

   b. Change to the Class directory or folder, if necessary.

Macintosh	Use the pop-up menu above the list of files to select your hard disk, and then double-click the Class folder.
Windows	In the right-hand list, double-click the C:\ folder, and then double-click the Class folder.
UNIX	Type: ~ and press Return (to return to your Home directory), and then double-click the Class directory.

   Note: Some UNIX users will need to type $HOME, rather than ~, depending on the shell they use. If necessary, ask your system administrator for help.

The Save Document dialog box indicates that the file will be saved in the `Class` directory or folder.

Macintosh

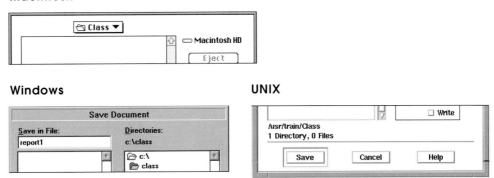

Windows   **UNIX**

c. In the Save in File text box (on the Macintosh, called Save Document As text box), delete any text that appears, and type: `report1`

d. Click **Save**.

2. From the File menu, choose **Close** to close the document.

3. In the FrameMaker samples window, click **Done** to close the FrameMaker samples window. (In UNIX, also close the blank document you opened in an earlier exercise.)

Exercise 7

Guided Tour

Opening a file and using the Save command

The Save command is used to save changes to an existing document. The table below describes when to use the Save command rather than the Save As command.

Use:	If:
Save	The document has been saved before, and you want to use the same directory or folder, filename, and permissions to save the document in Normal format.
Save As	This is the first time you've saved the document or you want to change its directory or folder, filename, or permissions. In addition, if you're saving a document in a format other than Normal, you need to use Save As.

1. Open the **report1** document you saved in the previous exercise:

   a. Open the Open Document dialog box.

      | **Macintosh** | From the File menu, choose **Open**. |
      | **Windows** | From the File menu, choose **Open**. |
      | **UNIX** | In the main FrameMaker window, click **OPEN**. |

   b. If necessary, change to the `Class` directory or folder.

   c. Double-click **report1**.

      The file you saved in the previous exercise appears.

      > **Tip:** A quick way to open a recently opened file is to select its name from the list of files that appears in the File menu.

2. Near the top of the second column of text, click to put the insertion point just before the word "United."

   ```
   nly seven years ago by an          Although corporate headquarters are in
   e team of biochemists, molecu-      the United States, considerable work
   sts, ethnobotanists, and phy-       occurs at the TerraMed branches
   'erraMed has become a major         located on every continent. Equipped
   :he field of biopharmaceuti-        with state-of-the-art biotechnology labo-
   ```

3. Make a simple change to the document by typing `southern` and then a space.

   ```
   nly seven years ago by an          Although corporate headquarters are in
   'e team of biochemists, molecu-     the southern United States, consider-
   ists, ethnobotanists, and phy-      able work occurs at the TerraMed
   'erraMed has become a major         branches located on every continent.
   the field of biopharmaceuti-        Equipped with state-of-the-art biotech-
   ```

   An asterisk (*) appears next to the page count in the status bar (at the bottom of the document window) to indicate that a change has been made to the file.

   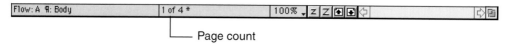

   Page count

4. From the File menu, choose **Save** to save the change to the file.

Notice the asterisk no longer appears in the status bar.

Automatically Saving and Backing Up

A FrameMaker document can be saved in three different ways.

■ You can use Save or Save As to save it manually.

■ FrameMaker can save a document automatically as you work, in case you forget to save regularly. You can set preferences for how often you would like files to be saved automatically. Then if you have a power failure, you can open the autosaved copy to recover the latest autosaved version.

■ When you save a document manually, you can tell FrameMaker to make a backup of the existing file *before* you save changes. Then if changes you save turn out to be incorrect, or you accidentally delete a document, you can open the backup file to retrieve the most recent old version.

Recovering After a Crash

If your system begins to crash, FrameMaker tries to create a file with your most recent changes before the system finishes crashing. This file is called a recover file. Usually after a system crash you can start working from the recover file and not lose any of your work.

Summary of Filenames

Platform	Autosave Files	Backup Files	Recover Files
Macintosh	filenameAutosave	filenameBackup	filenameRecover
Windows	filenam$.doc	filenam%.doc	filenam#.doc
UNIX	filename.auto	filename.backup	filename.recover

Exercise 8

Guided Tour

Setting backup and save preferences

In this exercise, you'll set backup and save preferences for working in all files.

1. From the File Menu, choose **Preferences**.

   The Preferences dialog box appears.

Macintosh

```
┌─────────────────────────────────────────┐
│              Preferences                 │
│ ┌─────────────────────────────────────┐ │
│ │ User Preferences:                   │ │
│ │ ┌─────────────────────────────────┐ │ │
│ │ │ ☒ Automatic Backup on Save      │ │ │
│ │ │ ☒ Automatic Save - Every: [5 ]  │ │ │
│ │ │                        Minutes  │ │ │
│ │ │ Greek Screen Text Smaller Than: │ │ │
│ │ │                       [7.0 pt]  │ │ │
│ │ └─────────────────────────────────┘ │ │
│ │ Compatibility Preferences:          │ │
│ │ ┌─────────────────────────────────┐ │ │
│ │ │ Cross-Platform: [Macintosh  ▼]  │ │ │
│ │ │ ☐ Save FrameImage with Imported │ │ │
│ │ │   Graphics                      │ │ │
│ │ │ ☒ Remember Missing Font Names   │ │ │
│ │ │ ☒ Show File Translation Errors  │ │ │
│ │ └─────────────────────────────────┘ │ │
│ │ Interface: [US EnglishInterface ▼]  │ │
│ │ ─────────────────────────────────── │ │
│ │     ( Set )  ( Cancel )  ( Help )   │ │
│ └─────────────────────────────────────┘ │
└─────────────────────────────────────────┘
```

Windows

```
┌──────────────────────────────────────┐
│             Preferences              │
│ User Preferences:                    │
│  ☒ Automatic Backup on Save          │
│  ☒ Automatic Save - Every: [5 ]      │
│                          Minutes     │
│  ☒ Show File Translation Errors      │
│  Greek Screen Text Smaller Than:     │
│                          [5.0 pt]    │
│ Compatibility Preferences:           │
│  ☐ Save FrameImage with Imported     │
│    Graphics                          │
│  ☒ Network File Locking              │
│    [ Set ]  [ Cancel ]  [ Help ]     │
└──────────────────────────────────────┘
```

UNIX

```
┌──────────────────────────────────────┐
│             Preferences              │
│ Preferences                          │
│                                      │
│  ☐ Automatic Backup on Save          │
│  ☐ Automatic Save--Every: [5 ]       │
│                          Minutes     │
│  Greek Screen Text Smaller Than:     │
│                          [7.0 pt]    │
│   [ Set ]   [ Cancel ]   [ Help ]    │
└──────────────────────────────────────┘
```

The Preferences dialog box sets operations for the entire editing session, not just for a single file.

2. Make sure **Automatic Backup on Save** is on (in UNIX, a setting is turned on if its checkbox appears filled or "pushed in").

3. Make sure **Automatic Save** is turned on.

4. Change the Automatic Save interval to **10** minutes:

   a. Double-click to select the number in the Minutes text box.

   b. Type `10` to change the setting to 10 minutes.

   c. Click **Set**.

Now, as you work, FrameMaker will write the most current contents of `report1`, the file you're working on, to an autosave file every 10 minutes. Whenever you use Save or Save As, the autosave file is deleted and the process starts over again at the specified 10-minute interval. This autosave process occurs not only for `report1`, but also for all other open documents.

> **Note:** An autosave document never overwrites the current version you're working on. You can always choose to save changes or revert to the last version you saved manually.

Zooming the Document

Also located in the status bar are zoom options that allow you to:

- Magnify text and objects (zooming in, making the display larger).
- Make text and objects appear smaller to fit more in the window (zooming out, making the display smaller).

Exercise 9

Guided Tour

Using preset zoom settings

In this exercise, you'll change the zoom using some preset zoom settings.

1. In the status bar at the bottom of the document window, click the **Zoom In** button (the uppercase Z).

                  Zoom Out ⎤ ⎣ Zoom In

The Zoom pop-up menu now indicates that the document has been enlarged to 120% of its original size.

                  ⎣ Zoom pop-up menu

The rulers at the top and left side of the document window have changed to show the true size of the document, but the window remains the same size.

> **Note:** Since zoom settings are saved with the document, an asterisk (*) will appear in the status bar when a change has been made to the zoom settings.

2. Press the **Zoom** pop-up menu to see the options.

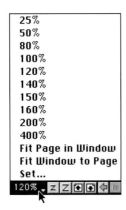

> **Note:** Your options may differ from those shown above, depending on your platform.

3. Move the pointer to choose **140%**, and release the mouse button.

   The document is enlarged to 140% of its original size.

4. Click the **Zoom Out** button (the lowercase z).

   └─ Zoom Out button

   The document reduces to 120% of its original size, and 120% appears in the Zoom pop-up menu.

   Because the window remains the same size, the page is cut off at the bottom and on the right side.

5. From the Zoom pop-up menu, choose **Fit Window to Page**.

   The document remains at 120% of its original size, but on wider monitors the width of the document window increases so that the page is no longer cut off.

6. From the Zoom pop-up menu, choose **25%**.

   Several pages of text are visible.

7. From the Zoom pop-up menu, choose **100%**.

   The document returns to 100% of its original size.

8. From the Zoom pop-up menu, choose **Fit Window to Page**.

   The zoom percentage remains the same, but on larger monitors the width of the window decreases to match the width of the document.

Window Guides and View Options

FrameMaker provides four types of document window guides—borders, text symbols, rulers, and grid lines—to help you work with a document. You can turn them on when you are working in a document, and off to see how a document will look when it is printed.

> **Note:** Regardless of whether borders, text symbols, rulers, and grid lines are turned on or off, they will not print out on paper.

Exercise 10

Guided Tour

Viewing borders and text symbols

In this exercise, you'll view a FrameMaker document using window guides. (On UNIX menus, the box preceding the choices represents the on/off toggle.)

1. Press your mouse button on the View menu, and determine whether your borders are already turned on.

   Your borders are turned on if a checkmark appears to the left of the Borders command (on UNIX, the checkbox to the left of Borders is selected if borders are on).

2. If your borders are *not* already turned on, from the View menu, choose **Borders** to turn on Borders.

The dotted lines that appear around the text show the borders of where the text will appear on the page. These rectangular, bordered objects are called *text frames*.

3. Move the pointer into a text frame without clicking anywhere.

   Notice that the pointer changes to an I-beam when moved inside a text frame.

4. From the View menu, choose **Text Symbols** to turn on text symbols.

   Text symbols appear throughout the document.

 — Text symbol

What the text symbols stand for and how they are used will be covered later in this workbook.

Exercise 11   Setting view options

Guided Tour

The settings in the View options dialog box affect how the document window and FrameMaker dialog boxes appear. The Display Units setting determines the default units of measurement that will appear in FrameMaker dialog boxes. The Rulers setting determines the units of measurement displayed by the document window rulers. Changing these settings affects only the current document.

In this exercise, you'll use the View Options dialog box to change the Display Units and the units displayed by the rulers.

1. Take a look at the rulers along the edge of the document window.

   The rulers currently measure in units of picas.

2. From the View menu, choose **Options**.

   The View Options dialog box appears.

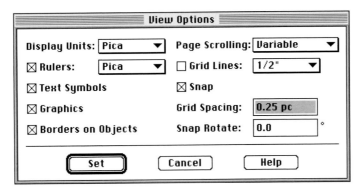

Notice that the units in the Grid Spacing text box are picas (pc).

3. From the Display Units pop-up menu, choose **Inch**.

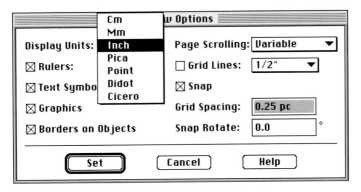

Note: The above change will not take effect until after you click Set in step 5.

4. From the Rulers pop-up menu, choose **1/8"**.

5. Click **Set**.

   The document rulers display ⅛-inch increments.

6. From the View menu, choose **Options**.

   Notice that the units displayed in the Grid Spacing text box have changed to inches.

7. Click **Cancel**.

Changing Pages

There are many ways to move through a document: scrolling, page buttons, the Go To dialog box, and keyboard shortcuts.

In the following table of keyboard shortcuts, a hyphen means that two keys should be pressed simultaneously and a space indicates that keys should be pressed in sequence.

Macintosh	
To Display	**Press**
Previous Page	Option-Pg Up or Esc p p
Next Page	Option-Pg Dn or Esc p n
First page in document	Home, or Command-Pg Up, or Esc p f
Last page in document	End, or Command-Pg Dn, or Esc p l (lowercase L)

Windows	
To display	**Press**
Previous page	Pg Up or Esc-p p
Next page	Pg Dn or Esc-p n
First page in document	Alt-Pg Up or Esc p f
Last page in document	Alt-Pg Dn or Esc p l

UNIX	
To display	**Press**
Previous page	F6, or Meta-v, or Esc p p
Next page	F7, or Control-v, or Esc p n
First page in document	Shift-F6 or Esc p f
Last page in document	Shift-F7 or Esc p l

Elaboration: Some keyboard shortcuts are specific to a certain platform to conform with the conventions of that platform. Shortcuts that begin with Esc are the same on all three platforms.

Exercise 12

Using scrolling features

To scroll through a document, use the scroll bar on the right side of the document window. The scroll bar is especially useful when you want to see an entire paragraph, a list, or other text that spans two pages.

Different parts of the scroll bar can be used to scroll through a document at varying rates.

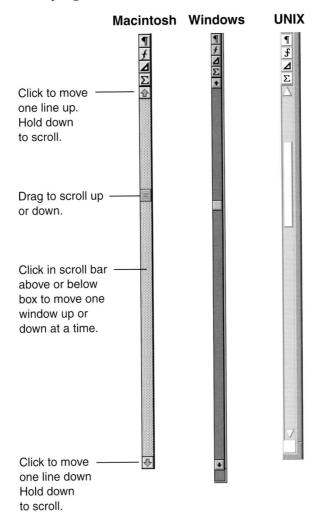

Macintosh   Windows   UNIX

Click to move one line up. Hold down to scroll.

Drag to scroll up or down.

Click in scroll bar above or below box to move one window up or down at a time.

Click to move one line down Hold down to scroll.

1. Press the **down scroll arrow**, and hold down the mouse button.

Down scroll arrow

The document scrolls down continuously.

2. Click the **up scroll arrow** at the top right of the document window.

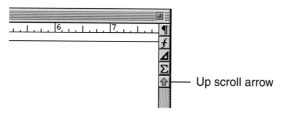
Up scroll arrow

The page moves up one line.

3. Press the **up scroll arrow** until the document scrolls all the way back to the top of page 1.

4. Locate the scroll box at the top right of the document window.

5. Drag the **scroll box** down to the bottom of the scroll bar.

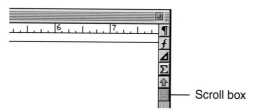
Scroll box

On UNIX and Windows, as you scroll, the page number in the status bar changes dynamically. When the scroll box reaches the bottom, the last page appears on the screen.

Note: On the Macintosh, after scrolling, you must click to put the insertion point on the page to make the current page number appear in the status bar.

6. Drag the **scroll box** back up to the top of the scroll bar.

   Page 1 appears, and 1 of 4 appears in the Page Status area of the status bar.

7. Click once in the **scroll bar** below the scroll box.

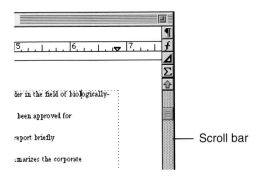

   Scroll bar

   The page advances one window. The page break between page 1 and page 2 may be visible at the top of the screen.

8. Click once in the **scroll bar** above the scroll box.

   The page scrolls back one window.

Exercise 13   **Using page buttons**

Guided Tour

Page buttons are quick and easy to use when you want to go forward or backward in a document.

1. Click the **Next Page** button (down arrow) in the status bar.

   └ Next Page button

Page 2 of the document appears, and "2 of 4" appears in the Page Status area.

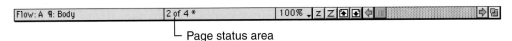

   └ Page status area

2. Click the **Previous Page** button (up arrow) in the status bar.

Previous Page button

Page 1 of the document appears, and "1 of 4" appears in the Page Status area.

3. Hold down **Shift**, and click the **Next Page** button (down arrow) in the status bar to see the last page of the document.

4. Hold down **Shift**, and click the **Previous Page** button (up arrow) in the status bar to return to the first page of the document.

Exercise 14

Guided Tour

Using the Go To dialog box

The Go To dialog box is used to move to a particular page—instead of continually clicking the page buttons until the desired page appears. There are several ways to display the Go To dialog box.

1. From the View menu, choose **Go to Page**.

The Go to Page dialog box appears.

2. In the Page Number text box, type: 3

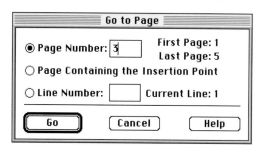

3. Click **Go**.

Page 3 of the document appears.

4. Click the Page Status area at the bottom of the document window to display the Go to Page dialog box, and go to page 2.

5. From the File menu, choose **Save**, and keep the document open.

Printing Documents

Exercise 15

Guided Tour

Using the Print dialog box

FrameMaker is preset to print one copy of the entire document on a pre-selected printer. You can customize printing by choosing settings in the Print dialog box.

1. From the File menu, choose **Print**.

   The Print dialog box appears.

> **Note:** The diagrams below are representative samples of the Print dialog boxes from each platform. The appearance of your Print dialog box may vary.

Macintosh

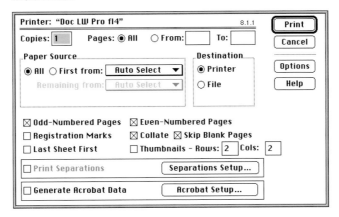

Windows

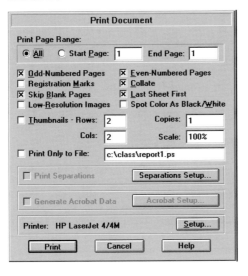

UNIX

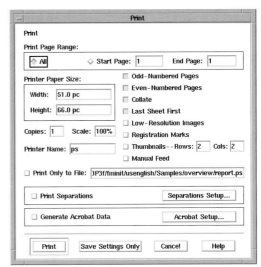

2. Click **Print** in the dialog box. (Click **Cancel** if you do not wish to print at this time.)

   FrameMaker prints the current document according to the current print settings.

Closing and Saving Documents

When you've finished using a document, you can close it to remove it from the desktop and the system's memory. Before closing you have the option to save or not save any changes you've made to the document.

Exercise 16   **Closing and saving changes**

Guided Tour

In this exercise, you'll close a document and save changes to it at the same time.

1. Go to page 2 in the document.

2. At the end of the first paragraph, put the insertion point between the word "development" and the period that follows it.

   > ments, and a percentage of profits is
   >
   > invested in local welfare and develop-
   >
   > ment. ¶

3. Type a space, then type: `program`

   Notice that an asterisk (*) appears in the status bar at the bottom of the window to indicate that a change has been made to the document.

4. From the File menu, choose **Close**.

The Unsaved Changes dialog box appears and asks if you want to save the changes before closing.

Macintosh

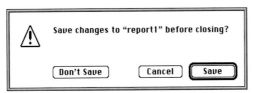

Windows

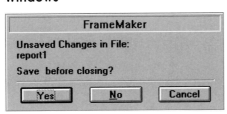

UNIX

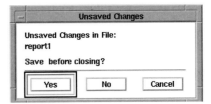

5. Click **Yes** (on the Macintosh, click **Save**).

The document disappears from the screen, and the changes are saved.

Exercise 17

Guided Tour

Not saving changes

In this exercise, you'll learn how *not* to save changes when closing a document, in case you make changes that you do not want to keep.

1. Open the document again:

a. From the File menu, choose **Open**. (In UNIX, in the main FrameMaker window, click **OPEN**.)

b. Double-click the filename **report1**.

2. On page 1, in the first paragraph, just before the word "large," type the word very and a space.

> TERRAMED ENTERS 1995 as a leader in the field of biologically-
>
> based pharmaceuticals. A v ery large number of new products have been approved
>
> for use in the past year and are being marketed worldwide. This report briefly

3. From the File menu, choose **Close**.

    The Unsaved Changes dialog box appears and asks if you want to save the changes before closing.

4. Click **Cancel**.

    The document remains on the screen, unsaved, with the changes intact.

5. Close the file and don't save the changes:

    a. From the File menu, choose **Close**.

    b. In the Unsaved Changes dialog box, click **No** (on the Macintosh, click **Don't Save**).

        The file is closed, the document disappears from the screen, and the changes made to the document are not saved.

6. Open the file again.

    Notice that the change you made was not saved.

7. Keep the document open if you plan to complete the optional exercise in this module. Otherwise, close the document.

Deleting Documents

You cannot delete a document from within FrameMaker. Delete files according to recommended procedures outlined in the user's guide for your system—Macintosh, Windows, or UNIX.

> **Note:** If you set your preferences to automatically create backup files (by choosing Preferences from the File menu and turning on Automatic Backup on Save), you will have to manually delete them as well.

Optional Exercise

The following exercise enables you to enhance your FrameMaker skills and to explore additional FrameMaker features. Some steps are intentionally brief, so that they require more independent thought on your part.

Exercise 18

Optional

Using keyboard shortcuts

In this optional exercise, you'll explore two keyboard shortcuts you can use when you have several files open at the same time.

1. Make a change to the report document, but do not save it.

2. Make the FrameMaker samples window appear, and then click **Resume**.

3. Change the name on the resume to your name.

4. To save all open documents, hold down **Shift**, and from the File menu, choose **Save All Open Files**.

   The Save All Open Files command replaces the Save command on the File menu when the Shift key is held down.

5. To close all open documents, hold down **Shift**, and from the File menu choose **Close All Open Files**.

   The Close All Open Files command replaces the Close command on the File menu when the Shift key is held down.

6. Click **No** (on the Macintosh, **Don't Save**) to avoid saving the changes.

Review   Test your understanding of the concepts and procedures covered in this module by answering the following review questions. You may check your answers with those listed after the questions.

Question 1: What is the meaning of the asterisk next to the page count in the Page Status area?

Question 2: How do you turn borders on/off? How about text symbols? Rulers?

Question 3: Which command do you use to save a document under a new name: Save or Save As?

Question 4: What happens when you click the uppercase Z button in the status bar?

Question 5: Describe at least two of the five ways to get from page 3 of a document to page 1.

Answer 1: The asterisk means that you have made changes to the document and they have not been saved.

Answer 2: Borders, text symbols, and rulers can be turned on and off from the View menu or in the View Options dialog box.

Answer 3: Save As.

Answer 4: The document's magnification increases.

Answer 5: To get from page 3 to page 5 of a document:

a. From the View menu, choose Go to Page (or click the Page Status to display the Go to Page dialog box), type 1, and click Go.

b. Use the up scroll arrow in the scroll bar.

c. Use the scroll box in the scroll bar.

d. Shift-click the Previous Page button.

e. Use the keyboard shortcut, Esc p f.

For more information

For more information about getting started with FrameMaker, see:

Chapter 2 of *Using FrameMaker*

Using Online Help

. . . .

Approximate time to complete: 15 minutes

Introduction

In this module, you'll become familiar with FrameMaker's online Help features. Online Help gives you access to information about the FrameMaker interface and functions, as well as access to in-depth online manuals.

Module Objectives

In this module, you'll learn how to

- Access Help from a menu or the main FrameMaker window
- Use the Help Index
- Use context-sensitive Help
- Locate FrameMaker shortcuts
- View online manuals
- Differentiate between general interface Help and in-depth online manuals

FrameMaker Model

When you use online Help you do not directly affect any particular component of the FrameMaker model. Instead, your interaction with Help assists you in learning more about the *FrameMaker application*, which increases productivity at all levels of the model.

Application Interface Help

FrameMaker online Help files provide information about commands and dialog boxes—and much more. Online Help provides information organized by topic and includes general descriptions—it does not provide step-by-step instructions.

Exercise 1   **Using Help**

Guided Tour

In this exercise, you'll become familiar with the Help window.

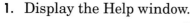

1. Display the Help window.

Macintosh	From the menu, choose **FrameMaker5 Help**.
Windows	From the Help menu, choose **Contents**.
UNIX	In the main FrameMaker window, click **HELP**.

The Help window appears displaying the Help Main Menu, a list of main topics.

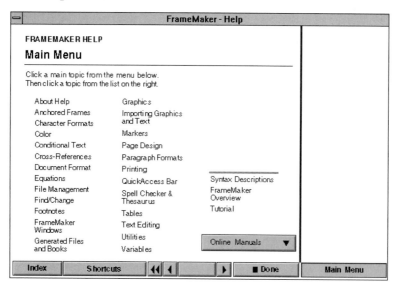

Tip: Another way to display the Help Main Menu is to click the question mark button in the QuickAccess bar, and then click Main Menu.

2. Click the first main topic in the left column, **About Help**.

   A list of subtopics for **About Help** appears on the right side of the Help window.

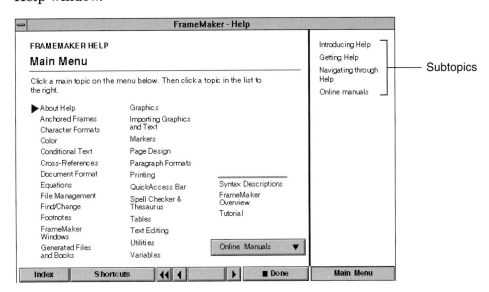

3. On the left side of the Help window, choose a new main topic from the following.

Macintosh	Document Window
Windows	FrameMaker Windows
UNIX	Document Window

The list of related subtopics on the right side of the Help window changes.

Windows

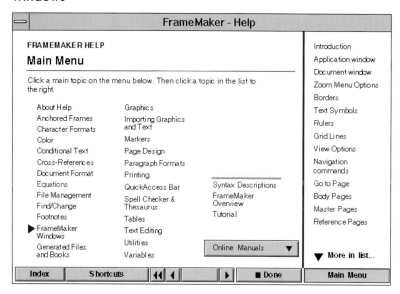

UNIX and Macintosh

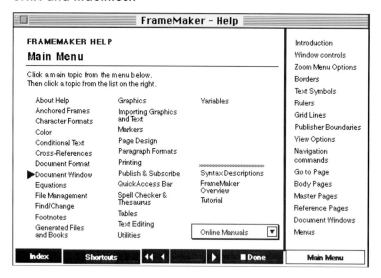

4. From the list of subtopics on the right side of the Help window, choose a topic from the following.

Macintosh	Window controls
Windows	Document window
UNIX	Window controls

A description of the document window and the window controls appears in the Help window.

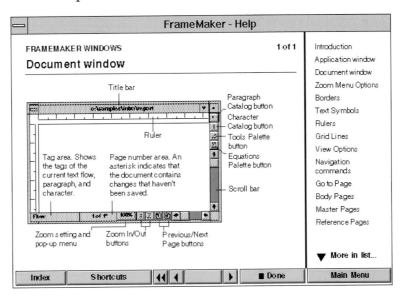

5. At the bottom of the Help window, click the **right arrow** and **left arrow** to move forward and backward through Help.

6. At the bottom of the Help window, click **Index**.

   The Help Index appears.

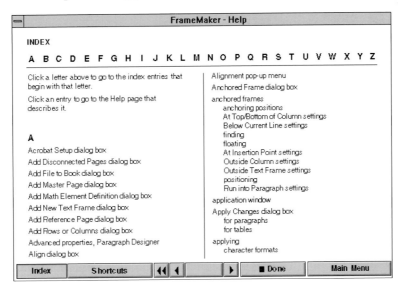

7. At the top of the Help window, click the letter **H.**

This displays the beginning of the list of topics that start with the letter "H."

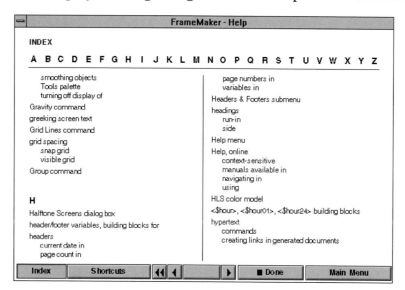

8. Under the **Help, online** topic, click **context-sensitive**.

   A description of context-sensitive Help appears.

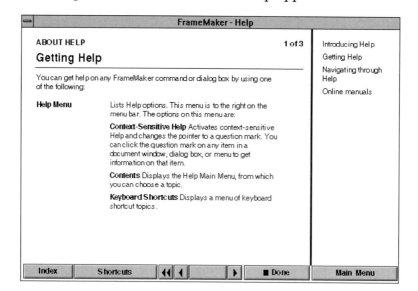

9. Read the description of context-sensitive Help.

10. At the bottom of the Help window, click **Main Menu** to return to the Help Main Menu.

   Tip: You can go to the Main Menu, Index, or Shortcuts at any time by clicking the appropriate button at the bottom of any Help window.

11. Click **Done** to close the Help window.

Exercise 2

Using context-sensitive Help

Context-sensitive Help provides information on any item in a document window, dialog box, or menu. In this exercise, you'll use context-sensitive Help to get information about the tab wells on the formatting bar.

1. If no documents are open, create a new **Portrait** document:

   a. Open the New dialog box.

Macintosh	From the File menu, choose **New**.
Windows	From the File menu, choose **New**.
UNIX	In the main FrameMaker window, click **NEW**.

   b. In the New dialog box, click **Portrait**.

2. Activate context-sensitive Help.

Macintosh	From the ⟨?⟩ menu, choose **Context-Sensitive Help** or From the Apple menu, choose **Context-Sensitive Help**.
Windows	From the Help menu, choose **Context-Sensitive Help**.
UNIX	From the Help menu, choose **Context-Sensitive Help**.

   The pointer changes to a question mark.

   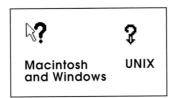

3. On the formatting bar, click one of the four **tab wells**.

   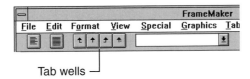

   Tab wells

A description of the tab wells appears in the Help window.

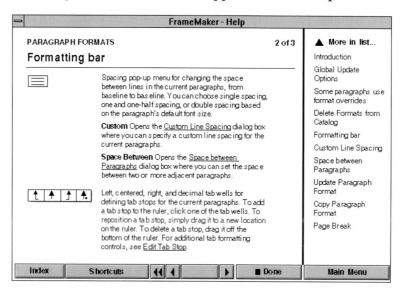

4. Review the function key shortcuts for your keyboard:

   a. At the bottom of the Help window, click **Shortcuts**.

      A list of topics appears for keyboard shortcuts.

   b. In the list of topics, click **Conventions and function keys**.

      A list of subtopics appears on the right side of the Help window.

   c. In the list of subtopics on the right, click **Function keys**.

      A list of function-key assignments appears.

Exercise 3

Guided Tour

Referencing online manuals

Similar to printed documentation, online manuals provide an in-depth approach to special topics.

In this exercise, you'll become familiar with the Help found in Framemaker online manuals.

1. From the Go To pop-up menu in the lower-right corner of the Help window, choose **Help Main Menu**.

2. From the Online Manuals pop-up menu in the lower-right corner, choose **What's New in FrameMaker**.

   A document window appears containing a table of contents for What's New in FrameMaker.

3. From the Go To pop-up menu in the upper-right corner of the window, choose **Using This Manual**.

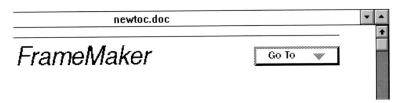

The document window shows a description of how to use online manuals.

4. When you have finished reading the information about online manuals, from the Go To menu, choose **Close**.

5. At the bottom of the Help window, click **Done** (Macintosh and UNIX).

6. **Close** any open documents at this time.

Optional Exercise

The following exercise enables you to enhance your FrameMaker skills and to explore additional FrameMaker features. Some steps are intentionally brief, so that they require more independent thought on your part.

Exercise 4

Optional

Understanding file management using Help

In this optional exercise, you'll use Help to review information on FrameMaker file management covered in the previous module.

1. In the Help Index under File Management (on the Macintosh, under Files, Management) view the help for the subtopics New and Save As.

    a. Open Help.

    b. Display the Index.

    c. Display the Index topics that begin with the letter "F."

    d. Click the desired subtopic.

Review   Test your understanding of the concepts and procedures covered in this module by answering the following review questions. You may check your answers with those listed after the questions.

Question 1: How do you display the main Help window?

Question 2: How do you use Context-Sensitive Help?

Question 3: How are online manuals different from items in the Help Main Menu?

_____

Answer 1: On the Macintosh, from the [?] menu, choose FrameMaker5 Help.
In Windows, from the Help menu, choose Contents.
On UNIX, in the main FrameMaker window, click HELP.

Answer 2: From the Help menu (on the Macintosh, from the [?] menu), choose Context-Sensitive Help, then click on the part of the window you want help with.

Answer 3: Online manuals provide in-depth information on special topics, while the other items in Help present only general descriptions.

For more information

For more information about getting started with FrameMaker, see:

Chapter 2 of *Using FrameMaker*

Editing Text

Approximate time to complete: 45 minutes

Introduction

In this module, you'll become familiar with the text editing capabilities of FrameMaker. Using these capabilities you can enter and manipulate text efficiently, and automatically make sure your document adheres to typographic conventions regarding quotation marks and extra spaces.

Module Objectives

In this module, you'll learn how to

- Enter text, including special characters
- Select and deselect text
- Undo changes to text
- Cut, copy, paste, move, and delete text
- Use Smart Quotes and Smart Spaces
- Use the Revert to Saved feature

FrameMaker Model

The operations you perform in this module will affect *text*, the primary building block of all FrameMaker documents.

Opening, Editing, and Saving Documents

In this module, you'll make changes to a sample letter to become familiar with editing a FrameMaker document.

Exercise 1

Guided Tour

Opening and saving a sample file

In this exercise, you'll open and save a sample letter before making changes to it.

1. From the FrameMaker list of sample documents, open the Letter sample:

   a. Display the FrameMaker list of sample documents.

Macintosh	From the [?] menu, choose **Samples & Clip Art**.
Windows	From the Help menu, choose **Samples & Clip Art**.
UNIX	From a document Help menu, choose **Samples & Clip Art**. (If there are no open documents, click **NEW**, then **Portrait**, first.)

   A window appears, showing a list of FrameMaker samples.

   b. In the FrameMaker samples list, click **Letter**.

   The sample letter appears.

2. Use the Save As dialog box to save the document in the Class directory or folder with the new filename bike:

   a. From the File menu, choose **Save As**.

   b. Change to the Class directory or folder if necessary.

   c. In the Save in File text box (on the Macintosh, called Save Document As text box), type: bike

   d. Click **Save**.

   The document is now saved as bike.

Text Symbols

Text symbols are visual cues that give you information about content, position, and format of objects in a document. FrameMaker uses text symbols to show tabs, ends of paragraphs and text flows, markers, and other items. The following is a list of the most common text symbols and their meanings.

¶ End of paragraph

§ End of flow

‹ Forced return

› Tab

T Marker

⊥ Anchored frame

Working with text symbols turned on can help you make precise editing changes—for example, selecting text at the end of a paragraph without selecting the end-or-paragraph symbol.

<table>
<tr><td>

Exercise 2

Guided Tour

</td><td>

Turning on text symbols and borders, and zooming in a document

In this exercise, you'll turn on the text symbols and borders and change zoom settings to prepare for editing a document.

1. Turn on borders and text symbols:

   a. From the View menu, choose **Borders**.

   b. From the View menu, choose **Text Symbols**.

The letter on your screen now shows dotted lines (borders) around the text and table, and text symbols appear in the text.

</td></tr>
</table>

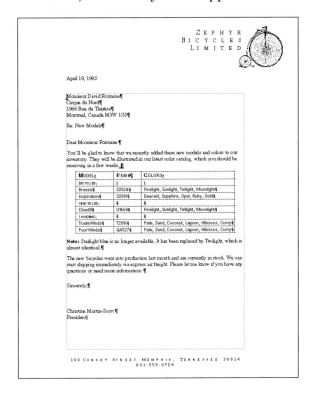

2. Zoom the document to **120%** and **Fit Window to Page**:

   a. In the status bar at the bottom of the document window, click the **Zoom In** button (the uppercase Z).

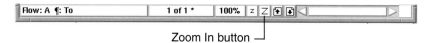

Zoom In button ⏤

The document enlarges to 120% of its original size.

   b. From the Zoom pop-up menu, choose **Fit Window to Page**.

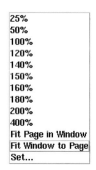

The window resizes to fit the new zoom setting.

Exercise 3   Adding and deleting text

Guided Tour

In the following exercise, you'll add text to and delete text from your document.

1. Put the insertion point after the period in the last paragraph.

> The new bicycles went into production last month and are currently in stock. We can start shipping immediately via express air freight. Please let me know if you have any questions or need more information. ¶

2. Type: It is our policy to provide the best possible service to our clients.

   Notice that you do not have to press Return to make the last few words appear on the next line, because the text wraps automatically to the width of the text frame. Press Return only when you want to start a new paragraph.

> The new bicycles went into production last month and are currently in stock. We can start shipping immediately via express air freight. Please let me know if you have any questions or need more information. It is our policy to provide the best possible service to our clients. ¶

3. In the second sentence of the last paragraph, put the insertion point after the word "freight" but before the period.

> The new bicycles went into production last month and are currently in stock. We can start shipping immediately via express air freight| Please let me know if you have any questions or need more information. It is our policy to provide the best possible service to our clients.¶

4. Type a space and then type: or ground carrier

    Make sure the sentence ends in a period.

> The new bicycles went into production last month and are currently in stock. We can start shipping immediately via express air freight or ground carrier| Please let me know if you have any questions or need more information. It is our policy to provide the best possible service to our clients.¶

5. In the "TradeWinds" row of the table, put the insertion point after the comma following the word "Lagoon."

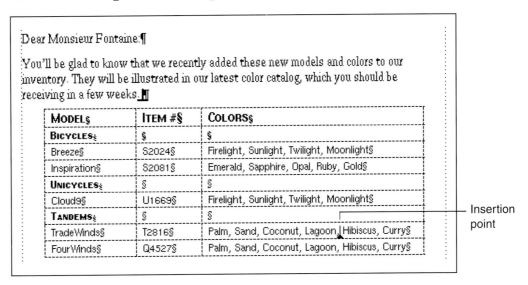

Insertion point

6. Press the **Backspace** or **Delete** key until the comma and the word "Lagoon" are deleted.

TANDEMS§	§	§
TradeWinds§	T2816§	Palm, Sand, Coconut, Hibiscus, Curry§
FourWinds§	Q4527§	Palm, Sand, Coconut, Lagoon, Hibiscus, Curry§

Exercise 4

Guided Tour

Selecting and deselecting text

In this exercise, you'll learn several ways to select and change text.

1. In the first paragraph, double-click the word "recently."

   The word is selected. Double-clicking selects a word.

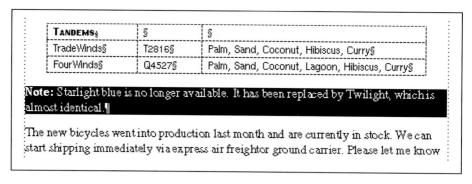

2. Press the **Backspace** or **Delete** key.

   The word "recently" is deleted, and the space following the word is also deleted because Smart Spaces is turned on. Smart Spaces prevents the typing of more than one consecutive space.

3. Triple-click the paragraph that begins with the word "Note" in bold letters. The paragraph, including the paragraph symbol, is selected. Triple-clicking selects a paragraph.

TANDEMS§	§	§
TradeWinds§	T2816§	Palm, Sand, Coconut, Hibiscus, Curry§
FourWinds§	Q4527§	Palm, Sand, Coconut, Lagoon, Hibiscus, Curry§

Note: Starlight blue is no longer available. It has been replaced by Twilight, which is almost identical.¶

The new bicycles went into production last month and are currently in stock. We can start shipping immediately via express air freighter ground carrier. Please let me know

4. Click anywhere in the document to deselect the paragraph.

5. Near the end of the first paragraph, put the insertion point before the words "in a few weeks."

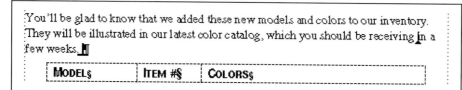

6. Hold down the **Shift** key and click before the period at the end of the same sentence.

This selects everything between the locations of the initial click and the Shift-click.

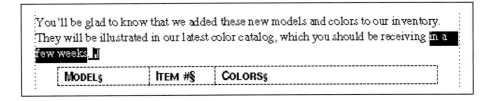

Note: You may also drag to select text.

7. Click anywhere to deselect the text.

Exercise 5

Guided Tour

Editing text

In this exercise, you'll select and replace text. Use the selection methods you learned in the previous exercise.

1. In the middle of the first paragraph, double-click the word "latest."

   The word is selected.

   Dear Monsieur Fontaine:¶

   You'll be glad to know that we added these new models and colors to our inventory. They will be illustrated in our latest color catalog, which you should be receiving in a few weeks.¶

2. Type: `twenty-page Spring` (follow the text with a space).

   The text "twenty-page Spring" now replaces the word "latest."

   Dear Monsieur Fontaine:¶

   You'll be glad to know that we added these new models and colors to our inventory. They will be illustrated in our twenty-page Spring color catalog, which you should be receiving in a few weeks.¶

3. At the end of the first paragraph, select the text "in a few weeks."

   Dear Monsieur Fontaine:¶

   You'll be glad to know that we added these new models and colors to our inventory. They will be illustrated in our twenty-page Spring color catalog, which you should be receiving in a few weeks.¶

4. Type: `by special delivery within the next 10 days`

> Dear Monsieur Fontaine:¶
>
> You'll be glad to know that we added these new models and colors to our inventory.
> They will be illustrated in our twenty-page Spring color catalog, which you should be
> receiving by special delivery within the next 10 days.¶

The text "by special delivery within the next 10 days" now replaces "in a few weeks."

Exercise 6   Using Clear and Undo

Guided Tour

The Clear command deletes selected text, just like pressing the Delete or Backspace key. When you use the Clear command, the selected text is not put on the Clipboard for later pasting (see explanation of the Clipboard in Exercise 7). The Undo command allows you to undo the previous action. This is helpful if you change your mind while editing a document.

In this exercise, you'll use the Clear and Undo commands, which are found on the Edit menu.

1. Triple-click to select the paragraph "Re: New Models."

> Monsieur David Fontaine¶
> Cirque du Nord¶
> 1966 Rue du Thérèse¶
> Montreal, Canada M3W 1G5¶
>
> Re: New Models¶

2. From the Edit menu, choose **Clear**.

   The sentence is removed from the document.

3. From the Edit menu, choose **Undo**.

   The Clear command is undone, so the sentence reappears.

> **Note:** Since the Undo command is applied only to your last action, make sure you use the Undo command *immediately* following the action you want to undo.

Exercise 7

Guided Tour

Cutting and pasting text

To move text, cut the selected text and paste it in a new location. When you cut text, it is placed on the Clipboard, an area in the computer's memory that serves as a holding place for what you last cut or copied. Once it's on the Clipboard, text can be pasted at another location in the same or a different document. The text stays on the Clipboard until you replace it by cutting or copying something else to the Clipboard.

In this exercise, you will cut and paste text to move it from one location to another in the document.

1. In the last cell of the table, select the word "Curry."

MODEL§	ITEM #§	COLORS§
BICYCLES§	§	§
Breeze§	S2024§	Firelight, Sunlight, Twilight, Moonlight§
Inspiration§	S2081§	Emerald, Sapphire, Opal, Ruby, Gold§
UNICYCLES§	§	§
Cloud9§	U1669§	Firelight, Sunlight, Twilight, Moonlight§
TANDEMS§	§	§
TradeWinds§	T2816§	Palm, Sand, Coconut, Hibiscus, Curry§
FourWinds§	Q4527§	Palm, Sand, Coconut, Lagoon, Hibiscus, **Curry**§

2. From the Edit menu, choose **Cut**.

   The word is cut from the document and placed on the Clipboard.

3. Press the **Backspace** or **Delete** key twice to delete the space and the comma.

4. In the "Breeze" row of the table, put the insertion point after the word "Moonlight."

MODEL§	ITEM #§	COLORS§
BICYCLES§	§	§
Breeze§	S2024§	Firelight, Sunlight, Twilight, Moonlight§
Inspiration§	S2081§	Emerald, Sapphire, Opal, Ruby, Gold§
UNICYCLES§	§	§
Cloud9§	U1669§	Firelight, Sunlight, Twilight, Moonlight§
TANDEMS§	§	§
TradeWinds§	T2816§	Palm, Sand, Coconut, Hibiscus, Curry§
FourWinds§	Q4527§	Palm, Sand, Coconut, Lagoon, Hibiscus, Curry§

5. Type a comma and a space.

6. From the Edit menu, choose **Paste**.

The word "Curry" is pasted in the document.

MODEL§	ITEM #§	COLORS§
BICYCLES§	§	§
Breeze§	S2024§	Firelight, Sunlight, Twilight, Moonlight, Curry§
Inspiration§	S2081§	Emerald, Sapphire, Opal, Ruby, Gold§
UNICYCLES§	§	§
Cloud9§	U1669§	Firelight, Sunlight, Twilight, Moonlight§
TANDEMS§	§	§
TradeWinds§	T2816§	Palm, Sand, Coconut, Hibiscus, Curry§
FourWinds§	Q4527§	Palm, Sand, Coconut, Lagoon, Hibiscus, §

7. In the "Cloud9" row of the table, put the insertion point after the word "Moonlight."

MODEL§	ITEM #§	COLORS§
BICYCLES§	§	§
Breeze§	S2024§	Firelight, Sunlight, Twilight, Moonlight, Curry§
Inspiration§	S2081§	Emerald, Sapphire, Opal, Ruby, Gold§
UNICYCLES§	§	§
Cloud9§	U1669§	Firelight, Sunlight, Twilight, Moonlight§
TANDEMS§	§	§
TradeWinds§	T2816§	Palm, Sand, Coconut, Hibiscus, Curry§

8. Type a comma and a space.

9. From the Edit menu, choose **Paste**.

The word "Curry" is again pasted in the document.

MODEL§	ITEM #§	COLORS§
BICYCLES§	§	§
Breeze§	S2024§	Firelight, Sunlight, Twilight, Moonlight, Curry§
Inspiration§	S2081§	Emerald, Sapphire, Opal, Ruby, Gold§
UNICYCLES§	§	§
Cloud9§	U1669§	Firelight, Sunlight, Twilight, Moonlight, Curry§
TANDEMS§	§	§
TradeWinds§	T2816§	Palm, Sand, Coconut, Hibiscus, Curry§

10. From the Edit menu, choose **Undo**.

The Paste command is undone.

11. From the Edit menu, choose **Redo**.

The Paste command is redone.

> **Elaboration:** When you choose the Undo command, its name changes to Redo on the Edit menu. If you then choose Redo, your document appears as it did before you chose Undo.

Exercise 8

Guided Tour

Copying and pasting text

To copy text to a new location, select text and use the Copy and Paste commands. When you use the Copy command, selected text is not removed when it is copied to the Clipboard.

In this exercise, you'll work with the Copy and Paste commands.

1. In the last row of the table, select the word "Coconut."

2. From the Edit menu, choose **Copy**.

   The word is copied and placed on the Clipboard.

3. In the "Inspiration" row of the table, put the insertion point after the word "Gold."

4. Type a comma and a space.

5. From the Edit menu, choose **Paste**.

   The word "Coconut" is pasted in the document.

Exercise 9

Guided Tour

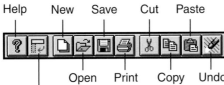

Using the QuickAccess bar

You can use the QuickAccess bar instead of the menu for many frequently used commands.

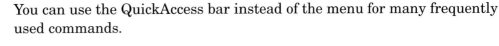

In this exercise, you'll use the QuickAccess bar to cut and paste text.

1. If the QuickAccess bar is not already visible, from the View menu, choose **QuickAccess Bar**.

2. In the "Inspiration" row of the table, select the word "Gold."

MODEL§	ITEM #§	COLORS§
BICYCLES§	§	§
Breeze§	S2024§	Firelight, Sunlight, Twilight, Moonlight, Curry§
Inspiration§	S2081§	Emerald, Sapphire, Opal, Ruby, Gold§
UNICYCLES§	§	§
Cloud9§	U1669§	Firelight, Sunlight, Twilight, Moonlight, Curry§
TANDEMS§	§	§
TradeWinds§	T2816§	Palm, Sand, Coconut, Hibiscus, Curry§
FourWinds§	Q4527§	Palm, Sand, Coconut, Lagoon, Hibiscus, Curry§

3. In the QuickAccess bar, click the **Cut** button.

    The word is cut from the document and placed on the Clipboard.

4. Press the **Backspace** or **Delete** key twice to delete the space and the comma.

5. In the "TradeWinds" row of the table, put the insertion point before the word "Coconut."

MODEL§	ITEM #§	COLORS§
BICYCLES§	§	§
Breeze§	S2024§	Firelight, Sunlight, Twilight, Moonlight, Curry§
Inspiration§	S2081§	Emerald, Sapphire, Opal, Ruby§
UNICYCLES§	§	§
Cloud9§	U1669§	Firelight, Sunlight, Twilight, Moonlight, Curry§
TANDEMS§	§	§
TradeWinds§	T2816§	Palm, Sand, Coconut, Hibiscus, Curry§
FourWinds§	Q4527§	Palm, Sand, Coconut, Lagoon, Hibiscus, Curry§

6. In the QuickAccess bar, click the **Paste** button.

    The word "Gold" is pasted in the document.

MODEL§	ITEM #§	COLORS§
BICYCLES§	§	§
Breeze§	S2024§	Firelight, Sunlight, Twilight, Moonlight, Curry§
Inspiration§	S2081§	Emerald, Sapphire, Opal, Ruby§
UNICYCLES§	§	§
Cloud9§	U1669§	Firelight, Sunlight, Twilight, Moonlight, Curry§
TANDEMS§	§	§
TradeWinds§	T2816§	Palm, Sand, GoldCoconut, Hibiscus, Curry§
FourWinds§	Q4527§	Palm, Sand, Coconut, Lagoon, Hibiscus, Curry§

7. Type a comma and a space.

Exercise 10

Guided Tour

Using the Maker menu (UNIX only)

You can use the Maker menu instead of the menu bar at the top of the document window to quickly select many editing commands. In this exercise, you'll use the Maker menu to copy and paste text.

1. In the "Breeze" row of the table, triple-click to select all the colors.

MODEL§	ITEM #§	COLORS§
BICYCLES:	§	§
Breeze§	S2024§	Firelight, Sunlight, Twilight, Moonlight, Curry§
Inspiration§	S2081§	Emerald, Sapphire, Opal, Ruby§
UNICYCLES:	§	§
Cloud9§	U1669§	Firelight, Sunlight, Twilight, Moonlight, Curry§
TANDEMS:	§	§
TradeWinds§	T2816§	Palm, Sand, Gold, Coconut, Hibiscus, Curry§
FourWinds§	Q4527§	Palm, Sand, Coconut, Lagoon, Hibiscus, Curry§

2. With the mouse pointer over any part of the document window, press your *right* mouse button.

3. The Maker menu appears.

MAKER	
Undo	!eu
Cut	!ex
Copy	!ec
Paste	!ep
Clear	!eb
Copy Paragraph Format	!eyp
Copy Character Format	!eyc
Copy Conditional Text Settings	!eyd
Copy Table Column Width	!eyw
Character Designer...	!ocd
Paragraph Designer...	!opd

4. From the Maker menu, choose **Copy**.

   The selected text is copied and placed on the Clipboard.

5. In the "FourWinds" row of the table, triple-click to select all the colors.

MODEL§	ITEM #§	COLORS§
BICYCLES:	§	§
Breeze§	S2024§	Firelight, Sunlight, Twilight, Moonlight, Curry§
Inspiration§	S2081§	Emerald, Sapphire, Opal, Ruby§
UNICYCLES:	§	§
Cloud9§	U1669§	Firelight, Sunlight, Twilight, Moonlight, Curry§
TANDEMS:	§	§
TradeWinds§	T2816§	Palm, Sand, Gold, Coconut, Hibiscus, Curry§
FourWinds§	Q4527§	Palm, Sand, Coconut, Lagoon, Hibiscus, Curry§

6. Press your right mouse button to make the Maker menu appear, and from the Maker menu, choose **Paste**.

The text on the Clipboard replaces the selected text.

MODEL§	ITEM #§	COLORS§
BICYCLES§	§	§
Breeze§	S2024§	Firelight, Sunlight, Twilight, Moonlight, Curry§
Inspiration§	S2081§	Emerald, Sapphire, Opal, Ruby§
UNICYCLES§	§	§
Cloud9§	U1669§	Firelight, Sunlight, Twilight, Moonlight, Curry§
TANDEMS§	§	§
TradeWinds§	T2816§	Palm, Sand, Gold, Coconut, Hibiscus, Curry§
FourWinds§	Q4527§	Firelight, Sunlight, Twilight, Moonlight, Curry◄
		§

7. Press **Backspace** or **Delete** just once to delete the extra space that appears.

Smart Spaces and Smart Quotes

Smart Spaces is a feature that prevents you from typing more than one consecutive space. If you want consistent spacing between words and sentences, turn on Smart Spaces. If you want to be able to type more than one space in a row, turn off Smart Spaces. When you delete a word while Smart Spaces is turned on, the extra space is deleted.

When Smart Quotes is turned on, FrameMaker uses curved left and right quotation marks (" "). If you prefer to use straight quotation marks (" "), turn off Smart Quotes.

Turning on Smart Spaces or Smart Quotes does not change any extra spaces or straight quotes already typed in the document, only spaces and quotes typed after turning on these features.

Likewise, turning off Smart Spaces or Smart Quotes does not change any text entered before turning off these features.

You can use the Find/Change command or the Spelling Checker to find extra spaces or straight quotation marks and change them. You will learn more about the Find/Change command in Module 5.

Exercise 11

Guided Tour

Using Smart Spaces

In this exercise, you'll work with Smart Spaces in a document. There is an optional exercise to learn more about Smart Quotes.

1. In the first paragraph, at the end of the first sentence, put the insertion point after the period. (The sentence ends with "...to our inventory.")

2. Press the **Space bar** several times.

   Because Smart Spaces is turned on, you cannot add extra spaces.

3. From the Format menu, choose **Document>Text Options.**

   The Text Options dialog box appears with Smart Spaces turned on.

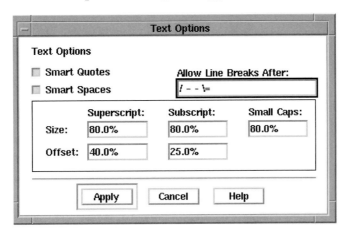

4. Click the **Smart Spaces** checkbox to turn off Smart Spaces.

5. Click **Apply.**

6. With the insertion point still in the same place, press the **Space bar** several times. Because Smart Spaces is turned off, you can add extra spaces.

7. Turn on **Smart Spaces** again:

   a. From the Format menu, choose **Document>Text Options.**

   b. Turn on **Smart Spaces.**

   c. Click **Apply.**

      Notice that turning on Smart Spaces did not remove the extra spaces that already exist in the document.

8. Press **Delete** just once.

   Because Smart Spaces is turned on, all the spaces but one have been deleted.

9. In the first sentence of the first paragraph, double-click the word "glad."

> You'll be glad to know that we added these new models and colors to our inventory. They will be illustrated in our twenty-page color catalog, which you should be receiving by special delivery within the next 10 days.¶

10. Press **Backspace** or **Delete** just once.

Because Smart Spaces is turned on, the word "glad" *and* the extra space are deleted.

> Dear Monsieur Fontaine:¶
>
> You'll be to know that we added these new models and colors to our inventory. They will be illustrated in our twenty-page Spring color catalog, which you should be receiving by special delivery within the next 10 days.¶

11. From the Edit menu, choose **Undo**.

The word "glad" and the extra space reappear.

Exercise 12 Adding special characters

Project

In addition to regular text, you can add special characters to a FrameMaker document. These include widely recognized symbols such as the em dash (—) and the trademark symbol(™).

> **Note:** For a complete list of special characters, see the *Quick Reference* document that came with your FrameMaker software.

In this exercise, you'll insert an em dash in your document.

1. In the second sentence of the last paragraph, put the insertion point after the word "immediately."

> The new bicycles went into production last month and are currently in stock. We can start shipping immediately|via express air freight or ground carrier. Please let me know if you have any questions or need more information. It is our policy to provide the best possible service to our clients.¶

2. Use the following keyboard shortcut to add an em dash after the word:
`Ctrl-q Q`

> **Tip:** A hyphen between keys in a keyboard shortcut means that you should press the keys simultaneously. A space between keys means you should release the first key before pressing the next key. If a letter in a shortcut is uppercase, hold down the Shift key while typing the letter.
>
> For the above shortcut:
>
> `Ctrl-q Q`
> └────┘
> └─── Press these two keys, then release...
>
> `Ctrl-q Q` ── ...and then hold down the Shift key while typing the letter Q
>
> On the Macintosh, you can also insert an em dash by pressing Shift-Option-hyphen.

An em dash appears after the word "immediately."

> The new bicycles went into production last month and are currently in stock. We can start shipping immediately—|via express air freight or ground carrier. Please let me know if you have any questions or need more information. It is our policy to provide the best possible service to our clients.¶

3. Delete the space after the em dash.

4. In the first column of the table, put the insertion point after the word "Cloud9."

5. Use the following keyboard shortcut to add a trademark symbol after the words: `Ctrl-q *`

> Cloud9™|

6. From the File menu, choose **Save** and keep the document open if you plan to complete the optional exercises in this module. Otherwise, close the document.

Optional Exercises

The following exercises enable you to enhance your FrameMaker skills and to explore additional FrameMaker features. Some steps are intentionally brief, so that they require more independent thought on your part.

Exercise 13

Optional

Using Revert to Saved

In this exercise, you make several minor changes to your `bike` document and then use the Revert to Saved command to return the document to its original condition.

1. Cut the Note paragraph from the letter.

2. In the closing of the letter, change the name Christine Martin-Scott to your name.

    An asterisk (*) appears after the page numbers in the status bar to indicate that changes have been made to the document since it was last saved.

1 of 1 *

3. From the File menu, choose **Revert to Saved** and click **OK** in the alert box that appears.

    After a few moments, FrameMaker restores the document to the last version you saved. Notice that the asterisk (*) has disappeared from the status bar.

    > **Tip:** If you think ahead, you can use Revert to Saved as a multiple-level Undo command. Just save your document before you perform steps you might want to undo. Then if necessary, use Revert to Saved to undo the steps since your last save.

Exercise 14

Optional

Adding quotation marks to a document

In this optional exercise, you'll use the Smart Quotes feature introduced earlier in this module to add curved quotation marks to your document.

1. In the last paragraph of the letter, in the last sentence, replace the words "provide the best possible service to our clients" with: `"go that extra mile"` for our customers

2. Save and close the document.

    > **Tip:** To type a straight quotation mark (as in the measurement 8") while Smart Quotes is turned on, press Shift-Control-'. (In Windows, type Esc-Shift-'.) To type a straight apostrophe, press Control-'.

Review

Test your understanding of the concepts and procedures covered in this module by answering the following review questions. You may check your answers with those listed after the questions.

Question 1: What is a quick way to select a word without dragging the mouse? A paragraph?

Question 2: If you want to type multiple spaces and FrameMaker won't allow you to do so, where do you find the option to turn this off, and what is it called?

Question 3: If you undo a change and then realize you should not have done so, what can you do?

Answer 1: Double-click a word to select it. Triple-click a paragraph to select it.

Answer 2: From the Format menu, choose Document>Text Options. This option is called Smart Spaces.

Answer 3: Immediately choose the Redo command from the Edit menu.

For more information

For more information about editing text in FrameMaker, see:

- Chapter 3 of *Using FrameMaker*
- Chapter 3, "Character Sets," in the *Quick Reference*

Finding Text, and Using the Spelling Checker and Thesaurus

Approximate time to complete: 1 hour

Introduction

In this module, you'll become familiar with the FrameMaker Find/Change, Spelling Checker, and Thesaurus features. You can find and change text, formats, and other items in a FrameMaker document. The Thesaurus provides synonyms, antonyms, and related words that you can select from and insert into your document. The Spelling Checker will check typing as well as spelling errors.

Module Objectives

In this module, you'll learn how to

- Use the Find/Change window to search for and change text
- Search through selected text and entire documents
- Use wildcards in a search
- Find and correct spelling errors
- Add words to document and personal dictionaries
- Use the Spelling Checker options and dictionaries
- Look up words in the FrameMaker Thesaurus

FrameMaker Model

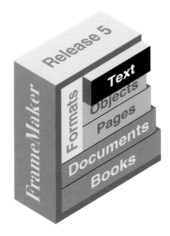

The commands in this module are primarily used to modify *text*. The Spelling Checker and Thesaurus act exclusively on the text in a document, but Find/Change can act on formats and objects as well.

Finding and Changing Text

In FrameMaker, use the Find/Change window to search for and change text. Searching begins at the insertion point and goes forward or backward, depending on which option you select.

By selecting different options, you can narrow your search. Consider the following example.

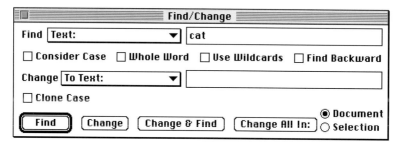

When the word "cat" is entered in the Find text box, the words found depend on which option is turned on.

Option turned on	Finds	Does not find
None	cat, Cat, catalog, duplicate	—
Consider Case	cat, catalog, duplicate	Cat
Whole Word	cat, Cat	catalog, duplicate

You can substitute wildcards for letters to broaden the search.

This	Finds
p?t	pat, pet, pit, pot, put
p*t	All of above plus: pact, peat, part, point, past

To search for a wildcard character (? or * for example), type a backslash before the wildcard character.

This	Finds
where\?	where?

You can also search for any of the following.

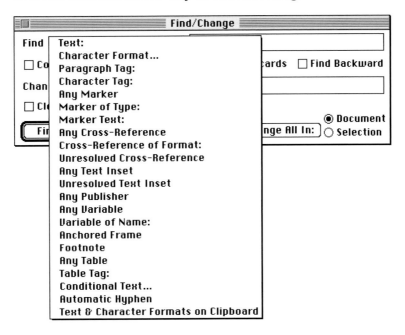

Exercise 1

Guided Tour

Finding text

In this exercise, you'll use the Find/Change window to find text. You will also use many of the options in the Find/Change window to narrow the scope of the search.

1. Use the Save As dialog box to save the bike document (created in the previous module) in the Class directory or folder with the new filename spell:

   a. Open the bike document.

   b. From the File menu, choose **Save As**.

   c. Change to the Class directory or folder if necessary.

   d. In the Save Document text box, type: spell

   e. Click **Save**.

2. If borders are not currently displayed, from View menu, choose **Borders** to turn borders on.

3. Put the insertion point at the beginning of the text frame in the document.

FrameMaker will start the search here.

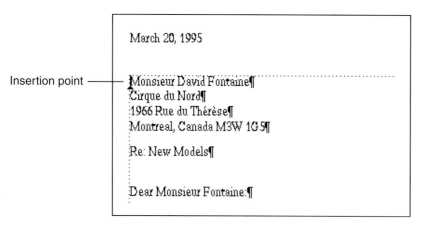

Insertion point ——

March 20, 1995

Monsieur David Fontaine¶
Cirque du Nord¶
1966 Rue du Thérèse¶
Montreal, Canada M3W 1G 5¶

Re: New Models¶

Dear Monsieur Fontaine:¶

4. From the Edit menu, choose **Find/Change**.

   The Find/Change window appears.

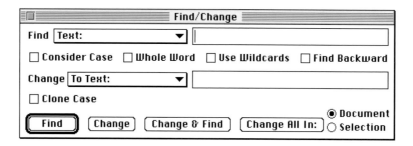

5. Move the window so you can see both the document and the Find/Change window.

6. Find the first occurrence of the word "Twilight" in the letter:

   a. In the Find text box, type: `Twilight`

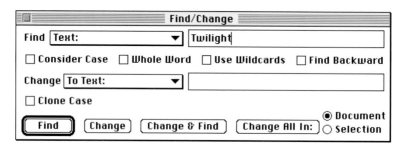

   b. Click **Find**.

The first occurrence of "Twilight" is selected.

7. Click **Find** again.

   The next occurrence of "Twilight" is selected.

   > **Tip:** You can also use the Find Next command on the Edit menu or the keyboard shortcuts to find the next occurrence of "Twilight."

8. Find each occurrence of the word "color:"

   a. In the Find text box, delete "Twilight" and type: color

   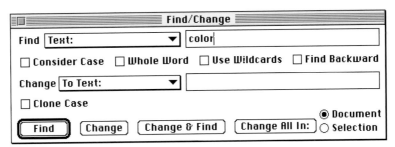

   b. Click **Find**.

   FrameMaker finds "color" as part of the word "colors."

   c. Click **Find** again.

   FrameMaker finds "color" as a whole word.

   d. Click **Find** again.

   FrameMaker finds "color" as part of the word "COLORS," not considering the difference in capitalization.

9. Find "color" as a whole word, not as part of a word:

    a. In the Find/Change window, turn on **Whole Word**.

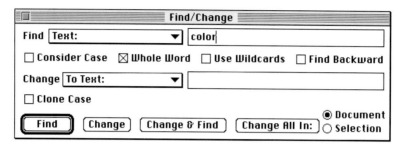

    b. Click **Find**.

    FrameMaker now finds "color" as a whole word, not when it appears as part of "colors" or "COLORS."

10. Find the word "Models:"

    a. In the Find text box, delete "color" and type: Models

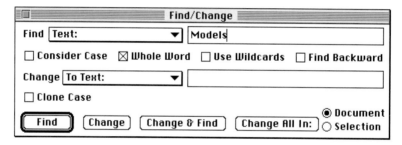

    b. Click **Find**.

    FrameMaker finds the first occurrence of "Models."

    c. Click **Find** again.

    FrameMaker finds the next occurrence of "Models." Notice that FrameMaker finds both uppercase and lowercase versions of the letter "M" in "Models."

11. Find "Models" with only an uppercase "M:"

    a. Turn on **Consider Case**.

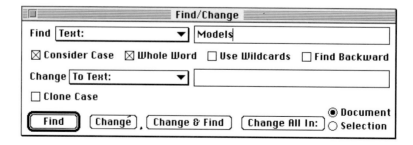

With Consider Case turned on, FrameMaker finds text matching the case entered in the Find text box.

b. Click **Find**.

FrameMaker finds only one occurrence of the word "Models" with an uppercase "M."

Changing found text

The Find/Change window allows you to replace several occurrences of the same word by entering the replacement text in the Change text box. In the following example, the word "cat" will be changed to "dog."

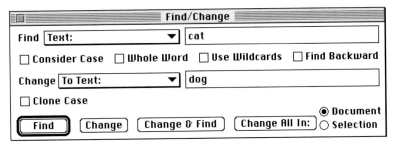

When you change a word without Clone Case turned on, the found word is replaced by the word in the Change text box exactly as it is typed.

This	Is replaced with
cat	dog
Cat	dog
CAT	dog

When you change a word with Clone Case turned on, the replacement is made using the same capitalization as the found word.

This	Is replaced with
cat	dog
Cat	Dog
CAT	DOG

The change pop-up menu gives you alternatives to replacing the found selection with text typed into the text box.

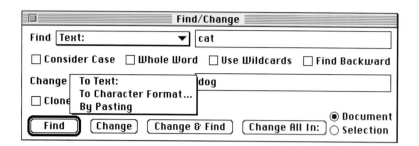

You can replace found text with a character format, or by pasting with any of the following stored on the Clipboard:

- Text
- Graphic
- Paragraph format
- Character format
- Table column width
- Conditional text setting

Pasting with a Paragraph format or Character format applies the format to the found text without changing the text itself. Pasting a table column width or conditional text setting works in a similar fashion.

Exercise 2

Guided Tour

Changing found text

In the following exercise, you'll find text and change it to the text in the change text box.

1. Find "Curry" and replace it with "Cornsilk:"

    a. In the Find text box, delete "Models" and type: Curry

    b. In the Change text box, type: Cornsilk

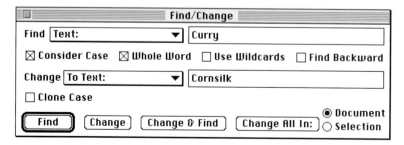

    c. Click **Find**.

The first occurrence of "Curry" is selected.

> Dear Monsieur Fontaine:¶
>
> You'll be glad to know that we added these new models and colors to our inventory. They will be illustrated in our 20 page Spring color catalog, which you should be receiving by special delivery within the next 10 days.¶
>
> | MODEL§ | ITEM #§ | COLORS§ |
> |---|---|---|
> | BICYCLES§ | § | § |
> | Breeze§ | S2024§ | Firelight, Sunlight, Twilight, Moonlight, Curry§ |
> | Inspiration§ | S2081§ | Emerald, Sapphire, Opal, Ruby, Gold, Coconut§ |

d. Click **Change**.

"Curry" is changed to "Cornsilk."

> Dear Monsieur Fontaine:¶
>
> You'll be glad to know that we recently added these new models and colors to our inventory. They will be illustrated in our 20 page Spring color catalog, which you should be receiving by special delivery within the next 10 days.¶
>
> | MODEL§ | ITEM #§ | COLORS§ |
> |---|---|---|
> | BICYCLES§ | § | § |
> | Breeze§ | S2024§ | Firelight, Sunlight, Twilight, Moonlight, Cornsilk§ |
> | Inspiration§ | S2081§ | Emerald, Sapphire, Opal, Ruby, Gold, Coconut§ |

2. Change the next occurrence of "Curry" to "Cornsilk:"

a. Click **Find**.

The next occurrence of "Curry" is selected.

> Dear Monsieur Fontaine:¶
>
> You'll be glad to know that we recently added these new models and colors to our inventory. They will be illustrated in our 20 page Spring color catalog, which you should be receiving by special delivery within the next 10 days.¶
>
> | MODEL§ | ITEM #§ | COLORS§ |
> |---|---|---|
> | BICYCLES§ | § | § |
> | Breeze§ | S2024§ | Firelight, Sunlight, Twilight, Moonlight, Cornsilk§ |
> | Inspiration§ | S2081§ | Emerald, Sapphire, Opal, Ruby, Gold, Coconut§ |
> | UNICYCLES§ | § | § |
> | Cloud9§ | U1669§ | Firelight, Sunlight, Twilight, Moonlight, Curry§ |

b. Click **Change & Find**.

"Curry" is changed to "Cornsilk" and the next occurrence of "Curry" is selected.

3. Use the **Change & Find** command to find the remaining occurrence of "Curry" and change it to "Cornsilk:"

   a. Click **Change & Find**.

   "Curry" is changed to "Cornsilk," and an alert box appears indicating that there isn't another occurrence of "Curry."

Macintosh

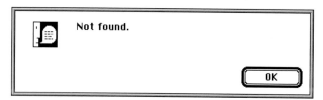

Windows

   b. Click **OK** (in UNIX, click **Continue**).

UNIX

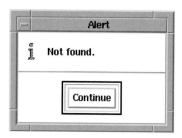

4. Change all occurrences of "Twilight" to "Midnight" using the **Change All In Document** command:

   a. In the Find text box, delete "Curry" and type: Twilight

   b. In the Change text box, delete "Cornsilk" and type: Midnight

c. In the Change All In: area in the lower-right corner of the window, turn on **Document**.

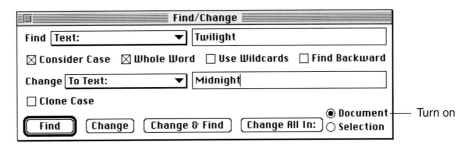

d. Click **Change All In**.

An alert box appears, indicating that you cannot use the Undo command to undo this global change.

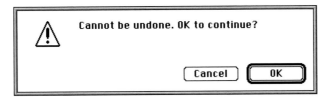

e. Click **OK**.

All occurrences of "Twilight" are changed to "Midnight."

> **Tip:** When a "Cannot be undone" message such as the one above appears, you can use the Revert to Saved command to undo the operation. First cancel out of the dialog box, save the document, and then perform the operation again, this time clicking OK. If you want to undo the operation, from the File menu, choose Revert to Saved.

5. Search backward from the current insertion point for "Sunlight" and replace it with "Daylight:"

a. In the Find text box, delete "Twilight" and type: Sunlight

b. In the Change text box, delete "Midnight" and type: Daylight

c. Turn on **Find Backward**.

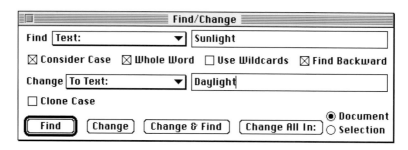

d. Click **Find**.

"Sunlight" is selected. Notice that FrameMaker searches backward from the insertion point.

e. Click **Change & Find**.

"Sunlight" is changed to "Daylight" and the next occurrence of "Sunlight" is selected.

f. Click **Change & Find** again.

"Sunlight" is changed to "Daylight," and an alert box appears indicating that there isn't another occurrence of "Sunlight."

g. Click **OK** (in UNIX, click **Continue**).

6. Find "10" and replace it with "tenn." This is intentionally misspelled. You will fix the misspelling in the next exercise:

a. In the Find text box, delete "Sunlight" and type: 10

b. In the Change text box, delete "Daylight" and type: tenn

c. Turn off **Consider Case**, **Whole Word**, and **Find Backward**.

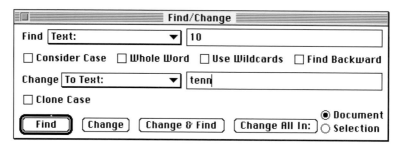

d. Click **Find**.

"10" is selected.

e. Click **Change**.

"10" is changed to "tenn."

Dear Monsieur Fontaine:¶

You'll be glad to know that we added these new models and colors to our inventory. They will be illustrated in our 20 page Spring color catalog, which you should be receiving by special delivery within the next tenn days.∎

7. Find "express air freight" and change it to "CycleTime Express:"

a. In the Find text box, delete "10" and type: express air freight

b. In the Change text box, delete "tenn" and type: CycleTime Express
   Be sure to type "CycleTime" without a space within it.

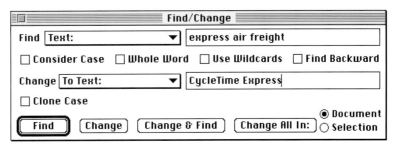

c. Click **Find**.

The text "express air freight" is selected.

d. Click **Change**.

The text "express air freight" is changed to "CycleTime Express.'

The new bicycles went into production last month and are currently in stock. We can start shipping immediately via CycleTime Express or ground carrier. Please let me know if you have any questions or need more information. It is our policy to provide the best possible service to our clients.¶

8. Close the Find/Change window.

9. From the File menu, choose **Save** and keep the document open.

Checking Spelling

The Spelling Checker checks your document for misspellings and common typing mistakes. It will also search for other items, such as repeated words, extra spaces, and straight quotation marks.

To spell-check a document, FrameMaker uses several dictionaries:

- A main dictionary that contains words found in a standard dictionary such as Webster's. You can't add words to or delete words from this dictionary.

- A site dictionary that contains some technical terms as well as words common to your site, such as the company name and product names. The system administrator can add or delete words.

Macintosh	The current site dictionary is displayed in the Site Dictionary pop-up menu.
Windows	The current site dictionary is specified in the maker.ini file.
UNIX	The current site dictionary is located in fminit directory, in site.dict file.

- A personal dictionary that contains words you use often. Regardless of the document you're spell-checking, FrameMaker uses this dictionary. You can add or delete words.

- A document dictionary that contains words specific to a single document. You can add or delete words. This dictionary is part of the document, not a separate file like the other dictionaries.

Exercise 3

Guided Tour

Using the Spelling Checker

In this exercise, you'll spell-check your document and work with the various dictionaries.

1. Put the insertion point at the beginning of the document.

March 20, 1995

Monsieur David Fontaine¶
Cirque du Nord¶
1966 Rue du Thérèse¶
Montreal, Canada M3W 1G 5¶

Re: New Models¶

Dear Monsieur Fontaine:¶

2. From the Edit menu, choose **Spelling Checker**.

   The Spelling Checker window appears.

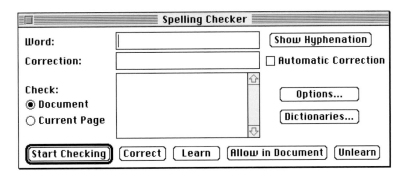

3. In the lower-left corner of the window, click **Start Checking**.

   The first word the Spelling Checker questions is "tenn." A list of possible corrections appears in the Correction scroll list.

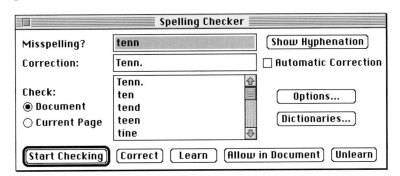

4. In the Correction scroll list, click **ten**.

   The word "ten" appears in the Correction text box.

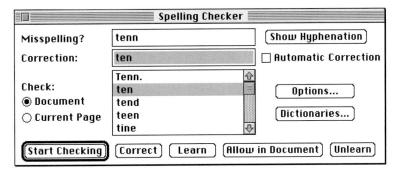

5. Click **Correct**.

   When you click Correct, the text in the Correction text box replaces the selected text in your document. The word "tenn" changes to "ten" and the next questioned word is selected in the document.

   FrameMaker questions the word "Cornsilk." Although "Cornsilk" is not in a FrameMaker dictionary, it *is* spelled correctly.

6. Click **Allow in Document**.

The word "Cornsilk" is added to the document dictionary. When you or anyone else spell-checks this document, FrameMaker will not question the word "Cornsilk."

Next, FrameMaker questions "CycleTime." This is a word you want to use in other documents, so you want to add this word to your personal dictionary.

7. Click **Learn** to add the word "CycleTime" to your personal dictionary.

The word "CycleTime" is added to your personal dictionary. FrameMaker will not question the word "CycleTime" in any document you spell-check.

> **Note:** To remove a word from your document dictionary or personal dictionary, type the word in the text box at the top of the Spelling Checker window and click Unlearn. You can also choose Open from the File menu, open the dictionary as a file, and then add or delete words directly.

Exercise 4

Guided Tour

Viewing Spelling Checker options and dictionary functions

In the following exercise, you'll look at ways to customize the functioning of the Spelling Checker. You will see options for the kinds of problems FrameMaker can find or ignore during the spell-check of a document. You will also view the Dictionary Functions dialog box to see other ways to work with dictionaries.

1. In the Spelling Checker window, click **Options**.

The Spelling Checker Options dialog box appears.

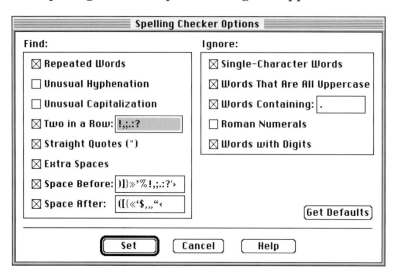

Notice the options you can choose when using the Spelling Checker.

2. Click **Cancel**.

3. In the Spelling Checker window, click **Dictionaries**.

The Dictionary Functions dialog box appears.

Macintosh

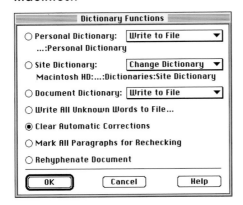

Windows

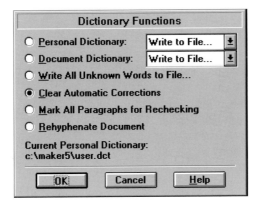

UNIX

Notice the dictionary functions you can use.

> **Tip:** You can use context-sensitive Help to learn more about any dictionary function listed in the dialog box.

4. Click **Cancel**.

5. Close the Spelling Checker window.

Using the FrameMaker Thesaurus

The Thesaurus helps you improve on a word already in a document, or search for the right word to express your idea. When you look up a word, you can replace it with any of the synonyms, related words, or antonyms shown in the Thesaurus window.

There are two ways to look up a word in the Thesaurus.

- Select a word in the document and open the Thesaurus window.

- With nothing selected in the document, type the word in the Thesaurus Look Up dialog box.

Exercise 5

Project

Using the Thesaurus

In the following exercise, you'll look up words in the Thesaurus. You'll also use a word you find in the Thesaurus to replace a word in your document.

1. In the first sentence of the last paragraph, double-click the word "stock" to select it.

> **Note:** Starlight blue is no longer available. It has been replaced by Midnight, which is almost identical.¶
>
> The new bicycles went into production last month and are currently in `stock`. We can start shipping immediately via CycleTime Express or ground carrier. Please let me know if you have any questions or need more information. It is our policy to provide the best possible service to our clients.¶
>
> Sincerely,¶

2. From the Edit menu, choose **Thesaurus**.

The Thesaurus window appears with "stock" in the Word pop-up menu in the upper-left corner. A list of definitions, synonyms, and related words appears in the window.

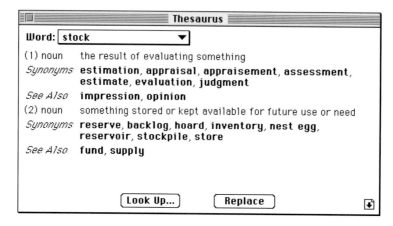

3. In the second list of synonyms, click **reserve**.

   The Thesaurus shows information for the word "reserve."

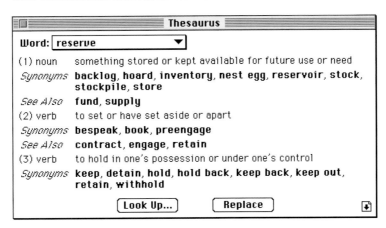

4. In the first See Also list, click **supply** to continue looking for a better word.

   The Thesaurus shows information for the word "supply."

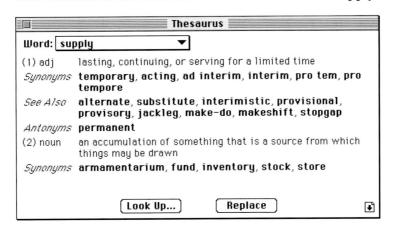

5. Press and hold down the **Word** pop-up menu in the upper-left corner.

   FrameMaker lists up to the last 10 words you looked up, in case you'd like to return to viewing the information for a previous word.

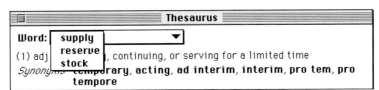

6. From the Word pop-up menu, choose **supply**.

   The Thesaurus again shows information for the word "supply."

7. At the bottom of the Thesaurus window, click **Replace**, and then close the Thesaurus window.

The word "supply" now replaces "stock" in the document.

> The new bicycles went into production last month and are currently in supply. We can start shipping immediately via CycleTime Express or ground carrier. Please let me know if you have any questions or need more information. It is our policy to provide the best possible service to our clients.¶
>
> Sincerely,¶

8. From the File menu, choose **Save** and keep the document open.

Exercise 6

Guided Tour

Looking up a word not in your document

In the following exercise, you'll look up a word in the Thesaurus that is not in your document.

1. With no text selected in your document, from the Edit menu, choose **Thesaurus**.

   The Thesaurus Look Up window appears.

   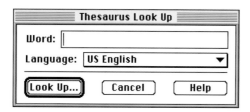

2. In the Word text box, type: clients

   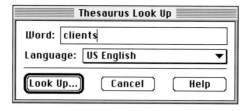

3. Click **Look Up**.

The Thesaurus window opens and shows information for the word "clients."

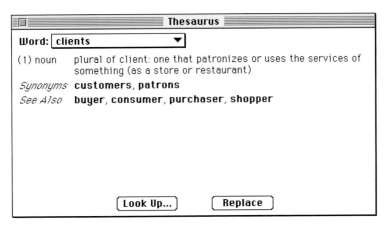

4. Close the Thesaurus window.

5. Save the file and keep the document open if you intend to complete the optional exercise in this module. Otherwise, close the document.

Optional Exercise

The following exercise enables you to enhance your FrameMaker skills and to explore additional FrameMaker features. Some steps are intentionally brief, so that they require more independent thought on your part.

Exercise 7

Optional

Using Find/Change with wildcards

You can use the asterisk (*) wildcard character in the Find/Change window as a substitute for zero or more characters, excluding punctuation.

In this optional exercise, you'll use wildcard characters to define your search parameters to find each item number that begins with S20 and then you'll modify the found item numbers manually.

1. In the Find/Change dialog box, turn on **Use Wildcards**.

2. In the Find text box, type: S20*

3. Click **Find** to find each number that begins with S20. Once you find each number, manually change them so they end with -A. For example, the number S2024 would be changed to S2024-A.

Review   Test your understanding of the concepts and procedures covered in this module by answering the following review questions. You may check your answers with those listed after the questions.

Question 1:   What Find/Change option should you turn on so FrameMaker will find "Catalog" but not "catalog"?

Question 2:   What items can you search for in a FrameMaker document besides text?

Question 3:   When the Spelling Checker questions a word in a document, how do you continue checking without changing that word?

Question 4:   How do you tell the Spelling Checker not to question a word in this document but to continue questioning it in other documents?

Question 5:   Besides spelling errors, the Spelling Checker can also correct repeated words and punctuation, and extra spaces, among other things. Where do you specify this?

Question 6:   How do you use the FrameMaker Thesaurus?

Answer 1:   Turn on Consider Case.

Answer 2:   You can also search for paragraph and character tags, markers, cross-references, and tables. (In the Find/Change window, display the Find pop-up menu to see a complete list.)

Answer 3:   Click Start Checking. The Spelling Checker will bypass the word but will return to the word after cycling through the document.

Answer 4:   Click Allow in Document.

Answer 5:   In the Spelling Checker window, click Options to display the Spelling Checker Options dialog box.

Answer 6:   Select a word and choose Thesaurus from the Edit menu. If you find a different word you would like to use in the Thesaurus window, click the word and click Replace.

For more information

For more information about searching for and replacing text, spell-checking, and using the Thesaurus, see:

Chapters 8 and 9 of *Using FrameMaker*

Using Templates

Approximate time to complete: 1 hour 15 minutes

Introduction

Templates contain formatting instructions to help keep the appearance of a document consistent from one page to another, and from one chapter to another. In this module, you'll become familiar with the FrameMaker templates and sample files and use them to create a document.

Module Objectives

In this module, you'll learn how to

- Preview templates
- Create a new document from a template
- Add and modify text in a template
- Apply paragraph and character formats
- Copy and paste paragraph formats
- Insert page breaks and forced returns
- Insert page numbers
- Import paragraph and character formats from another document

FrameMaker Model

To use a template as the basis for your own documents, you'll operate at several levels of the FrameMaker model. You'll issue commands to the *FrameMaker application*, adding and modifying the *text* of the template, and applying *formats* to text.

Creating Documents Using Templates

A template is any FrameMaker document you use as a foundation for creating or formatting other documents. Templates provide an easy way to ensure consistency from one document to another, and they can save you time because you do not have to start each document from scratch. You can use the standard templates that come with FrameMaker, or use any document you create as a template for creating other documents.

Exercise 1 | **Entering text into a template**

Guided Tour

With some templates much of the text of your document is already entered, so all you have to do is fill in the blanks to personalize the template. You'll work with this type of template in this exercise by using the Fax template to create a fax cover sheet.

1. Open the FrameMaker **Fax** template:

   a. Open the **New** dialog box.

Macintosh	From the File menu, choose **New**.
Windows	From the File menu, choose **New**.
UNIX	In the main FrameMaker window, click **NEW**.

   The New dialog box appears.

   b. At the bottom of the New dialog box, click **Explore Standard Templates**.

   The Standard Templates window appears.

   c. From the list of Business templates on the left, click **Fax**.

   The Standard Templates window displays a list of Fax template features and a miniature view of the Fax template.

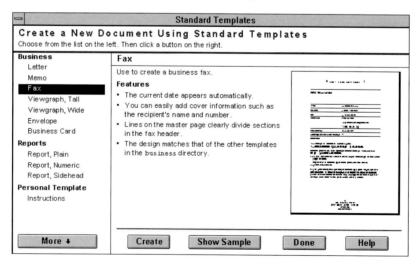

d. At the bottom of the window, click **Create.**

A copy of the Fax template appears. Notice that the current date is automatically inserted for you.

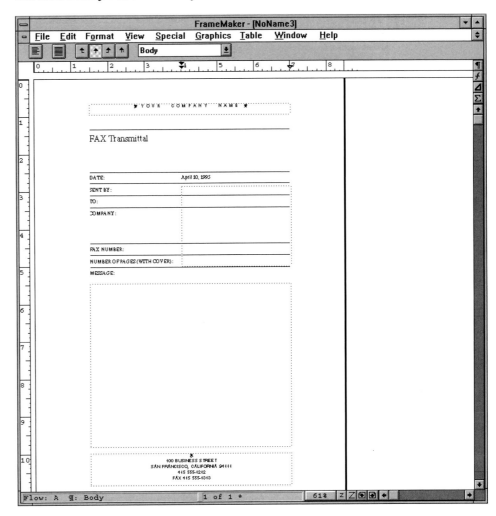

> **Elaboration:** When you click the Create button, a document containing blanks for you to fill in appears. When you click the Show Sample button, a sample that shows the document with the blanks filled appears.

2. Use the Save As dialog box to save the document in the `Class` directory or folder with the new filename `fax`.

3. Change the header to read `Campbell Software, Inc.`:

a. Highlight the words "YOUR COMPANY NAME."

b. Press the **Backspace** or **Delete** key to delete the words.

c. Type: Campbell Software, Inc.

4. Enter your name as the sender of the fax:

a. Put the insertion point in the line starting with "SENT BY:"

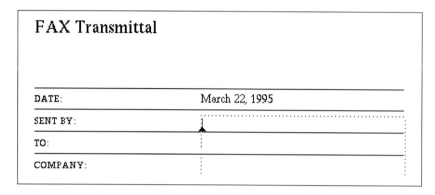

b. Type your name.

c. Press **Return** to go to the next line.

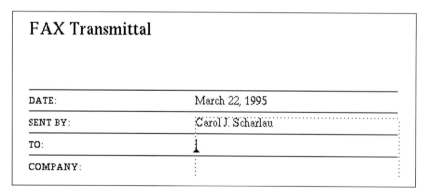

5. Using the same procedure, enter the following information in the template:

Barbara White
ABC Printing, Inc.
1234 First Street
San Jose, CA 95120
734-1234
1

Your fax should now be similar to this:

DATE:	June 26, 1995
SENT BY:	Carol J. Scharlau
TO:	Barbara White
COMPANY:	ABC Printing, Inc.
	1234 First Street
	San Jose, CA 95120
FAX NUMBER:	734-1234
NUMBER OF PAGES (WITH COVER):	1

6. Press **Return** to go to the message area of the template.

7. Type the following message:

```
Hi Barb:
Here's the information we discussed.
Call me with any questions.
```

8. Press **Return** twice, and then type your first name.

The message section should now be similar to this:

MESSAGE:

Hi Barb:

Here's the information we discussed.

Call me with any questions.

Carol

9. Change the street address, city, phone number, and fax number in the footer using the following text:

```
789 Barrett Drive
Sunnyvale, CA 94086
408 123-4586
FAX 408 123-4566
```

Your document should now be similar to this:

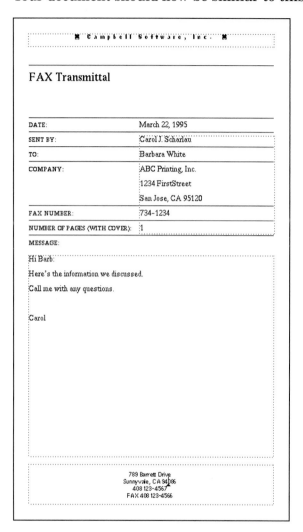

10. From the File menu, choose **Save**, close the document, and close the Standard Templates window.

Paragraph and Character Formats

You use paragraph and character formats to change the appearance of the text in your document, to give your document a more consistent, professional look.

A *paragraph format* is used to determine the appearance of all the text in a paragraph. In FrameMaker, a paragraph is defined as any text that ends with a ¶ symbol. A paragraph format includes layout information, such as indentation, alignment, tab stops, as well as information about the default font for text entered into the paragraph. Some typical names for paragraph tags in the FrameMaker templates are Title, Heading1, Body, and Bulleted.

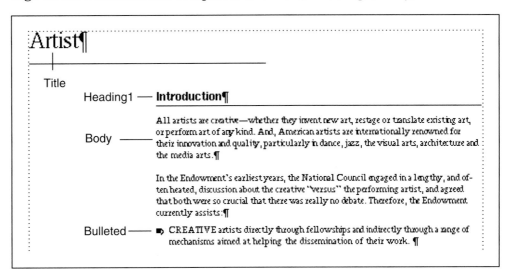

A *character format* is applied to a range of text within a paragraph, and is used to make a portion of a paragraph stand out. A character format includes information about text font family, style, and weight. Some typical names for character formats in the templates are Callout, Glossary, Emphasis, and FirstLetter.

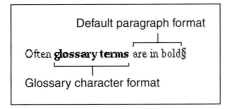

Paragraph formats are stored in a document's Paragraph Catalog, and character formats are stored in the Character Catalog. Each catalog contains formats specific to that document, and each format has its own name, called a *tag*.

Exercise 2

Guided Tour

Applying paragraph formats

In this exercise, you'll create a document from a template, and you'll apply various paragraph formats to the text you type in the document.

1. From the FrameMaker list of standard templates, open a copy of the **Memo** template:

    a. Open the New dialog box.

    b. Click **Explore Standard Templates**.

    c. In the Standard Templates window, in the list of templates, click **Memo**.

    The Standard Templates window displays a list of Memo features and a miniature view of the Memo template.

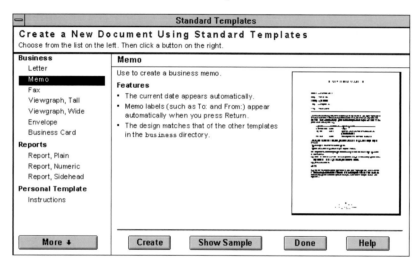

    d. At the bottom of the window, click **Create.**

A copy of the Memo template appears. Notice that the current date is automatically inserted for you and the insertion point is at the top of the document.

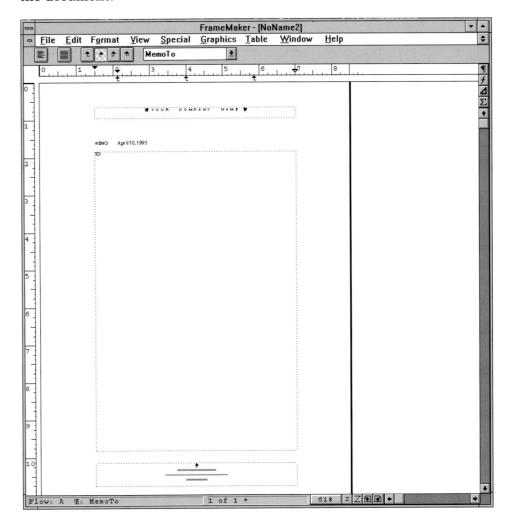

2. Use the Save As dialog box to save the document in the `Class` directory or folder with the new filename `memo`.

3. From the View menu, choose **Text Symbols**.

4. Zoom the document to **120%** and **Fit Window to Page**.

   a. At the bottom of the document, from the Zoom pop-up menu, choose **120%**.

   b. At the bottom of the document, from the Zoom pop-up menu, choose **Fit Window to Page**.

5. Make sure the insertion point appears after the word "To:".

6. In the lower-left corner of the document, look at the Tag area of the status bar.

   Notice the tag for the paragraph containing the insertion point (MemoTo) appears in the Tag area of the status bar.

Tag area ⸺⸺⸺⸺
Paragraph tag ⸺⸺⸺

7. Type: `All Staff`

8. Press **Return**.

   In the Tag area, notice that the new paragraph is automatically tagged MemoFrom.

9. Type: `Community Outreach, HR Dept.`

10. Press **Return**.

    Notice that the new paragraph is automatically tagged MemoSubject.

11. Type: `Holiday Food Drive`

12. Press **Return**.

    Notice that the paragraph is automatically tagged MemoCC.

13. Type: `Contractors, Vendors`

14. Press **Return**.

    Notice that the paragraph is automatically tagged Body.

15. Using the following example, enter the rest of the text into the memo.

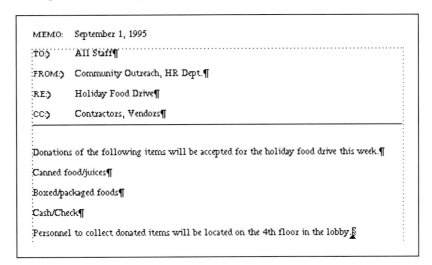

16. In the upper-right corner of the document window, click the **Paragraph Catalog** button.

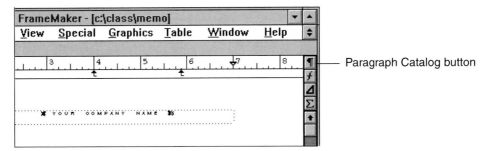

Paragraph Catalog button

The Paragraph Catalog appears. It contains many paragraph formats.

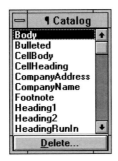

17. Resize the Paragraph Catalog so you can see all the formats:

    a. Move your pointer to the lower-right corner of the window.

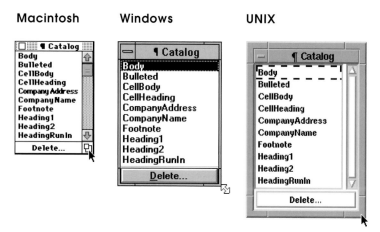

    b. Drag downward to resize the window so you can see all of the formats.

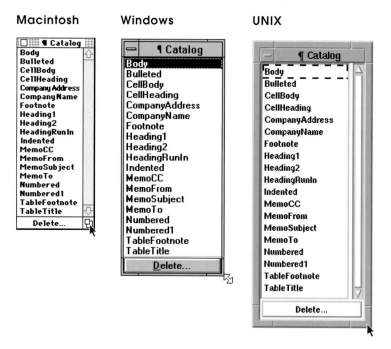

18. Apply the "Bulleted" paragraph format to the first item under the first paragraph:

    a. Put the insertion point in the paragraph that reads "Canned food/juices."

    b. In the Paragraph Catalog, click the word "Bulleted."

    The paragraph format changes to include a bullet.

    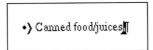

19. Apply the "Bulleted" tag to the two remaining items *at the same time*:

    a. Drag to select the two remaining items so they are both highlighted.

    b. In the Paragraph Catalog, click "Bulleted."

    "Bulleted" is applied to the selected paragraphs.

20. Close the Paragraph Catalog.

Different Ways to Apply Paragraph Formats

There are several ways to apply paragraph formats. No matter which method you use, the result is the same. After clicking in a paragraph or selecting multiple paragraphs, you can:

■ Choose the format from the Paragraph Catalog.

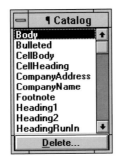

■ Choose the format from the Paragraph Format pop-up menu in the formatting bar at the top of the document.

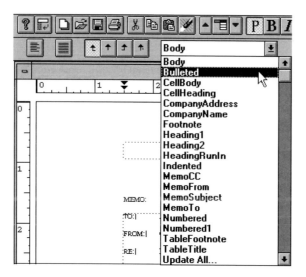

■ Choose the format from the Format>Paragraphs submenu.

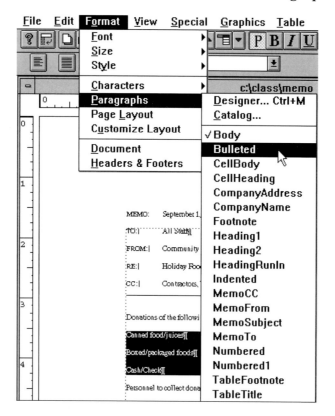

■ Choose the format from the Paragraph Tag pop-up menu in the Paragraph Designer and click Apply.

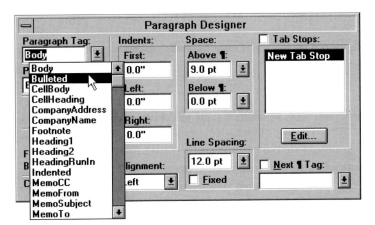

■ . Choose the format using the keyboard (see Optional Exercise 10 on page 6-34).

Exercise 3

Guided Tour

Applying character formats

In the previous exercise, you applied paragraph formats to text. The paragraph format controlled the layout of the entire paragraph, as well as the default font for the text in the paragraph. Character formats allow you to deviate from the default font for selected words in the text. In this exercise, you'll apply the Emphasis character format in the same document.

1. In the upper-right corner of the document window, click the **Character Catalog** button.

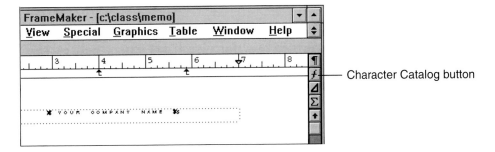

Character Catalog button

The Character Catalog appears.

2. Apply the **Emphasis** character tag to the words "this week:"

   a. In the first sentence, select the words "this week."

   MEMO: September 1, 1995
   TO:)   All Staff¶
   FROM:)   Community Outreach, HR Dept.¶
   RE:)   Holiday Food Drive¶
   CC:)   Contractors, Vendors¶

   Donations of the following items will be accepted for the holiday food drive **this week**.¶
   •} Canned food/juices¶

   b. In the Character Catalog, click **Emphasis**.

   The selected text changes to reflect the Emphasis character format, which is currently set to apply italics.

   MEMO: September 1, 1995
   TO:)   All Staff¶
   FROM:)   Community Outreach, HR Dept.¶
   RE:)   Holiday Food Drive¶
   CC:)   Contractors, Vendors¶

   Donations of the following items will be accepted for the holiday food drive *this week*.¶
   •} Canned food/juices¶

3. In the last paragraph of the memo, apply the Emphasis character tag to the text "4th floor lobby."

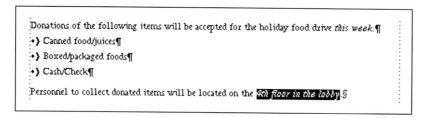

Donations of the following items will be accepted for the holiday food drive *this week*.¶
•} Canned food/juices¶
•} Boxed/packaged foods¶
•} Cash/Check¶
Personnel to collect donated items will be located on the *4th floor in the lobby*§

Tip: To remove a character format, highlight the text and then in the Character Catalog, click Default ¶ Font.

4. Close the Character Catalog.

5. From the File menu, choose **Save** and keep the document open.

Modifying Templates

Exercise 4

Guided Tour

Copying paragraph formats from another template

In this exercise, you'll copy a paragraph format from another document to add to the formats you have in the current document.

When you copy or cut selected text, it is stored on the Clipboard. In FrameMaker, you can also copy a paragraph's *format* to the Clipboard. When you copy a format, you store none of the paragraph's text, only its format, on the Clipboard. You can then use the Paste command to apply the format to one or more paragraphs in the same or another document, affecting only the format of the paragraph into which you are pasting.

When you copy and paste a paragraph format into a document, the format is *not* automatically added to the Paragraph Catalog. You must do this manually.

1. After the last sentence in the memo, using the paragraph tag Body, add the following text:

   ```
   To donate money:
   Make check payable to: DCL Assoc.
   Put check in green envelope
   Give envelope to receptionist
   ```

2. Open the sample book chapter, **resource.doc**:

   You'll copy a paragraph tag from this template into your memo.

   a. Display the FrameMaker list of sample documents.

Macintosh	From the ⟦?⟧ menu, choose **Samples & Clip Art**.
Windows	From the Help menu, choose **Samples & Clip Art**.
UNIX	From the document Help menu, choose **Samples & Clip Art**.

   The FrameMaker samples window appears.

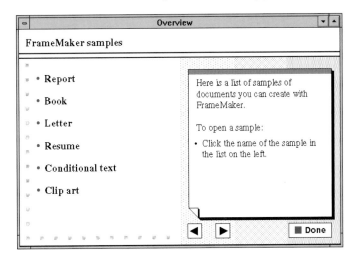

b. Click **Book**.

c. Double-click **resource.doc** to open the document.

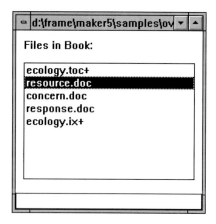

3. From the View menu, choose **Borders** to turn borders on.

4. In the upper-right corner of the document window, click the **Paragraph Catalog** button to open the Paragraph Catalog.

5. Go to page 2 in the document.

6. Put the insertion point in the paragraph that follows with the letter "a."

   This is the paragraph format you'll copy into your memo document.

   > **1.4   Gulf Coast Fisheries**
   >
   > a. Given the wide range of topics chosen by the authors, there is no attempt to synthesize the various ideas into a central theme.

   In the lower-left corner of the document, take a look at the Tag area. The paragraph format of this paragraph is Alpha.

7. From the Edit menu, choose **Copy Special>Paragraph Format**.

   The current paragraph's format (Alpha) is copied to the Clipboard.

8. In resource.doc, from the File menu, choose **Close** to close the document, and then close the book window and the FrameMaker samples window.

9. In your memo document, highlight the last three paragraphs.

10. From the Edit menu, choose **Paste** (*not* Paste Special).

   The Alpha format was applied to all three paragraphs, which now have alpha characters before the text.

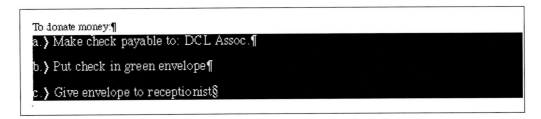

11. From the Format menu, choose **Size>10** to reduce the font size.

12. Notice that the Tag area of the status bar displays the new paragraph tag, Alpha.

   The asterisk (*) indicates an override, meaning that this tag is either different from the Alpha tag in the catalog, or that it is not in the catalog. In this case, the format is not stored in the catalog.

13. From the Paragraph Format pop-up menu on the formatting bar, choose **New Format**.

Macintosh

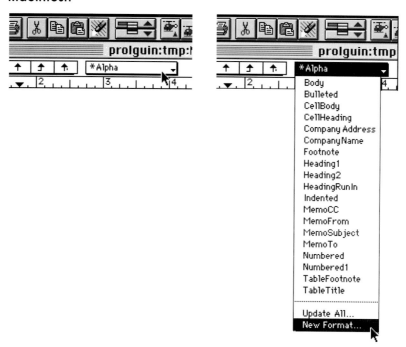

Windows

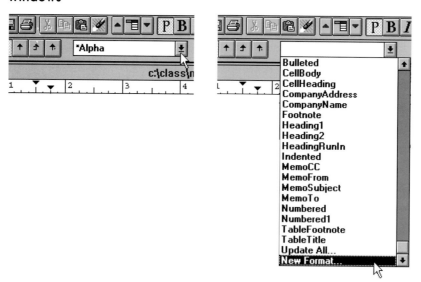

Note: In Windows, the New Format command may be off the bottom of the Paragraph Format pop-up menu. Click the menu's down scroll arrow to make the command visible.

UNIX

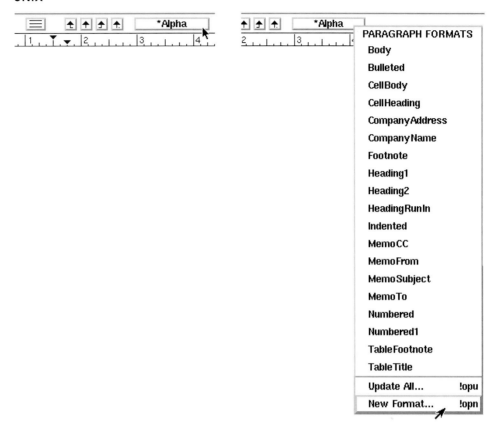

The New Format dialog box appears.

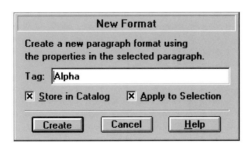

14. Click **Create**.

The paragraph format Alpha is added to the catalog. Because the Alpha tag has been added to the Paragraph Catalog, no overrides exist and the asterisk has disappeared from the status bar.

```
Flow: A   ¶: Alpha                          1 of 1 *
```

15. From the File menu, choose **Save**, close the document, and close the Standard Templates window.

Exercise 5

Tagging text as you type

Guided Tour

In this exercise, you'll create another document using a blank template, and then tag the text with paragraph formats as you type.

1. Create a new **Portrait** document:

   a. Open the New dialog box.

Macintosh	From the File menu, choose **New**.
Windows	From the File menu, choose **New**.
UNIX	In the main FrameMaker window, click **NEW**.

   b. Click **Portrait**.

   The new document appears.

2. Use the Save As dialog box to save the document in the `Class` directory or folder with the new filename `food`.

3. Before typing, apply the Title paragraph format to the first line, then type:
   `Annual Holiday Food Drive`

4. Enter the remaining text shown in the following example. Apply the paragraph tags shown at the left before typing the text.

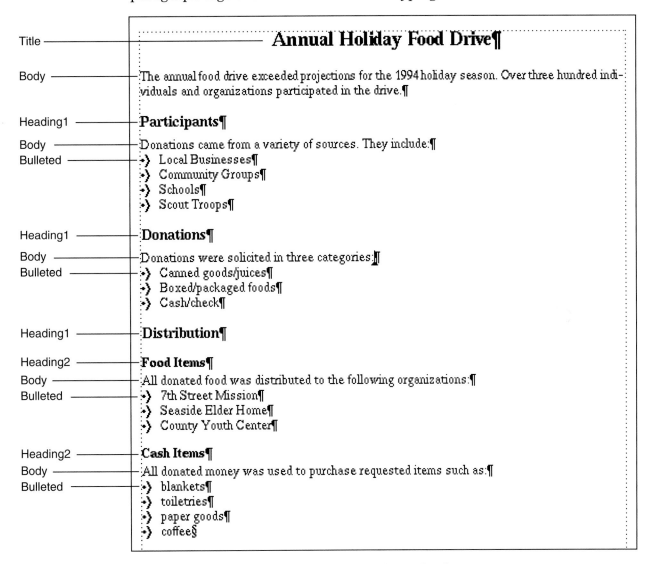

Title — **Annual Holiday Food Drive**¶

Body — The annual food drive exceeded projections for the 1994 holiday season. Over three hundred individuals and organizations participated in the drive.¶

Heading1 — **Participants**¶

Body — Donations came from a variety of sources. They include:¶
Bulleted — •) Local Businesses¶
•) Community Groups¶
•) Schools¶
•) Scout Troops¶

Heading1 — **Donations**¶

Body — Donations were solicited in three categories:¶
Bulleted — •) Canned goods/juices¶
•) Boxed/packaged foods¶
•) Cash/check¶

Heading1 — **Distribution**¶

Heading2 — **Food Items**¶
Body — All donated food was distributed to the following organizations:¶
Bulleted — •) 7th Street Mission¶
•) Seaside Elder Home¶
•) County Youth Center¶

Heading2 — **Cash Items**¶
Body — All donated money was used to purchase requested items such as:¶
Bulleted — •) blankets¶
•) toiletries¶
•) paper goods¶
•) coffee§

5. From the File menu, choose **Save** and keep the document open.

Exercise 6

Guided Tour

Adjusting the document

Some final adjustments are often necessary to complete a document. Such adjustments might include increasing the size of an initial capital letter for emphasis, changing where a line or page breaks, or adding the page number to the footer.

In this exercise, you'll make these adjustments to the document.

1. Change the size of the initial capital letter in the title to 54 points:

   a. Select the letter "A."

   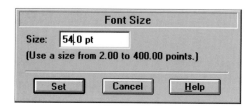

   b. From the Format menu, choose **Size>Other**.

      The Font Size dialog box appears.

   c. In the Size text box, delete 18 and type: 54

   ```
   ┌─────────────────────────────────────┐
   │              Font Size              │
   │  Size:  │54.0 pt        │            │
   │  (Use a size from 2.00 to 400.00 points.) │
   │   ┌─────┐   ┌────────┐   ┌──────┐    │
   │   │ Set │   │ Cancel │   │ Help │    │
   │   └─────┘   └────────┘   └──────┘    │
   └─────────────────────────────────────┘
   ```

   d. Click **Set**.

      The size of the letter "A" is now 54 points.

   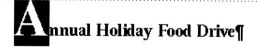

2. Add a forced return after the word "Annual" to make the title appear on two lines:

a. Click after the word "Annual."

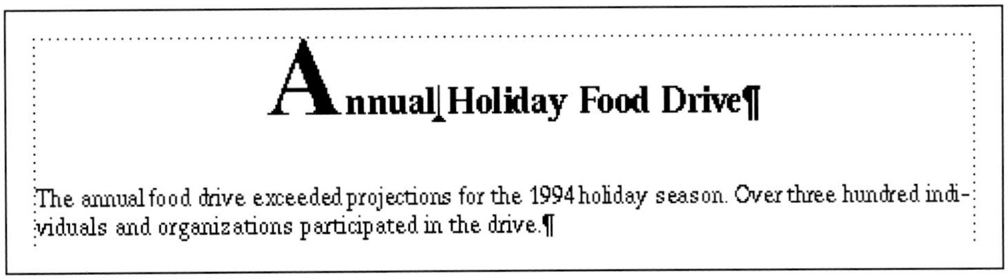

Annual⌷Holiday Food Drive¶

The annual food drive exceeded projections for the 1994 holiday season. Over three hundred individuals and organizations participated in the drive.¶

b. Press **Shift-Return**.

The title is now on two lines. Notice the text symbol (a left angle bracket) for the forced return.

Annual⟨

⌷Holiday Food Drive¶

Note: Although the title now appears on two lines, the second line is still part of the same paragraph as the first line.

3. Move the word "Distribution" to the top of the next page. This will create a second page for this document:

a. Put the insertion point in the paragraph with the word "Distribution."

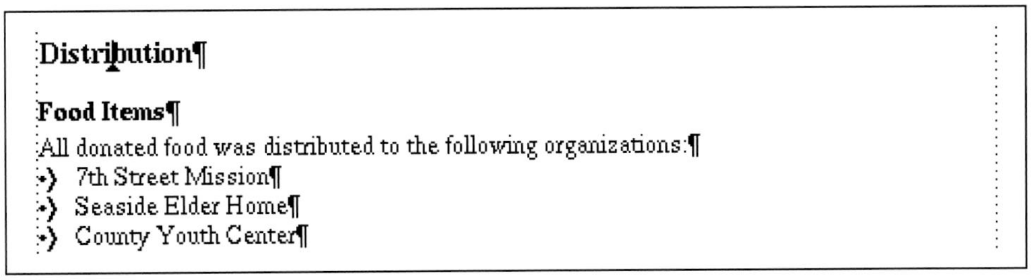

Distribution¶

Food Items¶
All donated food was distributed to the following organizations:¶
•) 7th Street Mission¶
•) Seaside Elder Home¶
•) County Youth Center¶

b. From the Special menu, choose **Page Break**.

The Page Break dialog box appears.

c. Turn on **At Top of Next Available**, and make sure **Page** is chosen from the pop-up menu to the right.

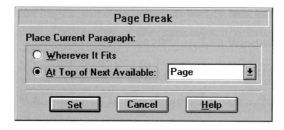

d. Click **Set**.

The paragraph moves to the top of the next page. A second page is created.

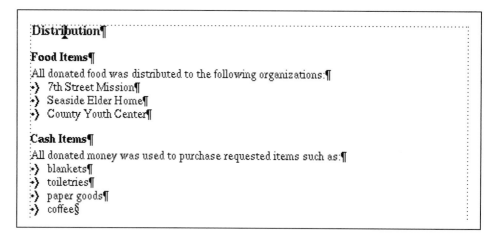

4. Add page numbers to the footer:

a. From the View menu, choose **Master Pages**.

The master page for this body page appears.

> **Elaboration:** The master page contains no text because it provides only the background for the page—in this case, text frames to contain a header, the body of the document, and a footer. These same elements appear on every page of the document. When you enter a page number on the master page, it will appear in the same position on every body page of the document.

b. Put the insertion point in the footer text frame.

Insertion point

c. Press **Tab** to move the insertion point to the center of the footer.

Insertion point —————

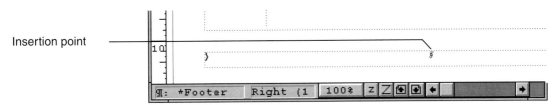

d. From the Format menu, choose **Headers & Footers>Insert Page #**.

The page number symbol (#) appears.

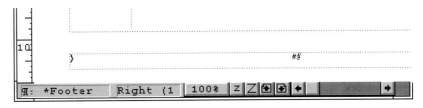

e. From the View menu, choose **Body Pages**, and look at both body pages.

The page number appears on both body pages.

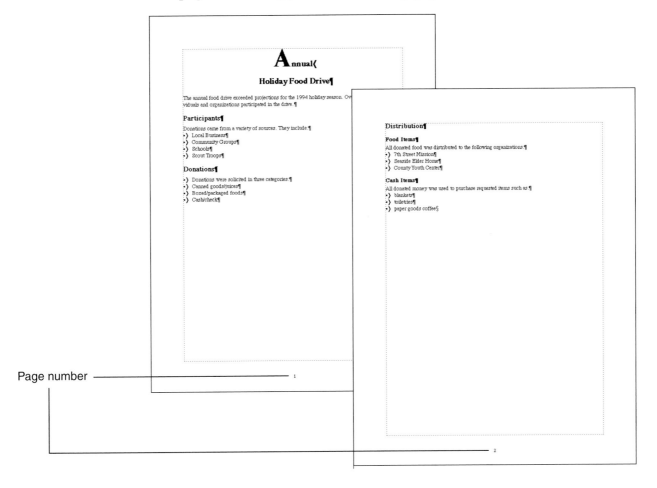

Page number —————

5. From the File menu, choose **Save** and keep the document open.

> **Elaboration:** When entered as described above, the # symbol represents the page number variable and will be replaced by the correct page number when viewing the Body Pages. Although the # symbol entered from the keyboard looks the same as the page number symbol, it will not be replaced by the page number.

Exercise 7

Guided Tour

Adding another page at the end of the document

In this exercise, you'll add another page at the end of the document by adding another paragraph and forcing a page break.

1. Put the insertion point at the end of the document, to the right of the word "coffee."

```
Cash Items¶
All donated money was used to purchase requested items such as:¶
•}  blankets¶
•}  toiletries¶
•}  paper goods¶
•}  coffee§
```

2. Press **Return**.

The new empty paragraph is using the same paragraph format as the paragraph "coffee" is using.

```
Cash Items¶
All donated money was used to purchase requested items such as:¶
•}  blankets¶
•}  toiletries¶
•}  paper goods¶
•}  coffee¶
•}  §
```

3. In the Paragraph Catalog, click **Heading1** to apply that format to the blank line before typing.

4. Type: `Plans for 1995 Food Drive`

Do not press Return.

> Cash Items¶
> All donated money was used to purchase requested items such as:¶
> •} blankets¶
> •} toiletries¶
> •} paper goods¶
> •} coffee¶
>
> **Plans for 1995 Food Drive**§

5. Move "Plans for 1995 Food Drive" to the top of the next page. This will create a third page for this document:

   a. From the Special menu, choose **Page Break**.

   b. Turn on **At Top of Next Available**, and make sure **Page** is chosen from the pop-up menu to the right.

   c. Click **Set**.

      The paragraph moves to the top of the next page. A third page is created for continuing your text.

> **Plans for 1995 Food Drive**§

6. From the File menu, choose **Save** and keep the document open.

Exercise 8

Guided Tour

Importing paragraph and character formats from another template

When you import paragraph formats from another document, FrameMaker merges the imported formats with the formats in the current document. If both documents contain a paragraph format with exactly the same tag, the imported format replaces the format with the same tag in the current document, and any text using the format is reformatted automatically.

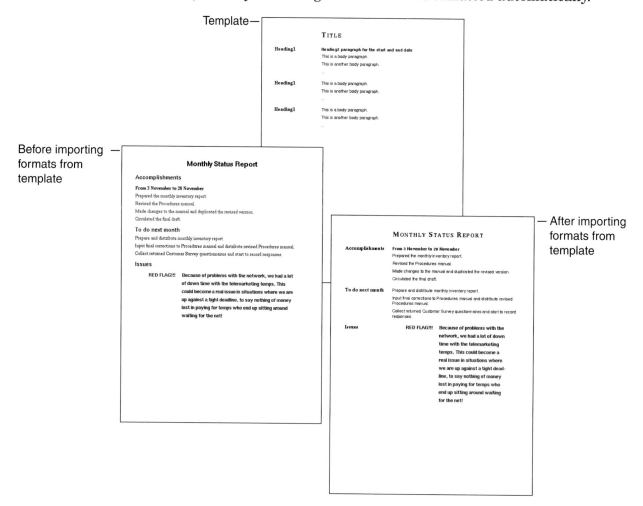

Template—

Before importing formats from template —

— After importing formats from template

Any paragraph tags unique to either document—the current document or the document from which you are importing—now appear in the Paragraph Catalog of the current document. (Importing character formats works the same way.)

In this exercise, you'll import formats into your document from a FrameMaker template.

1. Open the **Report, Numeric** template:

   a. From the File menu, choose **New.**

   b. At the bottom of the New dialog box, click **Explore Standard Templates.**

   c. In the list of report templates on the left, click **Report, Numeric.**

   d. At the bottom of the Standard Templates window, click **Show Sample.**

      The Numeric Report template appears, showing some sample text.

2. Use the Save As dialog box to save this document in the Class directory or folder with the new filename numrpt.

3. From the View menu, choose **Document Windows>food** (in Windows, from the Window menu, choose **food**) to bring the food document to the front.

4. From the File menu, choose **Import>Formats**.

   The Import Formats dialog box appears.

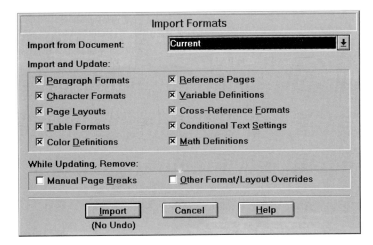

5. From the Import from Document pop-up menu, choose **numrpt**.

   This is the file from which you are importing paragraph and character formats.

6. In the Import and Update area, turn *off everything except* **Paragraph Formats** and **Character Formats**.

7. In the While Updating, Remove area, *turn on* **Manual Page Breaks** and make sure **Other Format/Layout Overrides** is *turned off.*

   The Import Formats dialog box should look like this:

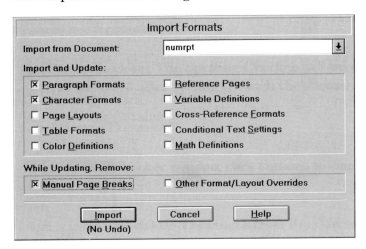

8. Click **Import**.

The text in your document is reformatted, based on the imported formats, and any additional formats are added to the Paragraph Catalog and Character Catalog. Because you removed manual page breaks when importing, "Distribution" and "Plans for 1995 Food Drive" no longer break to the tops of page 2 and page 3, respectively.

9. Page through your document to see the changes.

> **Note:** The name of the imported format must exactly match the name of the format in your document for reformatting to take place. For example, the format named "Body" in the template will replace "Body" in your document, but not "body" or "BODY".

10. From the File menu, choose **Save** and keep the document open if you intend to complete the optional exercises in this module. Otherwise, close all open documents.

Optional Exercises

The following exercises enable you to enhance your FrameMaker skills and to explore additional FrameMaker features. Some steps are intentionally brief, so that they require more independent thought on your part.

Exercise 9

Optional

Using report templates

Using the skills you learned in this module, use the report templates to give your food drive document a new look. There are three report templates from which to choose. The Plain Report is shown in the following example. Be sure to read the hints before you begin.

> **Report on the 1994**
> **Holiday Food Drive**
>
> **Submitted by Carol J. Scharlau**
>
> The annual food drive exceeded projections for the 1994 holiday season. Over three hundred individuals and organizations participated in the drive.
>
> **1.0 Participants**
>
> Donations came from a variety of sources. They include:
>
> - Local Businesses
> - Community Groups
> - Schools
> - Scout Troops
>
> **2.0 Donations**
>
> - Canned goods/juices
> - Boxed/packaged foods
> - Cash/check
>
> 1

Hints

- Save the "food" file with a new filename and work with that file rather than the original.

- Open the desired report template using the New dialog box.

- Save the report template with the new filename: `plain.rpt`

- Click on the lines of text in the report template to determine their formats so you will know what formats to apply to the corresponding paragraphs in the "food" file.

- After importing formats from `plain.rpt`, type the additional text at the beginning of your document and apply the appropriate paragraph formats.

Exercise 10

Optional

Applying paragraph formats from the keyboard

In this optional exercise, you'll apply paragraph formats from the keyboard.

1. Use the Save As window to save the report with the name `food3`.

2. Select all four bulleted paragraphs below the heading, "1.0 Participants."

3. Press the key combination from the following list.

Macintosh	Control-9 or Command-Space bar
Windows	Control-9
UNIX	Control-9 or F9

The Tag area of the status bar becomes active.

Macintosh   **Windows**   **UNIX**

4. Type the letter "N" to display the Numbered tag in the status bar.

> **Elaboration:** You only need to type enough letters of the paragraph format to identify the paragraph format uniquely. You can also press the down arrow key to scroll through the list of paragraph formats.

5. Press **Return** to apply the tag.

The highlighted paragraphs are now numbered.

Exercise 11   **Using Copy Special and Find/Change to change paragraph formats**

In this optional exercise, you'll use Copy Special and Find/Change to change all the bulleted lists to numbered lists.

1. Put the insertion point in one of the paragraphs of the numbered list.

2. From the Edit menu, choose **Copy Special>Paragraph Format**.

3. In the Find/Change window, find all occurrences of the paragraph tag named Bullet and change them by pasting.

4. Apply the Numbered1 paragraph format to the first paragraph of the second numbered list.

    The Numbered1 paragraph format is pasted and the first item in the list is now numbered 1.

5. Copy the Numbered1 paragraph format and paste it in the first paragraph of the remaining numbered lists.

Review   Test your understanding of the concepts and procedures covered in this module by answering the following review questions. You may check your answers with those listed after the questions.

Question 1:   How do you create a new document from a FrameMaker template?

Question 2:   How do you insert a page break in FrameMaker?

Question 3:   What are five ways to apply a paragraph format to text?

Question 4:   When a paragraph format named Heading1 is imported into a second document with a Heading1 format, what happens to the format in the second document?

Answer 1:   Open the template, save it with a new name, delete any sample text, and add text of your own.

Answer 2:   Put the insertion point in the paragraph you want to move to the next page. From the Special menu, choose Page Break. In the dialog box, turn on At Top of Next Available and choose Page from the pop-up menu.

Answer 3:   The five ways to apply a paragraph format to text are:

   a. Click a format in the Paragraph Catalog.

   b. Choose the format from the Format>Paragraphs submenu.

   c. Choose the format from the Paragraph Tag pop-up menu in the Paragraph Designer and click Apply.

   d. With the formatting bar displayed, choose the format from the ParagraphFormat pop-up menu.

   e. Press the appropriate keys to activate the Tag area of the status bar, type enough letters to uniquely identify the format (or press the up or down arrow keys to scroll through the formats), then press Return.

Answer 4:   The Heading1 format in the second document is reformatted to take on the characteristics of the imported Heading1 format.

For more information

For more information about creating documents from FrameMaker templates, see:

- Chapter 2 of *Using FrameMaker*

For more information about formatting text and applying formats, see:

- Chapters 4 and 5 of *Using FrameMaker*

For more information about importing formats from another document, see:

- Chapter 21 of *Using FrameMaker*

PART II

....

Character and

Paragraph Formats

Character Font Properties

Approximate time to complete: 45 minutes

Introduction

In this module, you'll become familiar with untagged font properties and character formats. A character format is a collection of properties that is stored in the Character Catalog under a name, or tag. Character formats allow for font consistency and manageability throughout a document, while untagged font properties allow you to make informal font changes to selected text.

Module Objectives

In this module, you'll learn how to

- Use untagged properties from the Format menu

- Compare untagged font properties to character formats

- Apply character formats in different ways

- Modify character formats

- Create character formats and store them in the Character Catalog

- Use the As Is setting in creating character formats

- Delete character formats from the Character Catalog

- Reapply a paragraph's default font

FrameMaker Model

FrameMaker *formats* help give documents a consistent appearance. There are formats for text, objects, and even entire pages. In this module, you'll work with character formats, which you'll apply to text.

Untagged Font Properties

In the last module of the previous volume, you applied paragraph and character formats to text. The paragraph format controlled the layout of the paragraph, as well as the default font for the text in the paragraph. The character format allowed you to deviate from the default font for selected words in the text.

In long, formal documents, such as books and manuals, it's best to deviate from the default paragraph font by tagging text with a character format, which helps you to apply fonts consistently throughout your document. However, for shorter, less formal documents, such as a fax or a memo, it's often easier to apply *untagged* font properties to change the appearance of text.

For example, when you want to emphasize a word in a memo by making it bold, instead of creating a new character tag for that font property and applying it, you can simply use the Format menu or the QuickAccess bar to select the desired font style. But untagged font properties should be used sparingly, since they cannot be globally modified as can fonts changed using character formats.

Exercise 1

Guided Tour

Applying untagged font properties

In this exercise, you'll become familiar with applying untagged font properties from the Format menu. Later in this module, you'll be able to compare this method of using untagged font properties with using character formats to deviate from the paragraph's default font for selected words.

1. From the FrameMaker list of sample documents, open the book chapter **resource.doc**:

   a. Display the FrameMaker list of sample documents.

Macintosh	From the **?** menu, choose **Samples & Clip Art**.
Windows	From the Help menu, choose **Samples & Clip Art**.
UNIX	From a document Help menu, choose **Samples & Clip Art**. (If there are no open documents, click **NEW**, then **Portrait**, first.)

   The FrameMaker samples window appears.

   b. Click **Book**.

   c. Double-click **resource.doc** to open the file.

2. Use the Save As dialog box to save the document in the `Class` directory or folder with the new filename `fonts`:

    a. From the File menu, choose **Save As**.

    b. Change to the `Class` directory or folder if necessary.

    c. In the Save Document text box, type: `fonts`

    d. Click **Save**.

3. From the View menu, turn on **Borders**.

4. Go to **page 2** in the document.

    The top of the page looks like this:

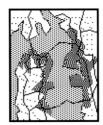

CHAPTER **1**   A Natural Source of Products

1.2   North American Wetlands

The symposium on Impact Assessment Study, was organized by the President's Council on Environmental Quality (CEQ). It was hosted by the Ecological Society American Institute of

b. The Impact Assessment Study, and the Michigan Environmental Review Board. Cooper uses his experience as Chairman of this Review Board in providing his views on environmental assessment.

5. Select the acronym "CEQ" on the third line of the first paragraph.

1.2   North American Wetlands

The symposium on Impact Assessment Study, was organized by the President's Council on Environmental Quality (CEQ). It was hosted by

6. From the Format menu, choose **Font>Courier**.

    The font changes from Times to Courier, and the text remains selected.

7. From the Format menu, choose **Size>14**.

    The size of the text increases to 14.

8. Make the same changes to the second occurrence of the acronym "CEQ" in the middle of the last paragraph in the second column.

> Environmental Policy Act. Smithy and Flame of **CEQ** review this history, pointing out both past progress and future potential. Several precedents were set in the hasty catchup phase for projects initiated but not completed prior to passage of the act: (a) the EIS was used to justify a decision already made, (b) alternatives were treated as

9. Apply the italic untagged font property to the words "importance" and "difficulty" in the two paragraphs immediately following the heading "1.5 Canadian Tundra:"

   a. At the beginning of the first paragraph following the heading "1.5 Canadian Tundra," double-click to select the word "importance."

   > **1.5   Canadian Tundra**
   > The **importance** and value of this process, as well

   b. From the Format menu, choose **Style>Italic**.

   c. At the beginning of the next paragraph, double-click to select the word "difficulty."

   > **1.5   Canadian Tundra**
   > The *importance* and value of this process, as well as its points of weakness, are well-known to the nation's ecologists—a sizable number of whom have participated in it. The symposium permitted ecologists to voice their views on improving the process.
   >
   > The **difficulty** to these questions (as well as their scope) is intimidating on both conceptual and practical grounds.

d. From the Format menu, choose **Style>Italic**.

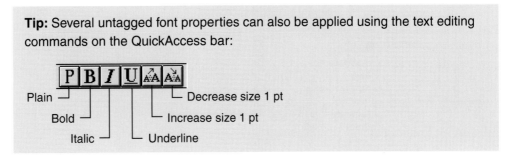

Tip: Several untagged font properties can also be applied using the text editing commands on the QuickAccess bar:

Plain — Decrease size 1 pt

Bold — Increase size 1 pt

Italic — Underline

Character Formats

You have seen that untagged font properties must be applied from the Format menu to selected text *individually*—first the font family, then the size, and then perhaps a style such as bold or italic. A character format is a *combination* of one or more font properties that has been assigned a name (character tag), such as *Emphasis*, and appears in the Character Catalog. Using character formats, rather than applying untagged font properties directly, makes it easier to apply special formatting quickly and consistently. For example, suppose that in your document, text that gives instructions should always appear in Courier font. Instead of using the Format menu to change the font in each instance, you can create a character format, and apply it from the Character Catalog with a single click.

Character formats make global updating easier as well. Suppose after you've already composed the workbook, you decide that text typed by the user should be in Courier font *and* bold. Instead of having to locate each instance of Courier font and change it to bold, as you would if you had used untagged font properties, you can simply update the definition of the character format.

Exercise 2

Guided Tour

Applying character formats

In this exercise, you'll apply character formats, and see how applying a character format differs from applying untagged font properties.

1. In the upper-right corner of the document window, click the **Character Catalog** button.

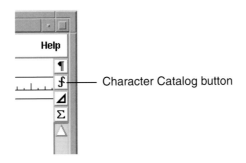

Character Catalog button

The Character Catalog appears.

> **Note:** You can also open the Character Catalog by choosing Characters>Catalog from the Format menu.

2. Select the text "new trends" in the seventh line of the first paragraph on page 2.

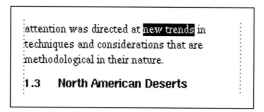

3. Look in the Tag area of the status bar.

   The paragraph format for this paragraph is Body.

4. In the Character Catalog, click **Emphasis**.

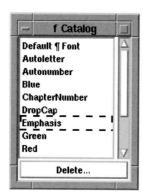

The Emphasis character format is applied to the selected text. Notice that the text is now in italics.

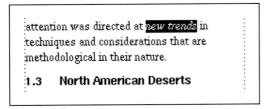

5. Look in the Tag area of the status bar.

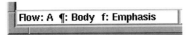

The Emphasis character format appears next to the Body paragraph format. Emphasis is·a deviation from the font properties of the Body paragraph.

6. Apply the Emphasis format to the words "no attempt" in the second line of the paragraph under the heading "1.4 Gulf Coast Fisheries."

> **1.4   Gulf Coast Fisheries**
>
> a.   Given the wide range of topics chosen by the authors, there is *no attempt* to synthesize the various ideas into a central theme.

7. Apply the Emphasis format to "Several precedents" in the last paragraph under the heading "1.5 Canadian Tundra."

> At a federal level many of the difficulties of the EIS process discussed by the authors of this symposium are a historical outgrowth of the initial implementation of the National Environmental Policy Act. Smithy and Flame of CEQ review this history, pointing out both past progress and future potential. *Several precedents* were set in the hasty catchup phase for projects initiated but not completed prior to passage of the act: (a) the EIS was used to justify a decision already made, (b) alternatives were treated as

The Emphasis format has now been applied to text in three separate areas of your document.

> **Tip:** If the Character Designer is open, that window can also be used to apply a character format to selected text. Just choose the desired character tag from the Character Tag pop-up menu, and click Apply. You'll learn more about the Character Designer in the following exercise.

Exercise 3

Guided Tour

Modifying character formats

In this exercise, you'll change the weight property of the Emphasis character format to have a weight of bold.

1. Make sure the words "Several precedents" are still highlighted.

2. From the Format menu, choose **Characters>Designer**.

   The Character Designer appears.

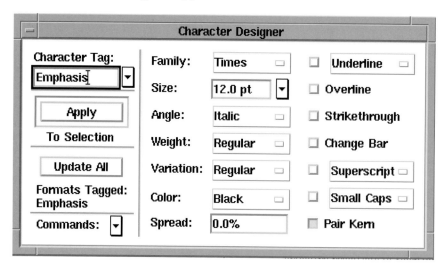

3. Use the Character Tag pop-up menu to see the list of character formats in the document. This is the same list that appears in the Character Catalog.

Character Tag pop-up menu

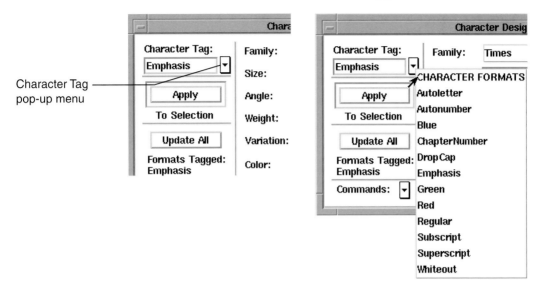

4. Globally update the **Emphasis** format to include the weight **Bold**:

   a. Make sure Emphasis appears in the Character Tag text box. If it doesn't, from the Character Tag pop-up menu, choose **Emphasis**.

   b. In the Character Designer, from the Weight pop-up menu, choose **Bold**.

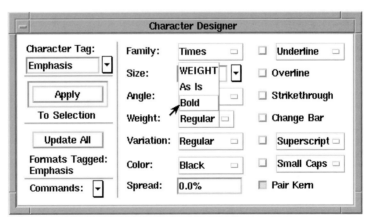

c. Click **Update All**.

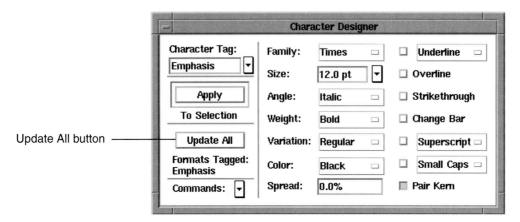

Update All button —————— Update All

The Emphasis format in the Character Catalog, and all instances where Emphasis was applied throughout the document, have been updated. Since the Character Catalog has also been updated, any text to which you apply the Emphasis format from now on will be bold as well as italic.

Notice that the text to which the untagged font property of italic was applied (the words "importance" and "difficulty" in the paragraphs above "Several precedents") did *not* change.

Exercise 4   Creating character formats

Guided Tour

In the previous exercise, you modified an existing character format. In this exercise, you'll create a new format and then apply it within the document.

1. At the top of page 2, in the left column, select the words "Impact Assessment Study."

You are now going to create a new character format specifically for the name Impact Assessment Study.

Notice the paragraph tag in the status bar is identified as Body.

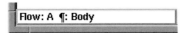

2. Create a new character format called **Name**:

   a. If the Character Designer isn't open, choose **Format>Characters>Designer**.

   b. From the Commands pop-up menu in the lower-left corner of the Character Designer window, choose **New Format**.

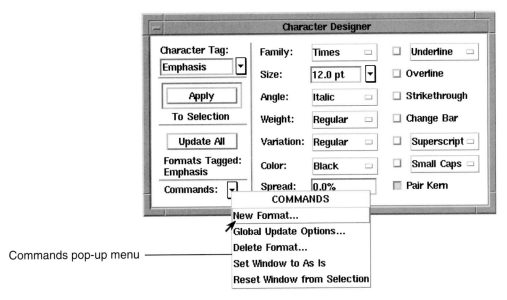

Commands pop-up menu

The New Format dialog box appears.

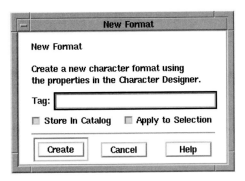

   c. In the Tag text box, type: Name

   d. Make sure **Store in Catalog** and **Apply to Selection** are turned on.

e. Click **Create**.

The new tag appears in the Character Catalog and in the
Character Designer.

> **Note:** On the Macintosh, you may need to click in the document window to
> activate it, and click inside the paragraph to make the tag name appear in the
> Character Designer.

3. Make the following changes to the Name format in the Character Designer:

   ■ Family: **Helvetica**

   ■ Size: **10** (type it in the Size text box or choose from the Size pop-up menu)

   ■ **Small Caps** (located in the lower-right corner of the window)

4. Click **Update All**.

   The new character format properties are applied to the selected text, and to
   the Name format in the Character Catalog.

5. Using the Character Catalog, apply the **Name** character format to the text
   "Impact Assessment Study" in the first bulleted paragraph near the
   bottom of the first column, and then in the first paragraph at the top of
   the second column.

Exercise 5

Guided Tour

Creating character formats using As Is

In this exercise, you'll create two character formats that include the strikethrough font property, which puts a line through text. Editors use this to indicate the part of a document that has been deleted. To demonstrate the use of the As Is setting, the first format you create will not use As Is, but the second will.

1. Select the word "Gulf" in the heading "Gulf Coast Fisheries."

> 1.4   **Gulf Coast Fisheries**
> a. Given the wide range of topics chosen by the

2. Create a new character format and name it **Edit**:

   a. From the Commands pop-up menu in the Character Designer, choose **New Format**.

   b. In the Character Tag text box, type: `Edit`

   c. Make sure **Store in Catalog** and **Apply to Selection** are turned on.

   d. Click **Create**.

   The Edit character format is added to the catalog and applied to the selected text. But it has the same font properties as the text selection before the format was applied.

3. In the Character Designer, turn on **Strikethrough**.

   Notice that bold is still the specified weight, because the default paragraph font of the heading is bold.

4. Click **Update All**.

   The Edit character format is updated so that the strikethrough line appears in the selected text.

> 1.4   **Gulf Coast Fisheries**
> a. Given the wide range of topics chosen by the

The Edit character format as it is currently defined will produce undesirable results if it is used on body text in the document. The following steps demonstrate the problem.

5. Select the heading and the body paragraph beneath "North American Wetlands" and apply the **Edit** character format from the Character Catalog:

   a. Select the text.

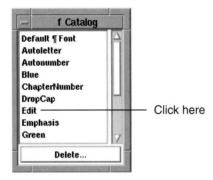

   b. In the Character Catalog, click **Edit**.

                                                 — Click here

Notice all the selected strikethrough text has become bold.

Elaboration: In addition to the strikethrough property, the Edit character format also changes other font properties, which makes the selected text appear the same as the original heading font on which Edit was based. To create a character format that changes only the strikethrough property without changing any other properties, As Is must be used.

6. From the Edit menu, choose **Undo**.

   The bold and strikethrough formatting are removed and the text is again displayed in the default font for the heading and body paragraphs.

   ## The As Is property

   From the previous steps, it is clear that we want a character format that will apply strikethrough to text, but not change any other text font properties. The As Is setting is used for this purpose. When the format is applied to selected text, those font properties left As Is will remain as they were prior to the application of the character format.

7. Make sure the heading and the body paragraph beneath "North American Wetlands" are still highlighted.

8. Setting the other properties to As Is, create a new format named **DeleteThis** and turn on the **Strikethrough** property:

   a. In the Character Designer, from the Commands pop-up menu, choose **New Format**.

   b. In the New Format text box, type: `DeleteThis`

   c. Click **Create**.

   d. From the Commands pop-up menu, choose **Set Window to As Is**.

   All properties for the DeleteThis format are set to As Is.

   > **Note:** The checkboxes for the properties on the right side have three settings: On, Off, and As Is. In UNIX, the As Is setting looks similar, but not identical, to the Off setting.

Macintosh

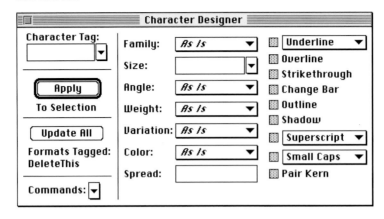

Windows

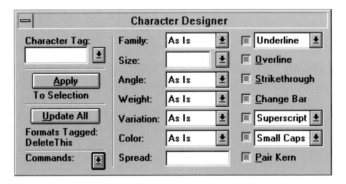

UNIX

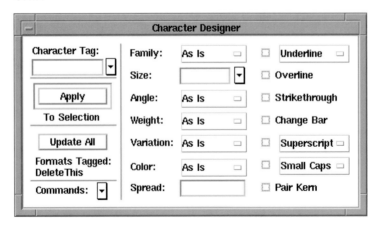

e. Turn on the **Strikethrough** property.

> **Note:** Clicking once on the checkbox changes the setting from As Is to Off. Clicking again will change the setting from Off to On.

f. Click **Update All**.

The DeleteThis character format is applied to the selected text. Notice that this time the Body text did not become bold.

> **Note:** After applying the DeleteThis character tag, the Character Designer will display the font as Helvetica, 12 pt, Regular, Bold, and so on. Instead of displaying the As Is settings of the format. The Character Designer is merely reflecting the properties of the currently selected text in the document and not those of the DeleteThis character format.

g. From the Character Tag pop-up menu in the upper-left corner of the Character Designer, choose **DeleteThis**.

The Character Designer displays the properties of the DeleteThis character format as it is defined in the Character Catalog.

Exercise 6

Project

Deleting a character format

In this exercise, you'll delete the Edit format from the Character Catalog, because you will not be using it in this document.

1. At the bottom of the Character Catalog, click **Delete**.

The Delete Formats from Catalog dialog box appears.

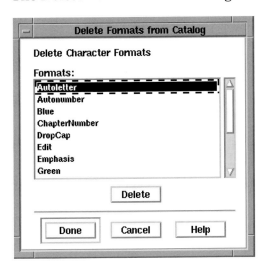

2. Click to select the **Edit** character format.

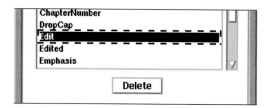

3. Click **Delete**.

4. Click **Done**.

   The Edit format is deleted from the Character Catalog.

> **Elaboration:** Deleting a format from the Catalog does not affect any text with the same tag already in the document; the text will simply have a tag that isn't stored in the Catalog.

Exercise 7

Project

Reapplying a paragraph's default font

To remove character formatting or untagged font properties from text, you use the Character Catalog to reapply the default paragraph font to the text. In this exercise, you'll reapply the default paragraph font to text that was previously tagged with the Edit character format.

1. Select the word "Gulf" in the heading "Gulf Coast Fisheries."

Notice that in the tag area of the status bar, the word is still tagged with the Edit character format.

```
Flow: A  ¶: Section  f: *Edit
```

> **Elaboration:** An asterisk (*) next to a format name indicates that the format of the currently selected text is either different from the format stored in the catalog, or that it is not stored in the catalog at all. In this case it is the latter, since the Edit format was removed from the Catalog in the previous exercise.

2. In the Character Catalog, click **Default ¶ Font**.

   The Edit character format is removed from the selected text.

   ```
   1.4   Gulf Coast Fisheries
   a.  Given the wide range of topics chosen by the
   ```

3. Save the file, and keep the document open if you intend to complete the optional exercise in this module. Otherwise, close the document, and if any other documents are open at this time, close them as well.

Optional Exercise

The following exercise enables you to enhance your FrameMaker skills and to explore additional FrameMaker features. Some steps are intentionally brief, so that they require more independent thought on your part.

Exercise 8

Project

Using the QuickAccess bar

In this optional exercise, you'll use the QuickAccess bar to apply untagged font properties to text, and then you'll create a character format based on the changed text.

1. Beneath the heading "North American Deserts," select the first letter in the word "This."

> **1.3   North American Deserts**
>
> ▊his symposium focused on how the biological significance of environmental impacts can be

2. If the QuickAccess bar is not already visible, from the View menu, choose **QuickAccess Bar** to display it.

3. If the text editing buttons (see following illustration) are not already displayed in the right half of the QuickAccess bar, click the **Page Up** or **Page Down** button until they appear.

Macintosh

Page Up/Down buttons

Windows

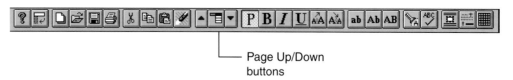

Page Up/Down buttons

UNIX

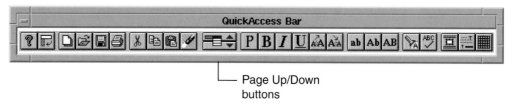

Page Up/Down buttons

4. Click the **B** button to make the letter bold.

5. Click the button 6 times to make the font 6 points larger.

> **1.3   North American Deserts**
>
> **T**his symposium focused on how the biological
> significance of environmental impacts can be

6. Use the Character Designer to create a new format named **Initial Cap**.

7. Apply the Initial Cap format to the letter "T" in the word "The" beneath the heading "Canadian Tundra" on the same page.

Review Test your understanding of the concepts and procedures covered in this module by answering the following review questions. You may check your answers with those listed after the questions.

Question 1: How do you apply an untagged font property to text?

Question 2: How do you apply a character tag to text?

Question 3: How do you create a new character format and add it to the Character Catalog?

Question 4: What are the advantages of using character formats to override the font properties of the default paragraph font versus applying untagged font properties?

Question 5: How do you remove a character format from text? From the Character Catalog?

Answer 1: Select the text, and then use the Format menu to change the font, size, or style of the text. Or use the QuickAccess bar to change the size or style of the text.

Answer 2: Select the text, and then click the tag in the Character Catalog. Or choose a tag from the Character Tag pop-up menu in the Character Designer, and click Apply.

Answer 3: In the Character Designer, from the Commands pop-up menu, choose New Format. Enter the character tag and make sure Store in Catalog is turned on. Make changes to the properties and click Update All.

Answer 4: A character format can apply multiple changes to selected text with a single click, and a character format can easily be updated globally.

Answer 5: To remove a character format from text, select the word or phrase using the format and apply the Default ¶ Font. To remove a character format from the Character Catalog, in the Character Catalog, click Delete. In the Delete Formats from Catalog dialog box, click the name of the format, click Delete, and then click Done.

For more information

For more information about character formats, see:

Chapter 5 of *Using FrameMaker*

Default Font and Basic Properties

Approximate time to complete: 45 minutes

Introduction

In this module, you'll become familiar with Default Font properties and Basic properties in the Paragraph Designer. The Basic property group is where you set a paragraph's indents, line and paragraph spacing, alignment, and tab stops. The Default Font property group is where you specify a paragraph's font properties.

Module Objectives

In this module, you'll learn how to

- Apply paragraph formats in different ways
- Modify the Basic and Default Font properties of paragraph formats
- Create paragraph formats and store them in the Paragraph Catalog
- Delete paragraph formats from the Paragraph Catalog
- Use the As Is setting when you make global paragraph formatting changes
- Use the Find/Change command to find a paragraph format

FrameMaker Model

In this module, you'll work with paragraph *formats*, which you'll apply to text.

Default Font Properties

In the previous module, you used untagged font properties and character formats to make selected text deviate from the paragraph's default font. In this module, you'll define the Default Font properties for a given paragraph. You'll notice that the Default Font properties in the Paragraph Designer look very similar to the properties in the Character Designer. You'll also define other Basic properties of a paragraph.

Exercise 1

Guided Tour

Modifying Default Font properties

In this exercise, you'll modify the Default Font properties of several paragraph formats.

1. From the FrameMaker list of sample documents, open the book chapter **resource.doc**:

    a. Display the FrameMaker list of sample documents.

    | **Macintosh** | From the [?] menu, choose **Samples & Clip Art**. |
    | **Windows** | From the Help menu, choose **Samples & Clip Art**. |
    | **UNIX** | In the main FrameMaker window, click **NEW**. |
    | | In the New dialog box, click **Portrait**. |
    | | From the Help menu, choose **Samples & Clip Art**. |

    b. Click **Book**.

    c. Double-click **resource.doc** to open the file.

2. Use the Save As window to save the file in the `Class` directory or folder with the name: `basic`

3. From the View menu, turn on **Borders** and **Rulers**.

4. Go to **page 12** in the document:

    a. From the View menu, choose **Go to Page**.

    b. In the Page Number text box, type: `12`

    c. Press **Return**.

5. Put the insertion point in the first Bullet paragraph under the heading "1.15 Resources."

First Bullet paragraph

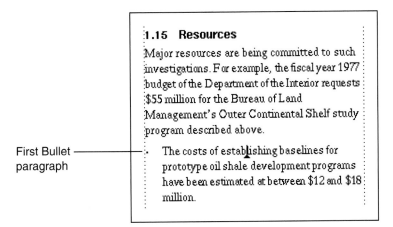

6. From the Format menu, choose **Paragraphs>Designer**.

The Paragraph Designer appears, displaying the Basic properties of the current Bullet paragraph.

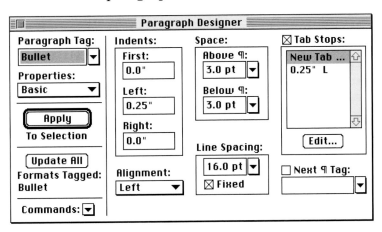

7. In the Paragraph Designer, from the Properties pop-up menu choose **Default Font**.

    The Paragraph Designer displays the Default Font properties of the current Bullet paragraph.

Properties pop-up menu

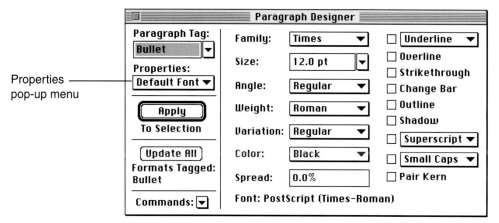

Notice that these Default Font properties in the Paragraph Designer look very similar to the properties in the Character Designer you used in the previous module.

8. Change the Bullet paragraph's default font size to **10 pt**:

    a. From the Size pop-up menu, choose **10 pt**.

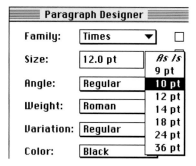

    b. Click **Update All**.

    All Bullet paragraphs in the document have changed to reflect the new point size.

9. Change the Section paragraph format's default font to size **14 pt** with **Small Caps**:

   a. Put the insertion point in the Section paragraph titled "1.15 RESOURCES."

   The Paragraph Designer now shows the Default Font properties of the Section paragraph format.

   b. From the Size pop-up menu, choose **14 pt**.

   c. Turn on **Small Caps**.

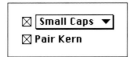

   d. Click **Update All**.

   All Section paragraphs in the document have changed to reflect the new point size and small caps setting.

   > **Elaboration:** Using Update All updates all paragraphs in the document that have the same tag. It also updates the Paragraph Catalog for future uses of the paragraph format.

Basic Properties

The Basic property group in the Paragraph Designer is where you can set a paragraph's indents, line and paragraph spacing, alignment, and tab stops.

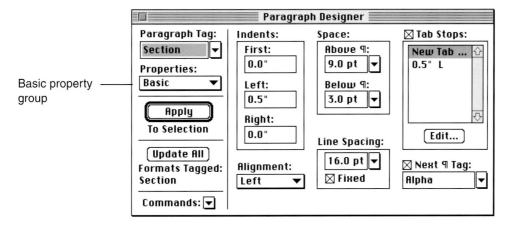

Basic property group

The Indents property sets the distances from the left and right edges of the text column to the text. The First indent setting affects only the first line of a paragraph. The Left indent setting affects all the lines after the first line. The Right indent setting affects the right indent of all the lines of a paragraph.

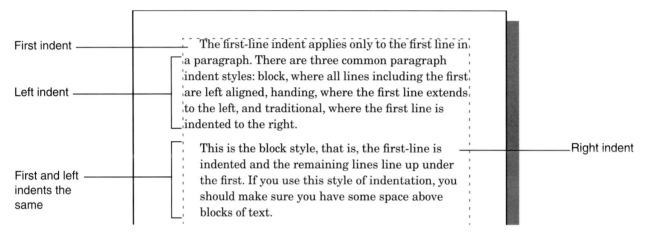

The indent settings are also displayed in the document ruler, and can be changed by dragging the appropriate marker in the ruler.

The Space Above and Space Below settings are also Basic properties. The Space Above setting determines how much white space will appear above a paragraph, however, white space does *not* appear if the paragraph is at the top of a column. The Space Below setting determines how much white space appears below a paragraph, and similar to Space Above, does not appear if the paragraph is at the bottom of a column.

The space between two paragraphs is *not* equal to the sum of the space below the top paragraph and the space above the bottom paragraph. Instead, the space between is determined by the larger of the two settings.

Exercise 2   Modifying Basic properties

Guided Tour

In this exercise, you'll continue to modify the Section paragraph format using Basic properties in the Paragraph Designer.

1. Make sure the insertion point is still in the Section paragraph titled "1.15 RESOURCES."

2. In the Paragraph Designer, from the Properties pop-up menu, choose **Basic**.

Properties pop-up menu ——

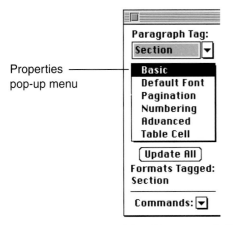

The Paragraph Designer displays the Basic properties of the current Section paragraph.

Section tag ——

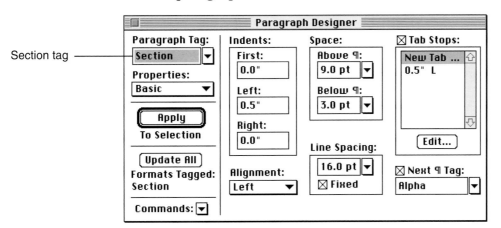

3. Change Space Above to **20 pt** and Space Below to **15 pt**.

4. Click **Apply**.

The new Space Above/Below properties are applied only to the Section paragraph that is currently selected, not to all Section paragraphs and not to the Section format that is stored in the Paragraph Catalog.

Notice that an asterisk (*) appears before the paragraph tag in the status bar.

> Flow: A ¶: *Section

The asterisk indicates that the current paragraph settings override (no longer match) the Paragraph Catalog format with the same name.

5. Click **Update All**.

The new Space Above/Below properties are applied to all Section paragraphs in the document and to the Section format that is stored in the Paragraph Catalog.

The asterisk before the paragraph tag in the status bar disappears.

Exercise 3   **Creating paragraph formats**

Guided Tour

In this exercise, you'll create two new paragraph formats named Quote and Author.

1. Go to **page 16** in the document.

2. In the second paragraph under the heading "1.19 DISCUSSION," put the Insertion point just before the quotation marks and the text "Specific baseline inventories."

Insertion point ————

> For example, in a memorandum on improving Environmental Impact Statements, the Chairman of the Council on Environmental Quality stated, "Specific baseline inventories and environmental research will often be needed initially to determine if there are environmental problems that should be analyzed in an impact statement" (Peterson 1976).

3. Press **Return** to start a new paragraph.

> For example, in a memorandum on improving Environmental Impact Statements, the Chairman of the Council on Environmental Quality stated,
>
> ["Specific baseline inventories and environmental research will often be needed initially to determine if there are environmental problems that should be analyzed in an impact statement" (Peterson 1976).

4. Click just before the quotation mark at the end of the entire quotation and type a period.

> determine if there are environmental problems that should be analyzed in an impact statement." ——— Insert period
> (Peterson 1976).

5. Delete the parentheses and period around the author's name and date.

6. Put the insertion point before the author's name.

> that should be analyzed in an impact statement."
> Peterson 1976

7. Press **Return** to start a new paragraph.

   The author's name and date are a separate paragraph.

> that should be analyzed in an impact statement."
> Peterson 1976

8. Create a new paragraph format named Author:

   a. In the Paragraph Designer, from the Commands pop-up menu, choose **New Format**.

   b. In the Tag text box, type: `Author`

   c. Make sure **Store in Catalog** and **Apply to Selection** are turned on.

   d. Click **Create**.

The Author paragraph format is applied to the current paragraph and is added to the Paragraph Catalog. Currently, the Author paragraph has the same properties as the Body paragraph where the insertion point was located when you created the Author paragraph.

9. In the Basic properties of the Paragraph Designer, change the **Indents** and **Alignment** to:

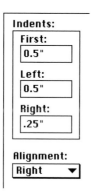

Note: On the Macintosh, you may need to click in the document window, and then click in the Author paragraph to make the Author paragraph settings appear in the Paragraph Designer.

10. Click **Update All**.

The Author paragraph moves to the right.

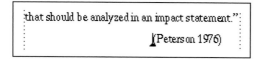

11. From the Properties pop-up menu in the Paragraph Designer, choose **Default Font**.

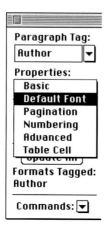

The Paragraph Designer displays the Default Font properties of the current Author paragraph.

12. From the Size pop-up menu, choose **10 pt**.

13. Click **Update All**.

   The Author paragraph is now smaller.

14. Put the insertion point in the paragraph with the quotation marks.

   "Specific baseline inventories and environmental research will often be needed initially to determine if there are environmental problems that should be analyzed in an impact statement."

   Peterson 1976

15. Create a new paragraph format named **Quote**:

   a. In the Paragraph Designer, from the Commands pop-up menu, choose **New Format**.

   b. In the Tag text box, type: `Quote`

   c. Make sure **Store in Catalog** and **Apply to Selection** are turned on.

   d. Click **Create**.

   The Quote paragraph format is applied to the current paragraph and is added to the Paragraph Catalog. Currently, the Quote paragraph has the same properties as the Body paragraph that the insertion point was in when you created the Quote paragraph.

16. Change the Quote format's size and angle to **10 pt Italic** and **Update All**:

   a. From the Size pop-up menu, choose **10 pt**.

   b. From the Angle pop-up menu, choose **Italic**.

   c. Click **Update All**.

   The Quote paragraph is now smaller and italic.

   "Specific baseline inventories and environmental research will often be needed initially to determine if there are environmental problems that should be analyzed in an impact statement."

   (Peterson 1976)

17. From the Properties pop-up menu in the Paragraph Designer, choose **Basic**.

   The Paragraph Designer displays the Basic properties of the Quote paragraph.

18. Specify the following **Indents** and **Space Above** and **Space Below** settings.

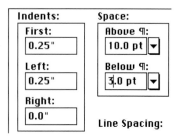

19. From the Next ¶ Tag pop-up menu, choose **Author**.

The Next ¶ Tag option allows you to specify which tag is automatically applied to the new paragraph that is created when you press Return in the current paragraph.

20. Click **Update All**.

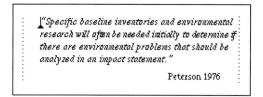

The Quote paragraph is now indented with different spacing above and below.

Now, you'll add new Quote and Author paragraphs to the document to see how the two paragraph formats work together.

21. On page 16, above the heading "1.20 PREDICTIVE VERSUS POST HOC STUDIES," add the quotation paragraph, "Discussion without action is wasteful:"

    a. Put the insertion point at the end of the paragraph above the heading "1.20 PREDICTIVE VERSUS POST HOC STUDIES."

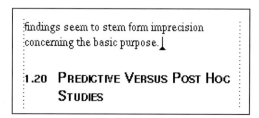

    b. Press **Return** to start a new paragraph.

c. Type: "Discussion without action is wasteful."

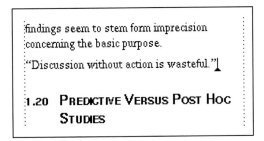

22. In the upper-right corner of the document window, click the **Paragraph Catalog** button.

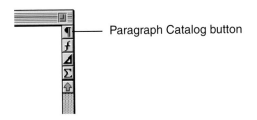

Paragraph Catalog button

Note: You can also open the Paragraph Catalog by choosing **Paragraphs>Catalog** from the Format menu.

23. In the Paragraph Catalog, click the **Quote** paragraph format.

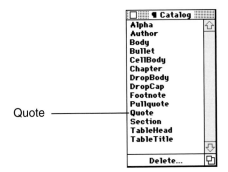

Quote

24. Press **Return**.

Because you defined Quote to have a Next ¶ Tag of Author, the insertion point moves to the right using the Author paragraph format you created.

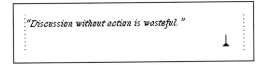

25. Type the author's name and date: `Blackburn, 1976`

> *"Discussion without action is wasteful."*
>
> Blackburn, 1976▮

As Is and Global Update Options

In FrameMaker, the term "As Is" is used in three different ways:

Use of As Is	Meaning	Example
When selecting items with different properties	If you select multiple paragraphs having different values for a property, the Paragraph Designer displays As Is for that property.	If you select two paragraphs, one centered and the other left-aligned, the Alignment pop-up menu will display As Is.
When changing properties of several formats	If you want to change some but not all of the properties, you can set the properties you don't want to change to As Is. When FrameMaker applies properties, it doesn't change properties set to As Is.	If you want to change all headings from centered to left-aligned but want to leave their other properties intact, you can set all properties to As Is, change only the alignment property, and then update all heading formats.
When creating a character format	When you create a character format, use As Is to set it up so that FrameMaker changes only the designated property when you apply the format to specific text within a paragraph. The As Is property is stored as part of the character format.	You can create a character format called Emphasis that changes selected text to italics while leaving the font family, size, and so on, intact.

In the previous module, you created a character format using the As Is setting, and then later applied the format to selected text. In this module, you will see how As Is is used for properties that have different settings in several paragraphs, and you will leave those properties As Is when making global updates.

Exercise 4

Guided Tour

Using As Is and global update options

In this exercise, you'll use As Is when you globally update the font properties for all paragraphs in the document.

1. Go to **page 12**.

2. Drag through several paragraphs to select them. It doesn't matter which paragraphs you select, as long as you select paragraphs with different properties.

environments, resource developments and potential impacts.

They include:

a. terrestrial,

b. freshwater,

c. and marine ecosystems.

As part of an accelerated program to develop geothermal resources in the western United States, U.S. Geological Survey regulations require a one-year environmental baseline study prior to initiation of geothermal production from federal leases. Bureau of Land Management lease stipulations governing a prototype oil shale development program in Colorado and Utah require the lessees to conduct two-year environmental baseline and monitoring studies prior to initiation of development.

The Department of the Interior has initiated an accelerated program to lease and develop Outer Continental Shelf oil and gas reserves in response to national energy needs. During the last two years, as part of that program, the Department's Bureau of Land Management has funded a wide ranging series of marine environmental baseline studies extending around the coasts of the United States from the Beaufort Sea in Arctic Alaska to the South Atlantic.

1.14 PREPARATIONS

a. In anticipation of probable need to prepare an Environmental Impact Statement on a program of deep ocean mining for manganese nodules, the National Oceanic and Atmospheric

b. Administration is undertaking baseline studies in the central Pacific Ocean.

c. Environmental baseline studies are being conducted by the electric utility industry in:

- rivers,
- estuaries,
- and coastal areas to meet Environmental Protection Agency and Nuclear Regulatory Commission requirements relating to power plants development.

An Environmental Protection Agency program to regulate ocean dumping of wastes has generated baseline surveys of various dump sites ranging from locations on the Outer Continental Shelf to a deep water dump site at the edge of the mid-Atlantic Continental Slope at depths extending to almost 3000 meters. The State of Washington is undertaking a program of baseline studies of Pugged Sound in advance of transshipment of Alaskan oil.

1.15 RESOURCES

Major resources are being committed to such investigations. For example, the fiscal year 1977

You'll change the font for *all* paragraphs in the document (not just the selected ones) at the *same* time, regardless of their paragraph tag.

3. In the Paragraph Designer, display the **Default Font** properties.

    As Is appears as a setting in the Paragraph Designer for the properties that are different across the selected paragraphs.

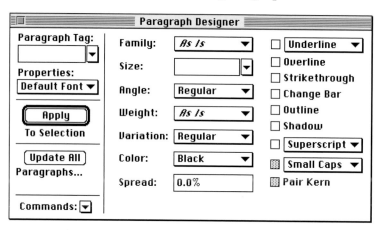

4. In the Paragraph Designer, from the Commands pop-up menu, choose **Set Window to As Is**.

    As Is appears as a setting for all the properties in the Paragraph Designer.

5. From the default font Family pop-up menu, choose **Helvetica**.

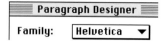

6. From the Commands pop-up menu, choose **Global Update Options**.

    The Global Update Options dialog box appears.

7. Make sure that **Default Font Properties Only** is turned on in the Use Properties in the Paragraph Designer area of the dialog box.

8. In the Update Paragraph Formats area, turn on **All Paragraphs and Catalog Entries**.

   This will change the font to Helvetica for all paragraph formats in the document.

   > **Tip:** It is also possible to globally update properties of only some of the paragraph formats by selecting those you'd like to change and turning on All Matching Tags in Selection.

9. Click **Update**.

   The default font family is now Helvetica for all paragraphs in the document, regardless of their paragraph tag, leaving all other properties As Is.

---

western United States, U.S. Geological Survey regulations require a one-year environmental baseline study prior to initiation of geothermal production from federal leases. Bureau of Land Management lease stipulations governing a prototype oil shale development program in Colorado and Utah require the lessees to conduct two-year environmental baseline and monitoring studies prior to initiation of development. The Department of the Interior has initiated an accelerated program to lease and develop Outer Continental Shelf oil and gas reserves in response to national energy needs. During the last two years, as part of that program, the Department's Bureau of Land Management has funded a wide ranging series of marine environmental baseline studies extending around the coasts of the United States from the Beaufort Sea in Arctic Alaska to the South Atlantic.

1.14 PREPARATIONS

a. In anticipation of probable need to prepare an Environmental Impact Statement on a program of deep ocean mining for manganese nodules, the National Oceanic and Atmospheric

b. Administration is undertaking baseline studies in the central Pacific Ocean.

c. Environmental baseline studies are being conducted by the electric utility industry in:

- rivers,
- estuaries,
- and coastal areas to meet Environmental Protection Agency and Nuclear Regulatory Commission requirements relating to power plants development.

An Environmental Protection Agency program to regulate ocean dumping of wastes has generated baseline surveys of various dump sites ranging from locations on the Outer Continental Shelf to a deep water dump site at the edge of the mid-Atlantic Continental Slope at depths extending to almost 3000 meters. The State of Washington is undertaking a program of baseline studies of Pugged Sound in advance of transshipment of Alaskan oil.

1.15 RESOURCES

Major resources are being committed to such investigations. For example, the fiscal year 1977 budget of the Department of the Interior requests $55 million for the Bureau of Land Management's Outer Continental Shelf study program described above.

---

10. Save the file, and keep the document open if you intend to complete the optional exercises in this module. Otherwise, close the document and any other open documents.

Optional Exercises

The following exercises enable you to enhance your FrameMaker skills and to explore additional FrameMaker features. Some steps are intentionally brief, so that they require more independent thought on your part.

Exercise 5

Optional

Deleting a paragraph format

In this exercise, you'll delete the **Pullquote** format from the Paragraph Catalog.

1. Click to make the insertion point appear anywhere on the page.

2. At the bottom of the Paragraph Catalog, click **Delete**.

   In the Delete Formats from Catalog dialog box, select the **Pullquote** paragraph format.

3. Click **Delete**.

4. Click **Done**.

> **Elaboration:** Deleting a format from the Catalog does not affect any text with the same tag already in the document; the text will simply have a format that isn't stored in the Catalog.

Exercise 6

Optional

Finding paragraph formats

In this optional exercise, you'll use the Find/Change window to find specified paragraph formats in your document. This is helpful when you want to change the properties of the paragraph format.

1. Use the Find/Change command to find the Author paragraph tag and change the default font to include small caps:

    a. From the Edit menu, choose **Find/Change**.

    b. From the Find pop-up menu, choose **Paragraph Tag**.

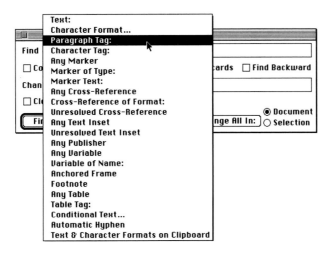

    c. In the Find text box, type: Author

    d. Click **Find**.

       The first occurrence of the Author paragraph tag is highlighted.

    e. Open the Paragraph Designer, change the Default Font to include small caps, and click **Update All**.

2. Follow steps similar to a-e in the preceding steps to change the default font size of the Bullet paragraph format to **11 pt**.

Review
Test your understanding of the concepts and procedures covered in this module by answering the following review questions. You may check your answers with those listed after the questions.

Question 1: How do you apply a paragraph format?

Question 2: Where do you make changes to paragraph format properties?

Question 3: How do you create a new paragraph format and add it to the Paragraph Catalog?

Question 4: When making a global paragraph formatting change, such as changing the font of all the text in the document, what Default Font properties should be set to As Is? Why?

Question 5: What happens to the paragraph format of selected text when you make changes in the Paragraph Designer and then click Update All? How is that different from what happens when you click Apply?

Answer 1: Put the insertion point in the paragraph and click a paragraph tag in the Paragraph Catalog. Or, in the Paragraph Designer, choose a tag from the Paragraph Tag pop-up menu and click Apply.

Answer 2: In the Paragraph Designer.

Answer 3: In the Paragraph Designer, choose New Format from the Commands pop-up menu. Type the paragraph tag, make sure Store in Catalog is turned on, and click Create. Make changes to the properties and click Update All.

Answer 4: All the Default Font properties *except* the font should be set to As Is, so only the font of each paragraph and paragraph tag will change and their other settings will remain the same.

Answer 5: When you click Update All, the appearance of the selected text *and* the definition of the paragraph format are updated to reflect the changes you made in the Paragraph Designer. When you click Apply, the changes are only applied to the selected text; the paragraph format itself remains unchanged.

For more information

For more information about formatting text and working with paragraph formats, see:

Chapters 4 and 5 of *Using FrameMaker*

Tab Properties

9

· ·

Approximate time to complete: 1 hour

Introduction

In this module, you'll practice setting and modifying tab properties. Tab stops can be used to create numbered and bulleted lists, outlines, and other text that must be aligned at specific places.

Module Objectives

In this module, you'll learn how to

- Add, edit, and delete tab stops using the formatting bar
- Add, edit, and delete tab stops using the Paragraph Designer
- Specify tab alignment
- Specify tab leaders

FrameMaker Model

Tab properties are included in paragraph *formats*.

Positioning Tab Stops with the Formatting Bar

Pressing the Tab key will only move the insertion point and text to the desired location when you have defined tab stops for the paragraph. The easiest way to create and position tab stops is to use the tab wells in the formatting bar.

Macintosh

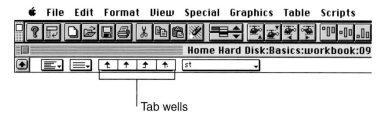

Tab wells

Windows

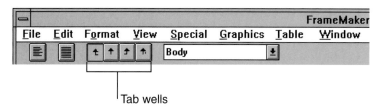

Tab wells

UNIX

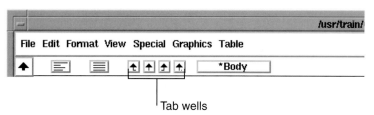

Tab wells

To set a tab stop using a tab well, drag the desired type of tab stop from the tab well to the appropriate position in the ruler.

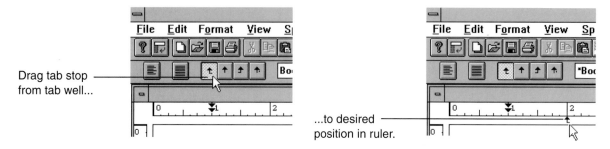

Drag tab stop from tab well...

...to desired position in ruler.

Each tab well sets a different kind of tab stop.

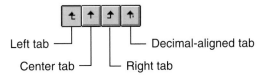

Left tab ⎯⎯⎯⎯⎯⎯ Decimal-aligned tab

Center tab ⎯⎯⎯ Right tab

Each kind of tab stop has a different effect on the alignment of text that follows a tab character.

Exercise 1

Project

Using the formatting bar to set tab stops

In this exercise, you'll create a list of Olympic swimmers, including each swimmer's ID number, trial day, best time, and country. Each line in the list will use a left, center, decimal, and right tab stop, and will look like the following:

0127	Pierre	Friday	9.5	France
1539	Johnathan	Saturday	10.05	USA
1383	Sven	Tuesday	8.959	Sweden
Left-aligned	Center-aligned	Decimal-aligned	Right-aligned

1. Create a new **Landscape** document:

   a. Open the **New** dialog box.

Macintosh	From the File menu, choose **New**.
Windows	From the File menu, choose **New**.
UNIX	In the main FrameMaker window, click **NEW**.

   b. Click **Landscape**.

2. Use the Save As dialog box to save the document in the `Class` directory or folder with the new filename `tabs`.

3. Display the formatting bar and rulers if they do not appear in your document window:

   a. If the rulers are not visible, from the View menu, choose **Rulers**.

   b. If the formatting bar is not visible:

Macintosh	Click the **formatting bar toggle**.
Windows	From the View menu, choose **Formatting Bar**.
UNIX	Click the **formatting bar toggle**.

Macintosh

Formatting bar toggle

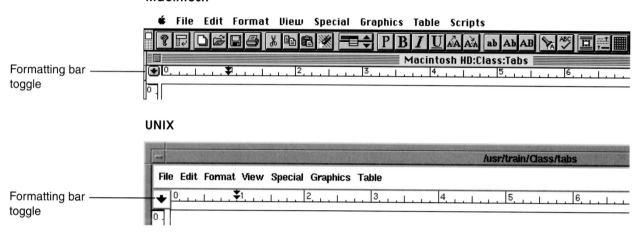

UNIX

Formatting bar toggle

4. Make sure **Snap** turned on:

   a. In the Graphics menu, locate the Snap command, and determine whether Snap is currently on or off.

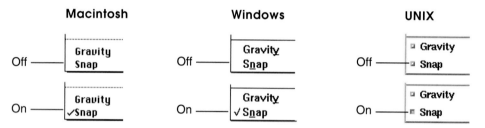

   b. If Snap is turned off, choose **Snap** to turn it on.

   > **Elaboration:** With Snap turned on, when you add or move a tab stop on the formatting bar, the tab symbol will automatically snap to the ⅛-inch ruler markings.

5. Click in the empty text frame and press **Tab** four times.

   Since no tab stops are defined, the insertion point does not move.

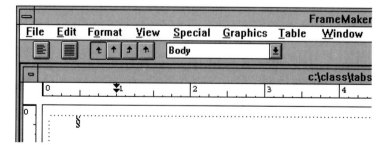

6. Create a **left**-aligned tab stop, **2 inches** from the left edge of the page:

   a. Hold down the mouse on the **left** tab well on the formatting bar.

   b. Drag a left tab symbol from the tab well to just under the **2-inch** mark on the ruler and release the mouse.

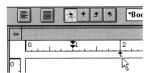

7. Create a **center**-aligned tab stop, **3¾ inches** from the left edge of the page.

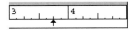

8. Create a **decimal**-aligned tab stop, **6¼ inches** from the left edge of the page.

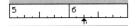

9. Create a **right**-aligned tab stop, **8½ inches** from the left edge of the page.

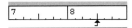

> **Tip:** You can delete a tab stop by dragging the tab symbol off the bottom of the ruler.

10. From the Format pop-up menu on the formatting bar (*not* the Format menu in the menu bar), choose **Update All**.

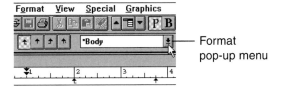

Format pop-up menu

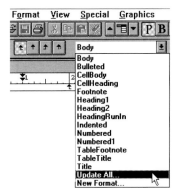

The Update Paragraph Format dialog box appears.

11. Click **Update**.

12. Add the following text to your document, typing **Tab** as appropriate:

0127	Pierre	Friday	9.5	France
1539	Johnathan	Saturday	10.05	USA
1383	Sven	Tuesday	8.959	Sweden

   a. Press **Backspace** four times to remove the tabs in the current paragraph.

   The insertion point is positioned in the first line of the document and you are ready to enter text.

   b. Type: 0127

   c. Press **Tab** to go to the first tab stop and type: Pierre

   d. Press **Tab** and type: Friday

   e. Press **Tab** and type: 9.5

   f. Press **Tab** and type: France

   g. Press **Return** to go to the next line.

   h. Enter the remaining two lines of text as follows.

13. Move the second tab stop to **4¼ inches** and **Update All** Body paragraphs and the Paragraph Catalog:

   a. Put the insertion point in the first line of text.

   b. Drag the **center**-aligned tab stop (currently set at 3¾ inches) to **4¼ inches**.

   The text moves and an asterisk appears before the paragraph tag, indicating there is an override in the paragraph.

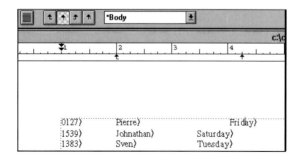

    c. From the Paragraph Format pop-up menu on the formatting bar, choose **Update All**.

      The Update Paragraph Format dialog box appears.

    d. Click **Update**.

      All Body paragraphs and the Paragraph Catalog are updated.

14. From the View menu, turn off **Text Symbols**.

    Your document should now look like this:

0127	Pierre	Friday	9.5	France
1539	Johnathan	Saturday	10.05	USA
1383	Sven	Tuesday	8.959	Sweden

Modifying Tab Properties

Exercise 2

Project

Modifying tab properties from the Formatting bar

Using the list you created in the previous exercise, you'll modify tab properties by adding a dot leader to the tab stops.

1. Turn on **Text Symbols**.

2. Make sure your insertion point is in the first line of text.

3. Double-click the **left-aligned** tab stop located at **2 inches** on the ruler.

    The Edit Tab Stop dialog box appears.

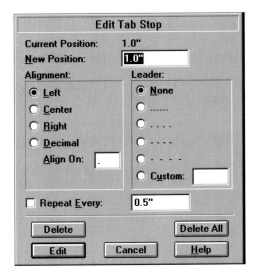

Notice that the current position in the Edit Tab Stop dialog box is 1.0" even though the tab stop in the ruler is at 2 inches.

> **Elaboration:** The positions displayed in the Edit Tab Stop dialog box are calculated from the left edge of the *text frame.* The values on the ruler are calculated from the left edge of the *page.*

4. In the Leader area, turn on the first leader character.

First leader character —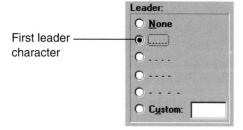

This will insert a line of dots (called a "dot leader") running up to the tab stop.

5. At the bottom of the dialog box, click **Edit**.

The leader appears in the document.

6. Add dot leaders to the tab stops located at **4¼, 6¼,** and **8½ inches** on the ruler:

   a. Double-click the **center**-aligned tab stop located at 4¼ inches.

   b. In the Edit Tab Stop dialog box, in the Leader area, turn on the first leader character.

   c. Click **Edit**.

   The leader appears in the document.

   d. Repeat steps a-c for the tab stops at **6¼ inches** and **8½ inches**.

7. Update all Body paragraphs and the Paragraph Catalog:

   a. From the Paragraph Format pop-up menu on the formatting bar, choose **Update All**.

   b. In the Update Paragraph Format dialog box, click **Update**.

   All Body paragraphs and the Paragraph Catalog are updated.

0127⟩	Pierre⟩	Friday⟩	9.5⟩	France¶
1539⟩	Johnathan⟩	Saturday⟩	10.05⟩	USA¶
1383⟩	Sven⟩	Tuesday⟩	8.959⟩	Sweden§

Line Spacing

The Line Spacing setting controls the amount of white space between the lines of a paragraph. The quickest way to change line spacing is to use the Line Spacing pop-up menu in the formatting bar. The preset values—Single, 1.5, or Double—are calculated based on the font size of the selected text; Single spacing means the distance from the baseline of one line of text to the next is 120% of the font size.

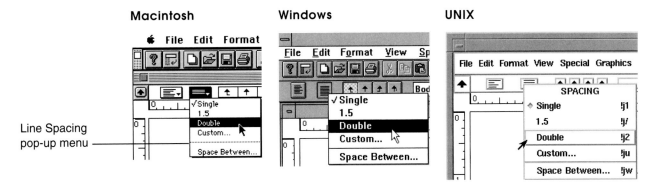

Line Spacing pop-up menu

To use line spacing that is different from the preset values, you can choose Custom from the pop-up menu, and then type in a value manually.

You can also change line spacing using the Line Spacing settings in the Basic properties of the Paragraph Designer.

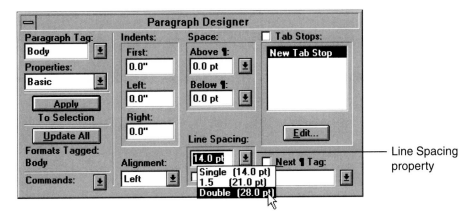

Line Spacing property

Exercise 3 Changing line spacing

Project

In this exercise, you'll use the formatting bar to change the line spacing between items in the list of athletes.

1. Put the insertion point in the first line of text.

2. From the Spacing pop-up menu on the formatting bar, choose **1.5**.

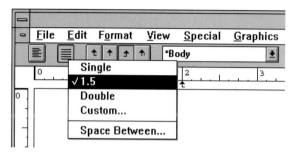

The distance between the first line and the second line of text increases.

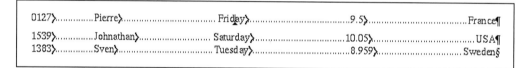

```
0127〉...........Pierre〉.....................................Friday〉...........................9.5〉............................France¶
1539〉...........Johnathan〉.......................Saturday〉.........................10.05〉........................USA¶
1383〉...........Sven〉.............................Tuesday〉..........................8.959〉......................Sweden§
```

3. From the Paragraph Format pop-up menu on the formatting bar, choose **Update All**.

4. In the Update Paragraph Format dialog box, click **Update**.

The Paragraph Catalog is updated with the new line spacing.

```
0127〉...........Pierre〉.....................................Friday〉...........................9.5〉............................France¶
1539〉...........Johnathan〉.......................Saturday〉.........................10.05〉........................USA¶
1383〉...........Sven〉.............................Tuesday〉..........................8.959〉......................Sweden§
```

Exercise 4 Modifying tab properties in the Paragraph Designer

Project

In the previous exercise, you used the formatting bar to display the Edit Tab Stop dialog box. In this exercise, you'll display that dialog box using the Paragraph Designer. You'll modify tab properties for only one paragraph, which will be the heading for your list.

```
ID#〉        Athlete〉        Practice Day〉            Personal Best〉        Country¶
```

1. Create an empty paragraph at the top of the document:

   a. Put the insertion point in the beginning of the line that starts with "0127."

   b. Press **Return**.

   c. Put the insertion point in the empty paragraph.

2. Type the heading text:

   a. Type: `ID#`

   b. Press **Tab** and type: `Athlete`

   c. Press **Tab** and type: `Practice Day`

   d. Press **Tab** and type: `Personal Best`

   e. Press **Tab** and type: `Country`

   Your document should now look like this:

ID#⟩...............Athlete⟩............................. Practice Day⟩..............Personal Best⟩................................... Country¶
0127⟩..............Pierre⟩............................. Friday⟩...................................9.5⟩...................................France¶
1539⟩..............Johnathan⟩......................... Saturday⟩..............................10.05⟩..................................USA¶
1383⟩..............Sven⟩............................. Tuesday⟩...................................8.959⟩.............................Sweden§

3. From the Format menu, choose **Paragraphs>Designer**.

   The Paragraph Designer appears.

4. In the Paragraph Designer, from the Properties pop-up menu, choose **Basic**.

   The Basic properties of the current Body paragraph are displayed.

5. In the Tab Stops scroll list, click the **5.25" .D** tab stop.

   > **Elaboration:** The list of tab stops displays not only the position of the tab stop, but also its alignment, and what type of leader, if any, has been assigned to it.

6. At the bottom of the Tab Stops scroll list, click **Edit**.

   The Edit Tab Stop dialog box appears.

7. In the Alignment area, turn on **Center**.

8. In the Leader area, turn on **None** to remove the dot leader.

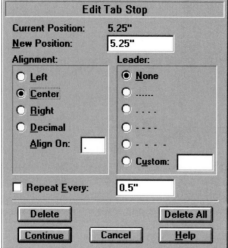

9. At the bottom of the dialog box, click **Continue**.

10. In the Paragraph Designer, click **Apply**.

> **Note:** Clicking Apply changes only the current Body paragraph.

The header "Personal Best" is now centered over the decimal-aligned numbers and the preceding dot leader has disappeared.

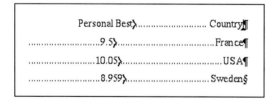

11. Remove the dot leaders from the three remaining tabs:

   a. In the Tab Stops scroll list, click the **1.0" L** tab stop.

   b. At the bottom of the Tab Stops scroll list, click **Edit**.

   c. In the Leader area, turn on **None**.

   d. At the bottom of the dialog box, click **Continue**.

   e. Repeat steps a-d for the **3.25" C** and the **7.5" R** tab stops.

   f. Click **Apply**.

Your document should now look like this:

ID#⟩	Athlete⟩	Practice Day⟩	Personal Best⟩	Country¶
0127⟩.............Pierre⟩..............................		Friday⟩..............................	.9.5⟩..............................	....France¶
1539⟩.............Johnathan⟩..................		Saturday⟩..............................	10.05⟩..............................	.....USA¶
1383⟩.............Sven⟩..............................		Tuesday⟩..............................	.8.959⟩..............................	.....Sweden§

12. Change the default font for this paragraph to **Bold**:

    a. In the Paragraph Designer, from the Properties pop-up menu, choose **Default Font**.

    b. From the Weight pop-up menu, choose **Bold**.

    c. Click **Apply**.

    d. Turn off **Text Symbols**.

    Your document should now look like this:

ID#	Athlete	Practice Day	Personal Best	Country
0127.............Pierre..............................		Friday..............................	.9.5..............................	....France
1539.............Johnathan..................		Saturday..............................	10.05..............................	.....USA
1383.............Sven..............................		Tuesday..............................	.8.959..............................	.....Sweden

13. Save the file and close the document. Keep the Paragraph Designer open if you intend to complete the optional exercises in this module. Otherwise, close the Paragraph Designer.

Optional Exercise

The following exercise enables you to enhance your FrameMaker skills and to explore additional FrameMaker features. Some steps are intentionally brief, so that they require more independent thought on your part.

Exercise 5

Optional

Creating a printed office form

In this optional exercise, you'll create paragraph formats with tab stops to replicate the following sample printed office form. All of the lines are set up with tab stops and underscore leader characters.

Change of Address Form

Name: _____

Address: _____

City: _____

State: _____

Zip: _____

Home Phone: _____

_____

Signature

1. Create a new **Portrait** document.

2. Save the document in the `Class` directory or folder with the name `form`.

3. Create the title using the **Heading2** paragraph format:

    a. Type: `Change of Address Form`

    b. Open the Paragraph Catalog, and apply the **Heading2** paragraph format to the text.

4. Press **Return** three times.

5. Type: `Name:`

6. Press **Tab** three times.

7. Create three **left**-aligned tab stops: one at **2 inches**, one at **4½ inches**, and one at **7 inches**.

8. Add an underscore leader to the tab stops at **4½ inches** and **7 inches**:

a. Double-click the tab stop at **4½ inches**.

b. In the Edit Tab Stop dialog box, in the Custom text box, type an underscore character (hold down **Shift** while typing a hyphen).

c. Click **Edit**.

A line appears between the tab stops at **2 inches** and **4½ inches**.

d. Repeat steps a-c with the tab stop at **7 inches**.

Your document should now look like this:

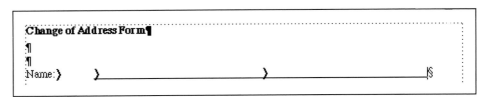

9. Define a new paragraph format named **TabLine**. Make sure it is stored in the catalog and applied to the selection.

10. Enter the Address and City lines:

a. Press **Return**.

b. Type: Address:

c. Press **Tab** three times.

The word "Address:" appears with a line after it.

d. Repeat steps a-c to create the City line.

Your document should now look like this:

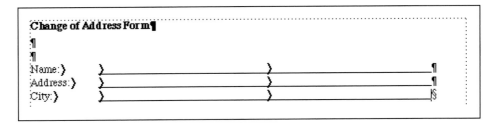

11. Increase the spacing between the lines:

    a. From the Spacing pop-up menu, choose **Double**.

       The spacing of the text does not change.

    > **Elaboration:** When you change the line spacing, it affects the space between the selected line and the line that follows. When there is no line after the selected line, there is no visible change in the line spacing.

    b. From the Paragraph Format pop-up menu, choose **Update All**.

    c. Click **Update**.

       Your document should now look like this:

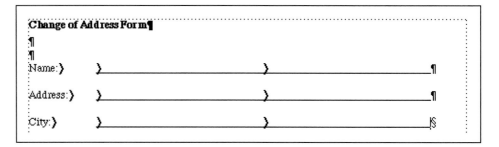

12. Enter the State, Zip, and Home Phone lines:

    a. Press **Return**.

    b. Type: State:

    c. Press **Tab** *twice*.

       A short line appears after the word "State:"

    d. Repeat steps a-c to create the Zip and Home Phone lines.

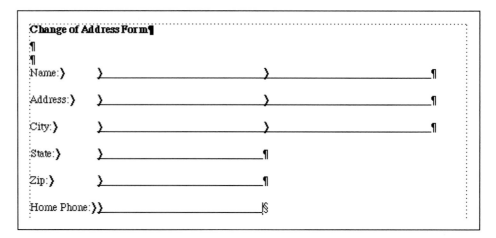

13. Add a line for the signature:

   a. Press **Return** twice.

   b. Press **Tab** three times.

14. Center the word "Signature" below the signature line:

   a. Press **Return**.

   b. Press **Tab** twice.

   c. Type: Signature

   d. Double-click the tab stop at **4½ inches**.

   e. In the Edit Tab Stops dialog box, change the alignment to **Center**, and the Leader to **None**.

   f. Click **Edit**.

   g. Turn off **Text Symbols**.

   Your document should now look like this:

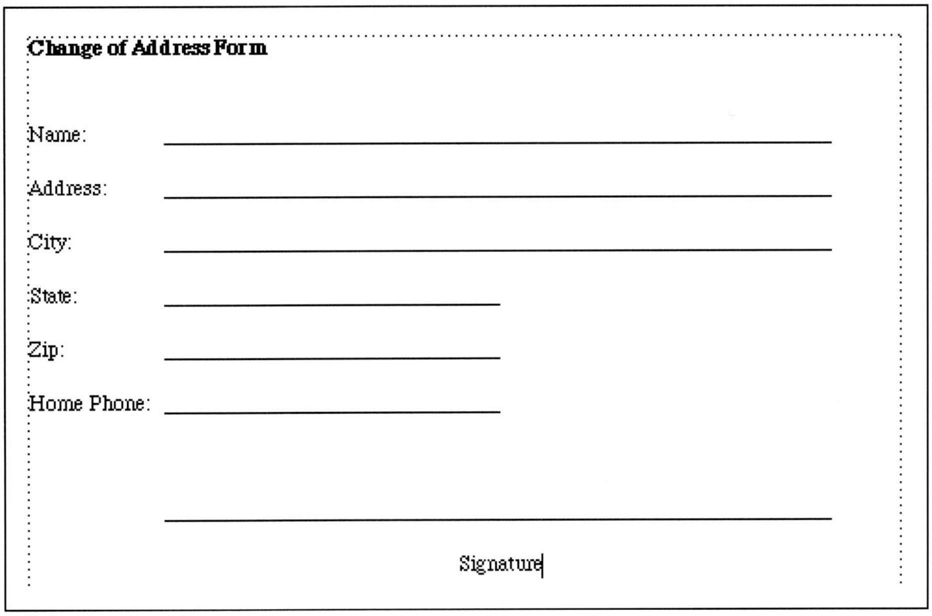

```
Change of Address Form


Name:              _____

Address:           _____

City:              _____

State:             _____

Zip:               _____

Home Phone:        _____


                   _____
                              Signature
```

Review Test your understanding of the concepts and procedures covered in this module by answering the following review questions. You may check your answers with those after the questions.

Question 1: How do you add tab stops to a paragraph?

Question 2: When you add a tab stop using the formatting bar, it applies to the current paragraph only. How do you add it to other paragraphs in the document with the same tag and to the Paragraph Catalog?

Question 3: How do you change the properties of an existing tab stop?

Question 4: How do you delete a tab stop?

Question 5: How do you add a tab stop that creates dots or an underline when you press Tab?

Answer 1: Drag a tab stop from a tab well on the formatting bar to the appropriate position on the ruler.

Answer 2: In the Paragraph Designer, click Update All. Or choose Update All from the Paragraph Format pop-up menu on the formatting bar.

Answer 3: You can change the position of a tab stop by dragging it in the ruler. To change other tab properties, use the Edit Tab Stop dialog box. To display the Edit Tab Stop dialog box, either double-click the tab stop in the formatting bar, or select the tab stop in the Tab Stops scroll list in the Paragraph Designer and click Edit.

Answer 4: Drag the tab stop symbol down off the bottom of the ruler.

Answer 5: In the Edit Tab Stop dialog box, change to the leader of the tab stop.

For more information

For more information about setting tab properties, see:

Chapter 4 of *Using FrameMaker*

Pagination and Advanced Properties

Approximate time to complete: 1 hour

Introduction

In this module, you'll become familiar with Pagination properties and Advanced properties in the Paragraph Designer. The Pagination property group specifies how and where a paragraph will appear on a page. The Advanced property group is where a paragraph's hyphenation is set.

Module Objectives

In this module, you'll learn how to:

- Use Start settings to control paragraph location.
- Use Keep With settings to control breaks between paragraphs.
- Set Widow and Orphan properties to control breaks within paragraphs.
- Identify and use In Column, Run-In Head, and Side Head settings for paragraph formats.
- Work with a straddle paragraph.
- Specify paragraph hyphenation.

FrameMaker Model

Pagination and Advanced properties are included in paragraph *formats*.

Keeping Paragraphs and Lines Together

The properties to determine paragraph location in a document are found in Pagination properties in the Paragraph Designer.

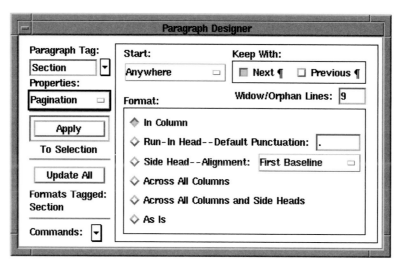

Most types of paragraphs by default are set to start anywhere on a page. To make sure the chapter titles or section headings always appear at the top of a page, you modify the Start property.

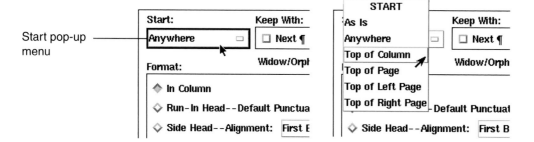

For multi-column layouts, the Start property can be set to start at the top of a column instead of at the top of a page. In documents that use separate left and right master pages, you can also make the paragraph start at the top of either a left or right-hand page.

A heading should normally appear just above the paragraph it describes, but occasionally a lone heading may appear at the bottom of a page or column, as shown below:

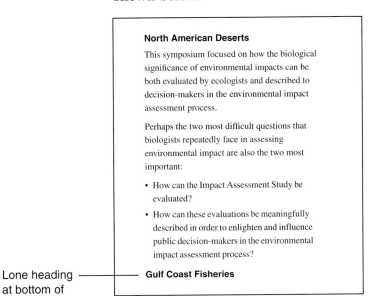

Lone heading at bottom of column

To force a heading to remain with the following paragraph, turn on the Keep With Next ¶ setting. When you want a paragraph to always appear with the paragraph that precedes it, turn on the Keep With Previous ¶ setting.

Single lines of body text—called widows and orphans—should not appear at the top or bottom of a page or column of a document.

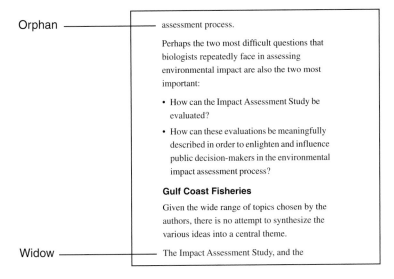

Orphan

Widow

The Widow/Orphan Lines setting controls how many lines of a paragraph can appear alone at the top or bottom of a text column. To avoid widows and orphans, make sure this property is set to at least 2.

Exercise 1

Guided Tour

Using Start and Keep With

In this exercise, you'll set properties to maintain paragraph integrity for a variety of paragraphs within a document.

1. From the FrameMaker list of sample documents, open the book chapter **resource.doc**:

   a. Display the FrameMaker list of sample documents.

Macintosh	From the [?] menu, choose **Samples & Clip Art**.
Windows	From the Help menu, choose **Samples & Clip Art**.
UNIX	From a document Help menu, choose **Samples & Clip Art**. (If there are no open documents, click **NEW**, then **Portrait**, first.)

   The FrameMaker samples window appears.

   b. Click **Book**.

   c. Double-click **resource.doc**.

2. Use the Save As dialog box to save the document in the Class directory or folder with the new filename pages.

3. Turn on **Borders**.

4. Go to **page 2**.

5. Put the insertion point in the heading "1.4 Gulf Coast Fisheries."

   > public decision-makers in the environmental impact assessment process?
   >
   > **1.4   Gulf Coast Fisheries**
   >
   > a. Given the wide range of topics chosen by the authors, there is no attempt to synthesize the various ideas into a central theme.

6. From the Format menu, choose **Paragraphs>Designer**.

   The Paragraph Designer appears.

7. From the Properties pop-up menu, choose **Pagination**.

   The Paragraph Designer displays the Pagination properties for the current Section paragraph.

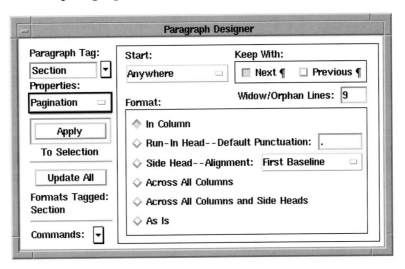

8. From the Start pop-up menu, choose **Top of Column.**

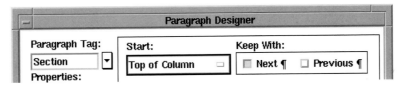

9. Click **Apply.**

   The Section paragraph moves to the top of the next column.

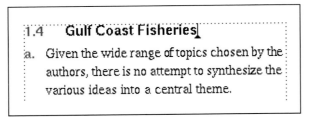

10. Go to **page 12.**

11. Under the heading "1.14 Preparations," put the insertion point in the third paragraph that begins with the text, "c. Environmental baseline."

12. In the Keep With area of the Paragraph Designer, turn on **Next ¶**.

13. Click **Apply**.

The paragraph moves to stay with the paragraph that follows it.

Elaboration: Although you *could* move the text in the above exercise to the top of the following column by adding extra Return characters above it, this is not recommended. If you subsequently delete or add text before the additional Returns, they would appear as unintended white space above the heading.

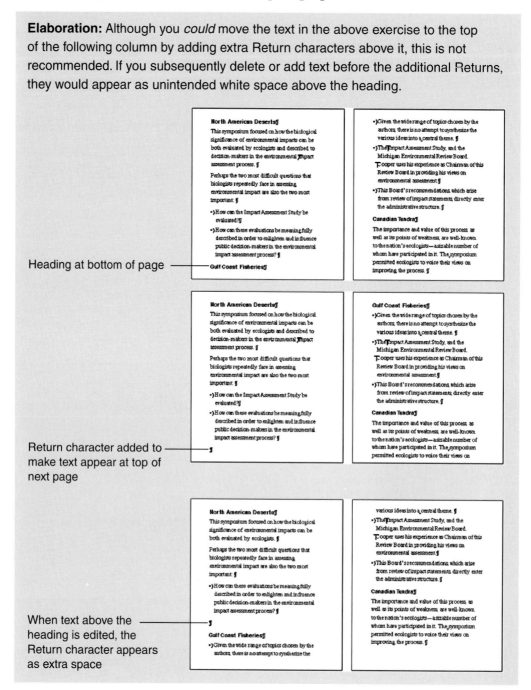

Heading at bottom of page

Return character added to make text appear at top of next page

When text above the heading is edited, the Return character appears as extra space

Exercise 2

Guided Tour

Making adjustments to widow and orphan settings

The body text of the document used in this exercise is already set up so that widows and orphans cannot be created. In this exercise, you'll modify the Widow/Orphan Lines property of the body text so you can see how widows and orphans are created. Then you'll see how to use the Widow/Orphan Lines property to avoid widows and orphans.

1. Go to **page 11**.

2. Put the insertion point in the paragraph at the bottom of the first column.

> Furthermore, "unreasonable pollution" was purposefully not defined.
>
> If formal standards do exist, they can be utilized as baseline measurements of reasonable

In the Paragraph Designer, notice that the current Widow/Orphan Lines setting is **2**.

3. Change the Widow/Orphan Lines setting to **1**.

4. Click **Apply**.

There is no visible change in the text. However, the widow/orphan property is now set to allow widows and orphans.

5. In the paragraph above, put the insertion point before the words "state legislator."

> through the efforts of Dr. Joseph Tax, law professor, and Tom Anderson, state legislator, that makes it legal for a citizen to sue any federal, state, industry, municipality or other individual for something called "unreasonable pollution." Furthermore, "unreasonable pollution" was purposefully not defined.
>
> If formal standards do exist, they can be utilized as baseline measurements of reasonable

6. Type: `an environmentally oriented` and then type a space.

> professor, and Tom Anderson, an
> environmentally oriented state legislator, that
> makes it legal for a citizen to sue any federal,
> state, industry, municipality or other individual
> for something called "unreasonable pollution."
> Furthermore, "unreasonable pollution" was
> purposefully not defined.
>
> If formal standards do exist, they can be utilized

Notice that adding text caused only one line of the following paragraph to appear at the bottom of the page.

7. Change the Widow/Orphan Lines property of the paragraph at the bottom of the first column back to **2**:

   a. Put the insertion point in the line at the bottom of the first column.

   > called "unreasonable pollution." Furthermore,
   > "unreasonable pollution" was purposefully not
   > defined.
   >
   > If formal standards do exist, they can be utilized

   b. Change the Widow/Orphan Lines setting to **2**.

   c. Click **Apply**.

   The single line of text at the bottom of the first column moves to the top of the second column.

   > If formal standards do exist, they can be utilized
   > as baseline measurements of reasonable
   > behavior, otherwise the judge may set standards

   Tip: When you want to make sure a paragraph will *always* stay together, change the Widow/Orphan Lines setting for the paragraph to 100, its maximum possible value.

8. Save the file, and close the document. Also close any other documents that are open at this time.

Using Special Formats for Headings

The Format setting of the Pagination properties specifies whether a heading is a normal paragraph, a run-in head, a side head, or straddles the columns in a multicolumn text frame.

FrameMaker provides three types of special headings—side heads, straddle heads, and run-in heads.

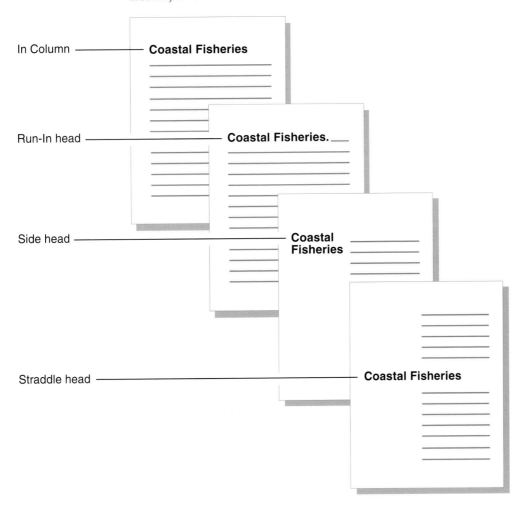

These special headings add to the appearance of the document, and serve as a navigation device when a reader's eye scans the page. You can use any combination of side heads, straddle heads, and run-in heads in a document.

Exercise 3

Guided Tour

Using side heads

A side head appears in the side head area of the current text flow.

In this exercise, you'll look at a side head paragraphs in a sample template, and then you'll apply the heading's paragraph format to text you add to the document.

1. From the FrameMaker list of standard templates, open a copy of the **Report, Sidehead** template with sample text:

   a. Open the New dialog box.

Macintosh	From the File menu, choose **New**.
Windows	From the File menu, choose **New**.
UNIX	In the main FrameMaker window, click **NEW.**

   b. Click **Explore Standard Templates**.

   The Standard Templates window appears.

   c. In the list of templates, click **Report, Sidehead**.

   d. At the bottom of the window, click **Show Sample**.

   The Sidehead Report template appears. Notice that the headings are in English and the body text is in Latin.

2. Use the Save As dialog box to save the document in the Class directory or folder with the new filename heading.

3. From the View menu, choose **Text Symbols** to turn on text symbols.

4. Put the insertion point in the side head on the left, "THE FLAMES FOLLOWED SOON AFTER."

Side head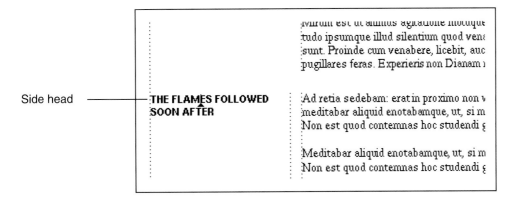

5. If it's not already open, open the Paragraph Designer and display the **Pagination** properties.

Look at the Pagination properties in the Paragraph Designer. The paragraph tag for the heading is Heading2. In the Format area, Side Head is turned on. This positions the heading in the side-head area to the left of the main text column.

6. Go to **page 2**.

7. Put the insertion point at the end of the paragraph starting with the number 3.

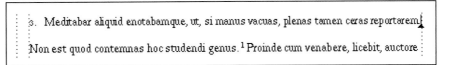

8. Press **Return**.

The number 4 appears at the beginning of the next paragraph.

> 3. Meditabar aliquid enotabamque, ut, si ma
> 4.

9. Open the **Paragraph Catalog**.

10. In the Paragraph Catalog, click **Heading2**.

   Because Heading2 is defined as a side-head paragraph, the insertion point appears in the side-head area to the left of the next paragraph.

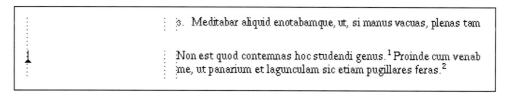

> 3. Meditabar aliquid enotabamque, ut, si manus vacuas, plenas tam
>
> Non est quod contemnas hoc studendi genus.[1] Proinde cum venab
> me, ut panarium et lagunculam sic etiam pugillares feras.[2]

11. Type: THIRTY DAYS LATER

> **THIRTY DAYS LATER**   Non est quod contemnas hoc studendi g&
>   me, ut panarium et lagunculam sic etiam

12. Press **Return**.

   The insertion point moves out of the side-head area, and the paragraph is tagged Body. Heading2 paragraphs are followed by Body paragraphs by default.

13. Type text until it wraps to become a two-line paragraph.

> **YS LATER**   Relief supplies from around the country poured in during the first few weeks following
>   the catastrophe.

Exercise 4   **Modifying a document using side heads**

In this exercise, you'll modify the heading document by removing the area for side heads and observing how text flows when the document's page layout does not allow room for side heads.

1. Go to **page 1**.

2. Put the insertion point in the heading "THE FLAMES FOLLOWED SOON AFTER."

> **THE FLAMES FOLLOWED**   Ad retia sedebam: erat in proximo non v
> **SOON AFTER**   meditabar aliquid enotabamque, ut, si m
>   Non est quod contemnas hoc studendi &

3. From the Format menu, choose **Page Layout>Column Layout**.

The Column Layout dialog box appears.

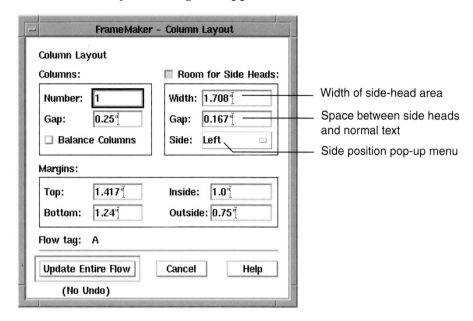

Currently the document is set up with Room for Side Heads turned on.

4. In the Column Layout dialog box, turn off **Room for Side Heads**.

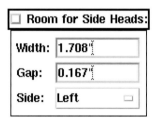

5. Click **Update Entire Flow**.

Notice the area for side heads disappears and the text now flows across the entire text frame.

> **Elaboration:** Although paragraph formats may be designated as side head paragraphs, these paragraphs will appear in the normal text flow until the document's column layout is set to leave room for side heads.

6. Turn **Room for Side Heads** back on:

a. From the Format menu, choose **Page Layout>Column Layout**.

b. In the Column Layout dialog box, turn *on* **Room for Side Heads**.

c. Click **Update Entire Flow**.

The document appears as it did before Room for Side Heads was turned off.

Exercise 5

Guided Tour

Punctuating run-in heads

A run-in head appears on the same line as the body text, but is still a separate paragraph. The punctuation of the heading is part of the heading format, so it does not appear when the run-in head is included in a generated file such as a table of contents.

In this exercise, you'll look at a run-in head in the `heading` document, and then you'll apply the heading's paragraph format to text you add to the document.

1. Put the insertion point in the bold word at the beginning of the last paragraph on page 1.

Run-In head ——

> **Ridebis.** Mirum est ut animus agitatione motuque corporis excitetur. Iam undique silvae et solitudo ipsumque illud silentium quod venationi datur magna cogitationis incitamenta sunt. Proinde cum venabere, licebit, auctore me, ut panarium et lagunculam sic etiam pugillares feras.

Look at the Pagination properties in the Paragraph Designer. The word "Ridebis" is actually a separate paragraph. The paragraph tag is HeadingRunIn.

In the Format area, Run-In Head is turned on. A period is set as the default punctuation following the heading.

> **Tip:** To override the default punctuation of a run-in head, type a punctuation character after the run-in heading text.

2. Go to **page 2**.

3. Put the insertion point at the end of the paragraph you typed in the previous exercise that starts with the words "Relief supplies."

> **THIRTY DAYS LATER**   Relief supplies from around the country poured in during the first few the catastrophe.

4. Press **Return**.

5. In the Paragraph Catalog, click **HeadingRunIn**.

Because HeadingRunIn is defined as a run-in head paragraph, the text in the paragraph below moves up so that insertion point appears at the beginning of the next paragraph.

> Non est quod contemnas hoc studendi genus.[1] Proinde cum venabere, licebit, auctore me, ut panarium et lagunculam sic etiam pugillares feras.[2]

6. Type: `Fires Extinguished`

Do not type a period. The punctuation (a period) is included in the paragraph format.

> **Fires Extinguished.** Non est quod contemnas hoc studendi genus.[1] Proinde cum venabere, licebit, auctore me, ut panarium et lagunculam sic etiam pugillares feras.[2]

The Body paragraph moves over to accommodate the text of the run-in head paragraph.

7. Save the file, and close the document. If any other documents are open at this time, close them as well.

Exercise 6

Guided Tour

Using Across All Columns formats

When you want text to span more than one column in a multicolumn document, you use a straddle head paragraph format. A straddle head can span either all the columns of a text flow, but not the side head area, or it can span both the side head area and all the columns.

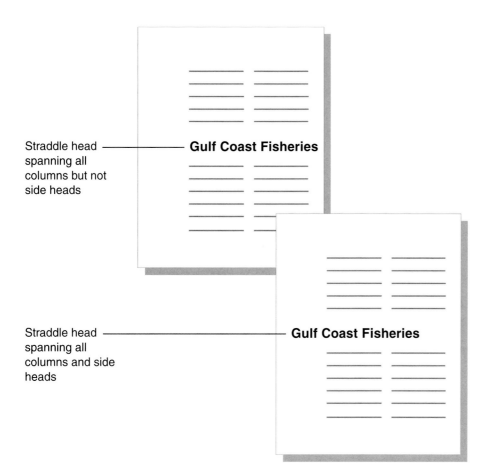

Straddle head spanning all columns but not side heads

Straddle head spanning all columns and side heads

In this exercise, you'll see what happens to text when a paragraph "straddles" two columns.

1. From the FrameMaker list of sample documents, open the **Report** sample:

   a. Display the FrameMaker list of sample documents.

Macintosh	From the [?] menu, choose **Samples & Clip Art**.
Windows	From the Help menu, choose **Samples & Clip Art**.
UNIX	From a document Help menu, choose **Samples & Clip Art**. (If there are no open documents, click **NEW**, then **Portrait**, first.)

   b. In the FrameMaker samples window, click **Report**.

   The sample report appears.

2. From the View menu, choose **Borders**.

3. Use the Save As dialog box to save the document in the `Class` directory or folder with the new filename `straddle`.

4. Go to **page 2**.

5. Put the insertion point in the paragraph that straddles both columns.

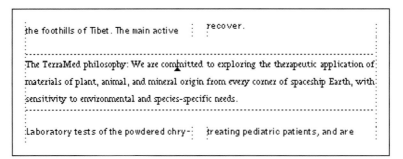

6. Display the **Pagination** properties in the Paragraph Designer.

   Notice in the Pagination properties that Across All Columns is turned on. This paragraph is a straddle head.

7. Put the insertion point between the words "Tibet" and "The" in the left column above the straddle.

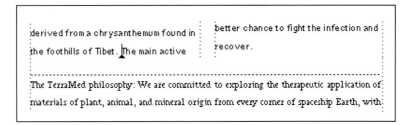

8. Type: `The medicinal properties of the chrysanthemum were first discovered by Tibetan monks in the 12th century.`

The text wraps *above* the straddle, and moves to the top of the next column, under the graphic.

> hailed by the international medical community as a life-saving intervention in the treatment of pneumonia. Res Pan is derived from a chrysanthemum found in the foothills of Tibet. The medicinal properties of the chrysanthemum were
>
> discovered by Tibetan monks in the 12th century. The main active ingredient, xanthistate, is effective in clearing the lungs of secretions produced by pneumonia, giving patients a better chance to fight the infection and recover.
>
> The TerraMed philosophy: We are committed to exploring the therapeutic application of materials of plant, animal, and mineral origin from every corner of spaceship Earth, with sensitivity to environmental and species-specific needs.

Note: If you add text above the straddle, the text will always stay above the straddle. If you want to add text under the straddle, put your insertion point under the straddle, and type text. Text will never automatically move from above the straddle to the leftmost column under the straddle.

9. Save the file, and close the document.

Setting Advanced Properties

In the Advanced properties of the Paragraph Designer, you determine how a paragraph hyphenates, specify a paragraph's word spacing, and specify a reference frame to appear above or below a paragraph. In this module, you'll focus primarily on the hyphenation properties.

When FrameMaker hyphenates text, it breaks words at the ends of lines so that the lines are approximately the same length. Without hyphenation, nonjustified paragraphs have more ragged (or uneven) lines, and justified paragraphs have more space between words.

Nonjustified, not hyphenated

If formal standards do exist, they can be utilized as baseline measurements of reasonable behavior, otherwise the judge may set standards based on social necessity. The wetlands were classified into types, mapped and areal extents determined. Total vegetated wetlands in Wallop Bay and its contiguous drainage area were estimated to be about 6,000 hectares. Of this total, about 2,500 hectares have been diked for various purposes. Some of the diked areas remain as agricultural grasslands still under some tidal influence, while others have been filled to become uplands. All are partially or even wholly removed form directly interacting as a part of the estuarine ecosystem. — Ragged edge

Nonjustified, hyphenated

If formal standards do exist, they can be utilized as baseline measurements of reasonable behavior, otherwise the judge may set standards based on social necessity. The wetlands were classified into types, mapped and areal extents determined. Total vegetated wetlands in Wallop Bay and its contiguous drainage area were estimated to be about 6,000 hectares. Of this total, about 2,500 hectares have been diked for various purposes. Some of the diked areas remain as agricultural grasslands still under some tidal influence, while others have been filled to become uplands. All are partially or even wholly removed form directly interacting as a part of the estuarine ecosystem. — Edge not as ragged

Justified, not hyphenated

If formal standards do exist, they can be utilized as baseline measurements of reasonable behavior, otherwise the judge may set standards based on social necessity. The wetlands were classified into types, mapped and areal extents determined. Total vegetated wetlands in Wallop Bay and its contiguous drainage area were estimated to be about 6,000 hectares. Of this total, about 2,500 hectares have been diked for various purposes. Some of the diked areas remain as agricultural grasslands still under some tidal influence, while others have been filled to become uplands. All are partially or even wholly removed form directly interacting as a part of the estuarine ecosystem. — More space between letters

Justified, hyphenated

If formal standards do exist, they can be utilized as baseline measurements of reasonable behavior, otherwise the judge may set standards based on social necessity. The wetlands were classified into types, mapped and areal extents determined. Total vegetated wetlands in Wallop Bay and its contiguous drainage area were estimated to be about 6,000 hectares. Of this total, about 2,500 hectares have been diked for various purposes. Some of the diked areas remain as agricultural grasslands still under some tidal influence, while others have been filled to become uplands. All are partially or even wholly removed form directly interacting as a part of the estuarine ecosystem. — Less space between letters

Exercise 7

Guided Tour

Using hyphenation

In this exercise, you'll turn on hyphenation in a paragraph. You'll also add a word to your personal dictionary that is designated as a word not to hyphenate.

1. From the FrameMaker list of sample documents, open the book chapter **resource.doc**:

   a. Display the FrameMaker list of sample documents.

Macintosh	From the [?] menu, choose **Samples & Clip Art**.
Windows	From the Help menu, choose **Samples & Clip Art**.
UNIX	In the main FrameMaker window, click **NEW**.
	In the New dialog box, click **Portrait**.
	From the Help menu, choose **Samples & Clip Art**.

   b. Click **Book**.

   c. Double-click **resource.doc** to open the file.

2. Use the Save As window to save the file in the `Class` directory or folder with the name: `hyphen`

3. From the View menu, turn on **Borders**.

4. Go to **page 11**.

5. Put the insertion point anywhere in the paragraph below the heading, "1.13 Conclusion."

> **1.13 Conclusion**
>
> With the advent of the environmental movement, and particularly in response to the National Environmental Policy Act and other legislation, the environmental baseline study has become an accepted element of many federal resource development and environmental protection programs. Currently, baseline studies conducted by various governmental agencies or required by regulations address a wide range of environments, resource developments and potential impacts.

6. From the Properties pop-up menu in the Paragraph Designer, choose **Advanced**.

   Notice that this is a Body paragraph, and that Hyphenation is turned off for this paragraph

7. Turn on **Hyphenation**.

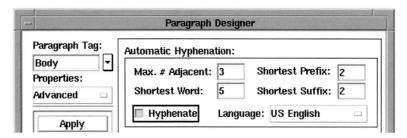

8. Click **Update All**.

   The following alert appears:

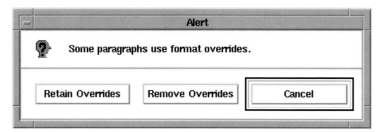

Elaboration: This alert frequently appears when you update the properties of a format used throughout a long document. One common reason a paragraph format is overridden is to make it either start at the top of the next column or page, or to keep it with the next or previous paragraph. In most circumstances, it is safest to retain the overrides.

9. Click **Retain Overrides.**

   All body text in the document is now hyphenated and the text adjusts.

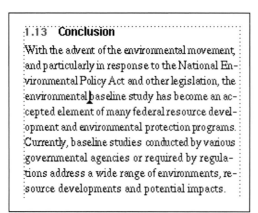

10. Save the file, and keep the document open if you intend to complete the optional exercises in this module. Otherwise, close the document and any other open documents.

Optional Exercises

The following exercises enable you to enhance your FrameMaker skills and to explore additional FrameMaker features. Some steps are intentionally brief, so that they require more independent thought on your part.

Exercise 8

Optional

Specifying that a word not be hyphenated

In this optional exercise, you'll specify that a particular word not be hyphenated when Hyphenation is turned on.

1. At the top of the right column, select the hyphenated word "Environmental."

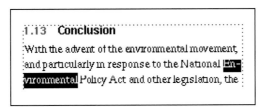

2. From the Edit menu, choose **Spelling Checker**.

3. In the text box at the top of the Spelling Checker, type: -Environmental

> **Note:** By placing the hyphen in front of this word, and clicking Learn, you add "Environmental" to your personal dictionary as a word not to hyphenate.

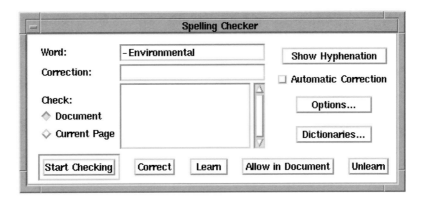

4. Click **Learn**.

The Spelling Checker continues to check the document.

5. In the Spelling Checker window, click **Dictionaries**.

6. In the Dictionary Functions dialog box, turn on **Rehyphenate Document**, and click **OK**.

The word Environmental now appears without hyphenation.

1.13 Conclusion

With the advent of the environmental movement, and particularly in response to the National Environmental Policy Act and other legislation,

---

Tip: To remove a custom hyphenation specification, follow the same steps as above, but click Unlearn.

Exercise 9

Optional

Justifying text

In this optional exercise, you'll justify the body text of the document.

1. Make sure the insertion point is anywhere in the first paragraph below the heading, "1.13 Conclusion."

1.13 Conclusion

With the advent of the environmental movement, and particularly in response to the National Environmental Policy Act and other legislation, the environmental baseline study has become an accepted element of many federal resource development and environmental protection programs. Currently, baseline studies conducted by various governmental agencies or required by regulations address a wide range of environments, resource developments and potential impacts.

---

2. In the Paragraph Designer, from the Properties pop-up menu, choose **Basic**.

3. From the Alignment pop-up menu, choose **Justified**.

4. Click **Update All**.

5. In the alert that appears, click **Retain Overrides**.

All the body text appears justified.

1.13 Conclusion

With the advent of the environmental movement, and particularly in response to the National Environmental Policy Act and other legislation, the environmental baseline study has become an accepted element of many federal resource development and environmental protection programs. Currently, baseline studies conducted by various governmental agencies or required by regulations address a wide range of environments, resource developments and potential impacts.

6. Save the file, and close the document.

Review   Test your understanding of the concepts and procedures covered in this module by answering the following review questions. You may check your answers with those listed below.

Question 1: How do you make a paragraph start at the top of the next page?

Question 2: How do you make sure that headings in a document will always stay with the following paragraph?

Question 3: What property do you modify to make sure that a single line of body text will not be left at the top or bottom of a column? What is a common value for the setting?

Question 4: How is a side head different from a run-in head?

Question 5: How do you hyphenate a paragraph?

Answer 1: In the Paragraph Designer, in the Pagination properties, change the Start setting to Top of Page.

Answer 2: In the Paragraph Designer, in the Pagination properties, turn on Keep with Next.

Answer 3: The widow/orphan property. The value of this property is typically set to ~ 2 lines.

Answer 4: A side head is located in the side head area to the left of paragraph that follows it. A run-in head appears in the same line as the paragraph that follows it.

Answer 5: In the Paragraph Designer, in the Advanced properties, turn on Hyphenate.

For more information

For more information about Pagination and Advanced properties in the FrameMaker Paragraph Designer, see:

Chapters 4 and 5 of *Using FrameMaker*

Numbering Properties

Approximate time to complete: 45 minutes

Introduction

In this module, you'll become familiar with using and modifying autonumber formats. Autonumbering is used to create numbered lists, bulleted items, table titles, and figure titles.

Module Objectives

In this module, you'll learn how to:

- Use and modify simple numbered lists.
- Use and modify simple lists with an alphabetic numbering style.
- Include text in numbered lists.
- Create a text-only autonumbered paragraph format.
- Use character formats with autonumbers.
- Create a special-character bullet.

FrameMaker Model

Numbering properties are included in paragraph *formats*.

Using Autonumbered Paragraph Formats

Lists in FrameMaker are created by setting up autonumber formats for paragraphs. As you add autonumbered paragraphs to your document, FrameMaker numbers them appropriately and renumbers those already in your document, if necessary.

An autonumbered list can be:

■ Numerically or alphabetically numbered paragraphs

1.
2.
3.

A.
B.
C.

■ Text and numbered paragraphs

Chapter 11
Section 2.3
Example 5:

Exercise 12:
Table C:
Figure 3b.

■ Text-only paragraphs:

•
Note:
Caution:

Hint:
To:
From:

Exercise 1

Project

Restarting autonumbered lists

In this exercise, you'll use autonumbering to create the list shown below:

> **Planning**
> 1. Lease
> 2. Permits
> 3. Contractors
>
> **Startup**
> 1. Vendors
> 2. Workforce

To do this, you'll use the two autonumbered paragraph formats, Numbered1 and Numbered, found in FrameMaker templates.

1. Create a new **Portrait** document:

   a. Open the New dialog box.

Macintosh	From the File menu, choose **New**.
Windows	From the File menu, choose **New**.
UNIX	In the main FrameMaker window, click **NEW**.

   b. Click **Portrait**.

2. Use the Save As dialog box to save the document in the Class directory or folder with the new filename number.

3. At the insertion point, type: Planning

4. Open the **Paragraph Catalog**.

5. Apply the **Heading2** paragraph format to the paragraph.

6. Press **Return**.

7. In the Paragraph Catalog, click **Numbered1**.

   FrameMaker automatically inserts the number 1, followed by a period and a tab.

> **Planning¶**
> 1. ⟩§

In the Paragraph Catalog, notice the two paragraph tags, Numbered1 and Numbered. Numbered1 restarts a list with the number 1, and Numbered increases the number incrementally to 2, 3, 4, etc.

8. Type: Lease

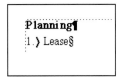

9. Press **Return**.

FrameMaker uses the Numbered paragraph format, and inserts the number 2 followed by a period and a tab.

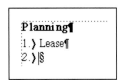

10. Enter the remaining items on the list as shown below.

11. Put the insertion point at the end of item number 3.

12. Press **Return**.

13. In the Paragraph Catalog, click **Heading2**.

14. Type: Startup

15. Put the insertion point in the paragraph that starts with the number 4, and then in the Paragraph Catalog, click **Numbered1**.

    The Numbered1 paragraph format is applied to the current paragraph, and the number 1 appears.

16. Press **Return**.

FrameMaker automatically inserts the number 2, using the Numbered paragraph format.

17. Press **Delete** to remove the extra number.

Modifying Autonumbered Paragraph Formats

Autonumber formats are created using the Numbering properties group of the Paragraph Designer. The Numbering properties of the Numbered1 format are shown below.

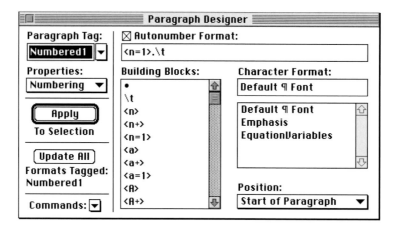

The individual elements of an autonumber are called *building blocks*. They can be typed into the Autonumber Format text box manually or they can be entered using the Building Blocks scroll list.

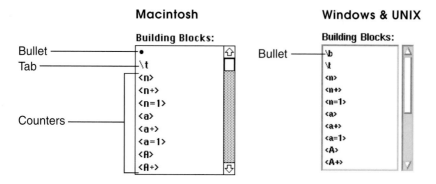

A *counter* is a placeholder that FrameMaker replaces with a number or letter in a sequence. For example, the counter <n+> incrementally increases the paragraph's number by one.

Each counter has a pair of angle brackets (< >) and information about the counter inside the brackets. Each counter is initially set to zero in the document. Thereafter, the counter can maintain its current value, or increase its value by 1.

Different types of numbered lists are created by using different counters. A list of autonumber counters and the type of autonumbered list they produce is shown below.

n = Arabic numbers (1, 2, 3, ...)

r = lowercase Roman (i, ii, iii, iv, ...)

R = uppercase Roman (I, II, III, IV, ...)

a = lowercase alphabetic (a, b, c, d, ...)

A = uppercase alphabetic (A, B, C, D, ...)

\t = insert tab character

Exercise 2

Project

Modifying the counter value

In this exercise, you'll see how autonumbered paragraph formats are defined in the Paragraph Designer, and you'll modify the counter value to make the list begin with capital letters, as shown below.

Planning
A. Lease
B. Permits
C. Contractors
Startup
A. Vendors
B. Workforce

1. Make sure the insertion point appears in the Numbered1 paragraph.

2. From the Format menu, choose **Paragraphs>Designer**.

   The Paragraph Designer appears.

3. From the Properties pop-up menu in the Paragraph Designer, choose **Numbering**.

The Numbering properties are displayed.

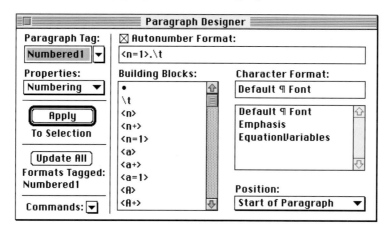

The building blocks for the Numbered1 paragraph format appear in the Autonumber Format text box. The building block <n=1> resets the counter to the number 1. There is also a period and a tab building block (\t) to make a period and some space appear after the number.

4. Put the insertion point in any Numbered paragraph (beginning with a number other than 1).

The Numbered paragraph tag appears in the Paragraph Designer.

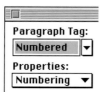

Notice the building block is <n+>, followed by a period and a tab.
The building block <n+> increments the previous number in the list.

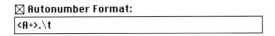

5. Change the autonumber format to use alphabetic characters:

    a. In the Autonumber Format text box, delete <n+> and type: <A+>

    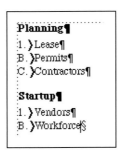

    > **Tip:** You can also enter <A+> by clicking that item in the Building Blocks scroll list.

    b. Click **Update All**.

    All Numbered paragraphs now begin with alpha characters.

    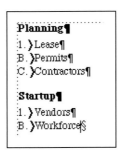

6. Change the Numbered1 format to use alphabetic characters:

    a. In the Paragraph Designer, from the Paragraph Tag pop-up menu, choose **Numbered1**.

    The autonumber format for the Numbered1 paragraph format appears in the Paragraph Designer.

    b. In the Autonumber Format text box, delete <n=1> and type: <A=1>

    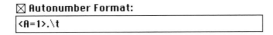

    c. Click **Update All**.

The Numbered1 paragraphs now begin with the letter A.

Exercise 3

Adding text to an autonumber format

In this exercise, you'll include text in the format to modify the autonumbering as shown below.

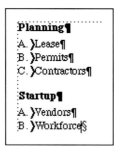

1. Make sure your insertion point is in a Numbered paragraph.

2. Change the autonumber format of the Numbered and Numbered1 paragraph formats to include the word "Step," followed by a space, before the building block:

   a. In the Paragraph Designer, in the Autonumber Format text box, click at the beginning of the text box and type: Step and then type a space.

b. Click **Update All**.

c. In the Paragraph Designer, from the Paragraph Tag pop-up menu, choose **Numbered1**.

d. Repeat steps a and b for the Numbered1 paragraph format.

Your document should now look like this:

Using Character Formats in Autonumber Formats

The character format for an autonumber can be different from the default font of the autonumbered paragraph. For example, you may want numbers or letters to be bold even though the text that follows it is not, or you may want the numbers in a list of steps to be in Helvetica font, and the text in Times.

In the Numbering properties of the Paragraph Designer there is a scroll list that you can use assign character formats to an autonumber. The list of character formats is the same as those found in the Character Catalog.

Exercise 4

Project

Changing character formats

In this exercise, you'll change the character format of the numbered paragraphs.

1. Change the autonumber character format of the Numbered and Numbered1 paragraph formats to **Emphasis**:

    a. Make sure the Numbering properties of the Numbered paragraph format are displayed in the Paragraph Designer.

    b. In the Paragraph Designer, in the Character Format scroll list, click **Emphasis**.

    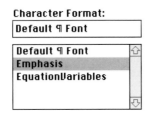

    c. Click **Update All**.

    The autonumbers of the Numbered paragraphs change to italics, the properties of the Emphasis character format.

    d. Use the Paragraph Tag pop-up menu to choose **Numbered1**.

    e. In the Character Format scroll list, click **Emphasis**, and then click **Update All**.

    Your document should now look like this:

Text-only Autonumber Formats

Previously, you included text with a counter in an autonumbered paragraph format. You can also use text alone—without a counter—in the format.

A Bulleted paragraph is one example of a text-only autonumbered paragraph format. The building blocks for a Bulleted paragraph include a bullet character (on the Macintosh, a bullet symbol: •) followed by a tab (\t).

Autonumber format of Bulleted paragraph format

Bulleted tag applied to paragraph

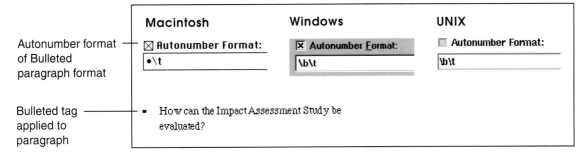

When a tab is used in the autonumber and you want the text in subsequent lines of the paragraph to wrap under the text of the first line, the Tab Stop and the Left Indent settings must be identical. This type of indentation is called a "hanging" indent.

Left Indent setting

Hanging indent

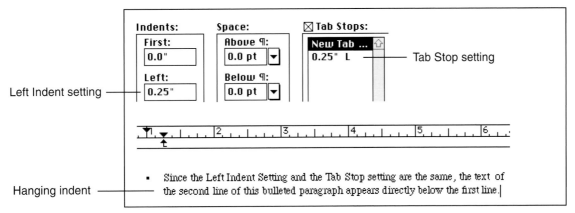

The following examples show some uses of text-only autonumbered paragraph formats.

Note: Take with plenty of food.

WARNING! Harmful or fatal if swallowed.

Exercise 5

Project

Creating a text-only autonumbered paragraph format

In this exercise, you'll create a text-only autonumbered paragraph form at that displays the word "note" at the beginning of the paragraph, as shown below.

> **Note:** Hourly plant personnel will be hired locally. Some exempt employees may need to be recruited from out of the area.

You'll start by looking at an existing text-only autonumbered format, and then you'll modify that format by changing its autonumber text, assigning it a character format, and changing its tab settings.

1. Put the insertion point at the end of the last Numbered paragraph in the document.

2. Press **Return**.

3. In the Paragraph Designer, from the Paragraph Tag pop-up menu, choose **Bulleted**.

4. Click **Apply**.

The Bulleted format is applied to the current paragraph. The Bulleted paragraph tag and the corresponding autonumber format appear in the Paragraph Designer. Notice that the Bulleted tag contains no counter, only a bullet symbol and a tab character.

Macintosh

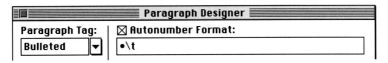

Windows and UNIX

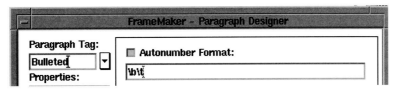

Note: In UNIX and Windows, a bullet is represented by \b in the Autonumber Format text box and in the Building Blocks scroll list.

5. Type:

   Hourly plant personnel will be hired locally. Some exempt employees may need to be recruited from out of the area.

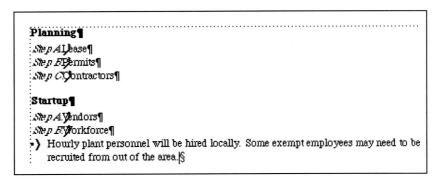

6. Create a new text-only autonumber format named **Note**:

   a. With the insertion point in the Bulleted paragraph, in the Paragraph Designer, from the Commands pop-up menu, choose **New Format**.

   The New Format dialog box appears.

b. In the Tag text box, type: `Note`

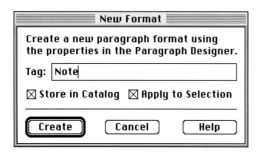

c. Make sure **Store in Catalog** and **Apply to Selection** are turned on.

d. Click **Create**.

The Note paragraph format is applied to the current paragraph and Note is added to the Paragraph Catalog.

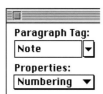

7. Replace the Bulleted autonumber format with the word `Note`, followed by a colon and a tab building block:

a. In the Paragraph Designer, in the Autonumber Format text box, delete the **\b** building block (• on the Macintosh).

b. In the same location as the deleted building block, type: `Note:` (don't forget the colon)

c. Click **Update All**.

> Note:Hourly plant personnel will be hired locally. Some exempt employees may need to be
> recruited from out of the area.§

Next, you'll adjust the tabs and indents of the Note paragraph format to move the text in the first line farther away from the word "Note," and to make the second line of text appear below the first line.

8. In the Paragraph Designer, change the left indent and left tab stop to **.4"**:

a. From the Properties pop-up menu, choose **Basic**.

b. Change the number in the Left Indent text box to **.4"**.

c. In the Tab Stops scroll list, click the **0.25" L** tab.

d. At the bottom of the Tab Stops scroll list, click **Edit**.

The Edit Tab Stop dialog box appears.

e. In the New Position text box, change the number to **.4"**

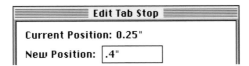

f. Click **Continue**.

g. In the Paragraph Designer, click **Update All**.

Space is added between the word "Note:" and the text of the note. Text in the second line is aligned with the text in the first line.

> Note: Hourly plant personnel will be hired locally. Some exempt employees may need to be recruited from out of the area.§

Next, you'll create a bold character format to apply to the autonumber text, the word "Note."

9. Create a new character format named **Bold**:

a. From the Format menu, choose **Characters>Designer**.

The Character Designer appears.

b. From the Commands pop-up menu, choose **Set Window to As Is**.

c. From the Weight pop-up menu, choose **Bold**.

d. From the Commands pop-up menu, choose **New Format**.

The New Format dialog box appears.

e. In the Tag text box, type: Bold

f. Make sure **Store in Catalog** is turned on, but turn *off* **Apply to Selection**.

g. Click **Create**.

> **Elaboration:** Apply to Selection is turned off because the Bold character format can only be applied to the autonumbered text through the Numbering properties of the Paragraph Designer. Leaving Apply to Selection turned on would assign the character format to whatever text is currently selected in the document, which is not desirable.

10. Apply the **Bold** character format to the autonumber of the Note paragraph:

    a. In the Paragraph Designer, from the Properties pop-up menu, choose **Numbering**.

    b. In the Character Format scroll list, click **Bold**.

    c. Click **Update All**.

    The word "Note:" becomes bold.

    > **Note:** Hourly plant personnel will be hired locally. Some exempt employees may need to be recruited from out of the area. §

11. Save the file, and keep the document open if you intend to complete the optional exercise in this module. Otherwise, close the document.

Optional Exercise

The following exercise enables you to enhance your FrameMaker skills and to explore additional FrameMaker features. Some steps are intentionally brief, so that they require more independent thought on your part.

Exercise 6

Optional

Creating a bulleted list using a Symbol character

You can use characters other than a round bullet in your autonumbered lists. In this exercise, you'll create an autonumber format that uses a character in the Symbol font, the diamond (♦).

1. Put the insertion point at the end of the first Numbered1 paragraph.

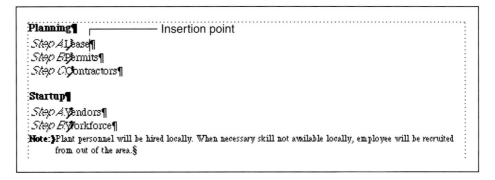

2. Set the Character Designer properties to **As Is**, change the font family to **Symbol**, and the Size to **14 pt**:

   a. In the Character Designer, from the Commands pop-up menu, choose **Set Window to As Is**.

   b. From the Family pop-up menu, choose **Symbol**.

   c. From the Size pop-up menu, choose **14 pt**.

3. Create a new character format named **BulletSymbol**, and store it in the Character Catalog, but *don't* apply it to the current selection:

   a. From the Commands pop-up menu, choose **New Format**.

   b. In the Tag text box, type: `BulletSymbol`

   c. Make sure **Store in Catalog** is turned on and **Apply to Selection** is turned *off*.

   d. Click **Create**.

4. Create a new paragraph format named **BulletDiamond**. Store it in the Paragraph Catalog and apply it to the current selection:

   a. In the Paragraph Designer, from the Commands pop-up menu, choose **New Format**.

   b. In the Tag text box, type: `BulletDiamond`

   c. Make sure **Store in Catalog** and **Apply to Selection** are turned on.

   d. Click **Create**.

5. Change the autonumbering of the BulletDiamond paragraph format so that it displays a diamond-shaped bullet:

   a. In the Paragraph Designer, from the Properties pop-up menu, choose **Numbering**.

   b. Delete the contents of the Autonumber Format text box, and type: ®\t

Macintosh	To enter ®, press **Option-r**
Windows	To enter ®, hold down the **Alt** key while typing **0174**
UNIX	To enter ®, press **Control-q**, and then hold down Shift while typing **(**

   The Autonumber Format should look like this:

   ⊠ **Autonumber Format:**

   ®\t

   c. In the Character Format scroll list, click **BulletSymbol**, and click **Update All**.

   A diamond-shaped bullet, followed by a tab, appears in the BulletDiamond paragraph in the document.

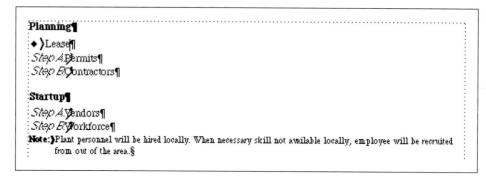

6. Indent the text of the BulletDiamond paragraph format to **0.5"**:

   a. From the Properties pop-up menu, choose **Basic**.

   b. Change the indents to those shown below:

   Indents:

   First:
   .25"

   Left:
   .5"

   Right:
   0.0"

   c. In the Tab Stops list, select the tab stop at **0.25"**.

   d. Click **Edit**.

   e. Delete the contents of the New Position text box, and type: . 5

   f. Click **Continue**.

   g. Click **Update All**.

   The bullet is indented.

7. Apply the BulletDiamond paragraph format to the remaining Numbered and Numbered1 paragraphs in the document:

   a. Select the two Numbered paragraphs below the heading "Planning."

   b. In the Paragraph Designer, from the Paragraph Tag pop-up menu, choose **BulletDiamond**.

   c. Click **Apply**.

   d. Repeat steps a-c with the Numbered1 and Numbered paragraphs below the heading "Startup."

8. From the View menu, turn off **Text Symbols**.

   Your document should now look like this:

   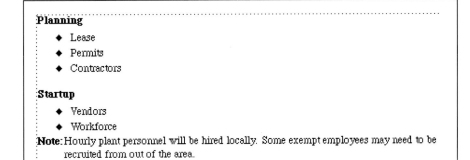

   Planning
   - Lease
   - Permits
   - Contractors

   Startup
   - Vendors
   - Workforce

   Note: Hourly plant personnel will be hired locally. Some exempt employees may need to be recruited from out of the area.

9. Save the file, and close the document.

Review Test your understanding of the concepts and procedures covered in this module by answering the following review questions. You may check your answers with those listed below.

Question 1: What two built-in paragraph formats do you use to create a simple autonumbered list? Why do you need to use two different formats?

Question 2: What building blocks do you use to make an autonumbered list alphabetic?

Question 3: What two Autonumber formats do you use to create the following autonumbered list: Question 1:, Question 2:, Question 3:?

Question 4: How do you make only the number of an autonumbered paragraph bold?

Question 5: How is a text-only autonumbered paragraph different from other autonumbered paragraphs? What are some examples of when to use a text-only autonumbered paragraph?

Answer 1: The Numbered1 and Numbered formats are used to create a simple autonumbered list. You apply the Numbered1 format to the first paragraph in a numbered list, because it makes the paragraph start with the number one. You apply the Numbered format to the remaining paragraphs in the list to make each paragraph increase incrementally by one.

Answer 2: The <A=1> and <A+> building blocks.

Answer 3: Question <n=1>: is the first autonumber format.
Question <n+>: is the autonumber format for the rest of the list.

Answer 4: Create a character tag that is bold. In the Numbering properties of the Paragraph Designer, in the Character Format scroll list, click the bold character tag.

Answer 5: Text-only autonumbered paragraphs do not contain any numbers. Examples of text-only paragraphs are bullets, notes, warnings, cautions, and so on.

For more information

For more information about autonumbering, see:

Chapter 4 of *Using FrameMaker*

Multiple Autonumbers

Approximate time to complete: 45 minutes

Introduction

In this module, you'll create some autonumber formats that automatically reset and others that are made up of multiple counters. FrameMaker's autonumbering capabilities allow you to identify multiple levels as well as different series of autonumbers within the same text flow.

Module Objectives

In this module, you'll learn how to:

- Automatically reset counters
- Use series labels
- Use multiple counters

FrameMaker Model

Multiple autonumbers are created using the numbering properties included in paragraph *formats*.

Resetting Autonumbered Paragraphs

In the previous module, you created autonumbered lists using two paragraph formats. The Numbered1 format set the first item in the list to number 1, and the Numbered format was used to create the consecutive numbers after that, as shown in the example below.

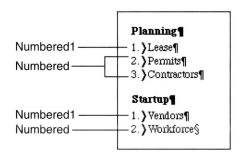

Another way to reset the counter in a list uses only one paragraph format. If your document includes a particular paragraph that always precedes a numbered list (for example, a first-level heading), you can use its autonumber to reset the count to zero, and create a single paragraph format for all numbered steps, as shown below.

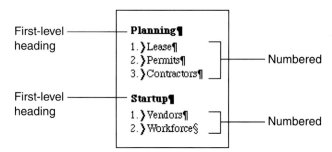

Exercise 1

Project

Automatically resetting autonumbered paragraphs

In this exercise, you'll create a single autonumbered paragraph format that will automatically reset when preceded by a Heading1 paragraph. An example is shown below.

1. Create a new **Portrait** document:

   a. Open the New dialog box.

Macintosh	From the File menu, choose **New**.
Windows	From the File menu, choose **New**.
UNIX	In the main FrameMaker window, click **NEW**.

   b. Click **Portrait**.

2. Use the Save As dialog box to save the document in the Class directory or folder with the new filename multnum.

3. Type: Screening

4. Open the **Paragraph Catalog**.

5. Apply the **Heading1** paragraph format to the paragraph.

6. Press **Return**.

7. Apply the **Bulleted** paragraph format to the paragraph.

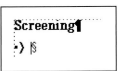

8. Create a new paragraph format named **AlphaStep**. Be sure to store it in the Paragraph Catalog and apply it to the current selection:

   a. In the Paragraph Designer, from the Commands pop-up menu, choose **New Format.**

   The New Format dialog box appears.

   b. In the Tag text box, type: AlphaStep

   c. Make sure **Store in Catalog** and **Apply to Selection** are turned on.

   d. Click **Create**.

   The AlphaStep paragraph format is applied to the current paragraph and added to the Paragraph Catalog.

9. Change the autonumber format to <A+>.\t:

   a. From the Properties pop-up menu in the Paragraph Designer, choose **Numbering**.

   b. Delete the text in the Autonumber Format text box.

c. In the Building Blocks scroll list, click **<A+>**, type a **period** (.), and click **\t** in the scroll list.

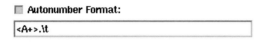

d. Click **Update All**.

The paragraph changes to include an alphabetic character.

10. Enter the additional text as shown below. Be sure to apply the **Heading1** format to the heading "Implementation," and the **AlphaStep** format to the paragraph that follows it.

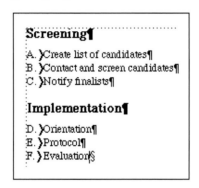

11. Change the Heading1 paragraph's autonumber format to < =0> to reset the autonumbering to zero:

a. Put the insertion point in one of the Heading1 paragraphs.

b. In the Paragraph Designer, display the **Numbering** properties.

c. In the Autonumber Format text box, type: < =0>

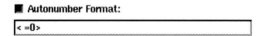

> **Note:** Make sure the left bracket is followed by a space. This is so the counter will be reset, but no number will appear in the Heading1 paragraph in the document.

d. Click **Update All**.

The counter is reset to zero for the numbered list that follows the Heading1 paragraph.

> **Screening¶**
>
> A.)Create list of candidates¶
> B.)Contact and screen candidates¶
> C.)Notify finalists¶
>
> **Implementation¶**
>
> A.)Orientation¶
> B.)Protocol¶
> C.)Evaluation§

Series Labels in Autonumbered Paragraphs

An autonumber series label distinguishes one series of autonumbering from another within the same flow of text. For example, to number figures and tables independently of each other, you could use the letters F and T as the series labels for figure and table numbering. FrameMaker permits one series of numbers or letters in a flow without a series label. Each additional series must have a series label to keep its numbering independent.

Exercise 2

Project

Using a series label in an autonumber format

In this exercise, you'll create an autonumber paragraph format that contains a series label and text. An example is shown below.

> **Screening**
>
> A. Create list of candidates
>   Figure 1:   Diagram of filtering process used to create list.
> B. Contact and screen candidates
> C. Notify finalists
>
> **Implementation**
>
> A. Orientation
> B. Protocol
>   Figure 2:   List of procedures used in protocol.
> C. Evaluation

1. Put the insertion point at the end of the first line below the Screening heading.

> **Screening¶**
>
> A.)Create list of candidates¶
> B.)Contact and screen candidates¶
> C.)Notify finalists¶

2. Press **Return**.

```
Screening¶
A.)Create list of candidates¶
B.)¶
C.)Contact and screen candidates¶
D.)Notify finalists¶
```

3. Create a new paragraph format named **Figure**. Make sure to store it in the Paragraph Catalog and apply it to the current selection:

   a. In the Paragraph Designer, from the Commands pop-up menu, choose **New Format.**

      The New Format dialog box appears.

   b. In the Tag text box, type: `Figure`

   c. Make sure **Store in Catalog** and **Apply to Selection** are turned on.

   d. Click **Create**.

      The Figure paragraph format is applied to the current paragraph and added to the Paragraph Catalog.

4. In the Paragraph Designer, display the **Numbering** properties.

5. In the Autonumber Format text box, delete the contents and type:
   `Figure <n+>:\t`

6. Click **Update All**.

   The paragraph is numbered "Figure 2:" It is numbering consecutively from the last AlphaStep paragraph.

```
Screening¶
A.)Create list of candidates¶
Figure 2:¶
C.)Contact and screen candidates¶
D.)Notify finalists¶
```

7. Display the **Basic** properties, change the **First** indent to **0.25"**, and the **Left** indent to **1.0"**.

8. Change the position of the Tab Stop at 0.25" to **1.0"** to match the Left indent.

9. Click **Update All**.

   The Figure paragraph is indented.

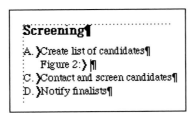

10. Display the **Numbering** properties, and type F : at the beginning of the Autonumber Format text box.

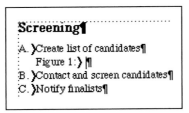

11. Click **Update All**.

    The paragraph autonumbering changes to "Figure 1." This is because you have specified the series label "F."

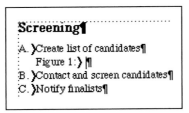

12. In the Figure 1 paragraph, type: Diagram of filtering process used to create list.

13. Below the Implementation heading, click after the word Protocol.

14. Press **Return**, apply the Figure paragraph format, and type:

    List of procedures used in protocol.

The new Figure paragraph is labeled "Figure 2."

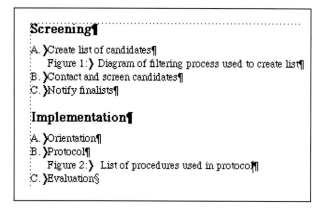

> **Elaboration:** The Heading1 format resets only the unlabeled series of the Alpha Step format. The Figure format continues the numbering sequence under the "F" series label.

15. Save the file, and close the document.

Multiple Counters in Autonumber Formats

An autonumber can have more than one counter. For example, autonumbers for a series of section titles might each have 2 or 3 counters, as follows.

This format	Appears as	And might be tagged as
<n+>.<n=0>	1.0	1Level
<n>.<n+>	1.1	2Level
<n>.<n+>	1.2	2Level
<n+>.<n=0>	2.0	1Level
<n>.<n+>	2.1	2Level
<n>.<n>.<n+>.	2.1.1	3Level

The counters in each format are independent of each other. A counter's position in the string determines how it is displayed and incremented. When incrementing a counter, FrameMaker bases its value on the corresponding counter in the previous autonumber paragraph in the same series, where:

- <n=0> resets the value to zero and displays it.

- <n+> increments the value and displays it.

- <n> carries the value and displays it.

- < > carries the value but doesn't display it.

The < > counter (angle brackets with a space between them) tells FrameMaker to keep the value the same but not to display it. This counter is used because a counter's position in the string determines how it is displayed and incremented. For example, autonumbers for an outline might use the following formats.

This format	Appears as	And might be tagged as
<R+>	I	1stLevel
< ><A+>	A	2ndLevel
< >< ><n+>	1	3rdLevel
< >< >< ><a+>	a	4thLevel
< ><A+>	B	2ndLevel
< >< ><n+>	1	3rdLevel

where:

- <R+> is uppercase Roman numerals incremented by the value of 1.

- < > carries the value but does not display it.

- <A+> is uppercase letters incremented by the value of 1.

- <a+> is lowercase letters incremented by the value of 1.

- <n+> is numbers incremented by the value of 1.

When working with multiple counters, keep these basic concepts in mind:

- A counter is a placeholder in an autonumber string.

- The value of a counter is determined by looking backward. In other words, a counter's value is derived from the previous paragraph's autonumber in the same series.

Exercise 3

Project

Using multiple counters in an autonumber format

In this exercise, you'll use multiple counters in an autonumber format. An example is shown below.

> **1.0   Overview of FrameMaker**
>   1.1   How to think about FrameMaker
>   1.2   Features
> **2.0   Working with Documents**
>   2.1   Opening files
> **3.0   Online Help**
> **4.0   Editing Text**

1. Create a new **Portrait** document, and save it in the `Class` directory or folder with the filename `numprac`.

2. Create a new paragraph format named **1Level**. Make sure to store it in the Paragraph Catalog and apply it to the current selection.

3. Change the properties of the 1Level format to add autonumbering, adjust indents, tab stops and space above, and change the weight to Bold:

   a. Display the **Numbering** properties, and in the Autonumber Format text box, type: `S:<n+>.<n=0>\t`

   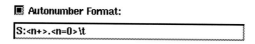

   b. Click **Update All**.

      The paragraph now begins with 1.0.

   c. In the **Basic** properties, change the space above to **6.0 pt**, and add a **Left** tab stop **0.5"** from the left edge of the text column.

   d. Click **Update All**.

   e. Display the **Default Font** properties, change the Weight to **Bold**, and click **Update All**.

4. In the document, type: `Overview of FrameMaker`

5. Press **Return**.

   The new paragraph begins with 2.0.

6. Add the remaining text as shown below.

   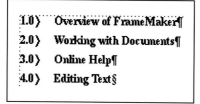

7. Put the insertion point at the end of the first line, and press **Return**.

```
1.0)   Overview of FrameMaker¶
2.0)   ¶
3.0)   Working with Documents¶
4.0)   Online Help¶
5.0)   Editing Text§
```

8. Create a new paragraph format named **2Level**. Be sure to store it in the Paragraph Catalog and apply it to the current selection.

9. Change the properties of the 2Level format to adjust the autonumbering, indents, and tab stops, and change the weight to Roman:

   a. In the Numbering properties, change the autonumber format to:
   S:<n>.<n+>\t

   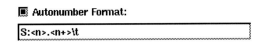

   ▣ Autonumber Format:

   S:<n>.<n+>\t

   b. Click **Update All**.

   The paragraph now begins with 1.1.

   c. Display the **Basic** properties, change the **First** indent to **0.5"**, the **Left** indent and the existing **Tab Stop** to **1.0"**, and then click **Update All**.

   d. In the **Default Font** properties, change the Weight to **Regular** (on the Macintosh, **Roman**), and click **Update All**.

10. In the document, type: How to think about FrameMaker

11. Press **Return**.

    The current paragraph now begins with 1.2.

    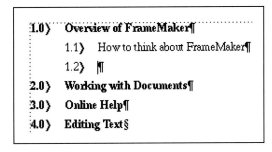

    ```
    1.0)   Overview of FrameMaker¶
           1.1)   How to think about FrameMaker¶
           1.2)   ¶
    2.0)   Working with Documents¶
    3.0)   Online Help¶
    4.0)   Editing Text§
    ```

12. Type: `Features`

13. Put the insertion point at the end of line 2.0, press **Return**, and apply the **2Level** paragraph format.

    The paragraph begins with 2.1.

14. Type: `Opening files`

    Your document should now look like this:

    1.0) **Overview of FrameMaker**¶

        1.1) How to think about FrameMaker¶

        1.2) Features¶

    2.0) **Working with Documents**¶

        2.1) Opening files¶

    3.0) **Online Help**¶

    4.0) **Editing Text**§

    ---

15. Save the file and keep the document open if you intend to complete the optional exercises in this module. Otherwise, close the document.

Optional Exercises

The following exercises enable you to enhance your FrameMaker skills and to explore additional FrameMaker features. Some steps are intentionally brief, so that they require more independent thought on your part.

Exercise 4

Optional

Creating a more complex autonumbered series

In this optional exercise, you'll modify the autonumber formats from the previous exercise and add a new autonumber format to create the list shown below.

> **1.** Overview of FrameMaker
>
> Exercise 1:   How to think about Frame
>
> Exercise 2:   Features
>
> **2.** Working with Documents
>
> Exercise 1:   Opening files
>
> **3.** Online Help
>
> **4.** Editing Text

1. Change the autonumber format of the 1Level paragraph format to:
   `S:<n+>.\t`

   The zero is removed from the 1Level autonumber.

> **1.)** Overview of FrameMaker¶
>
>   1.1)   How to think about FrameMaker¶
>
>   1.2)   Features¶
>
> **2.)** Working with Documents¶
>
>   2.1)   Opening files¶
>
> **3.)** Online Help¶
>
> **4.)** Editing Text§

2. Change the autonumber format of the 2Level paragraph format to:
   `S:Exercise < ><n+>:\t`

> **Note:** Be sure to type a space between the empty angle brackets (< >).

Notice that the 2Level headings are numbered consecutively below the heading, "Overview of FrameMaker," and that the 2Level counter is reset below the heading, "Working with Documents."

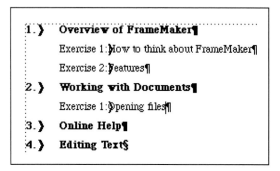

Elaboration: The 2Level autonumber is reset following a 1Level heading because the 2Level autonumber is in the second position in the autonumber string, and the 1Level heading has no placeholder in the second position of its autonumber format.

1Level autonumber format:

```
S:<n+>.\t
```
        └── Displays 1Level autonumber; no placeholder for 2Level autonumber

2Level autonumber format:

```
S:Exercise < ><n+>:\t
```
              │   └── Displays 2Level autonumber
              └── Placeholder for 1Level autonumber

The empty angle brackets (< >) are present in the 2Level autonumber to carry forward the number in the first position of the autonumber string, but not display it in the 2Level autonumber.

3. Change the position of the tab in the 2Level paragraph format to **1.5"**.

   The text appears farther away from the autonumber.

   > 1.)   **Overview of FrameMaker**¶
   >
   >   Exercise 1:)   How to think about Frame
   >
   >   Exercise 2:)   Features¶
   >
   > 2.)   **Working with Documents**¶
   >
   >   Exercise 1:)   Opening files¶
   >
   > 3.)   **Online Help**¶
   >
   > 4.)   **Editing Text**§

4. Save the file, and close the document.

Exercise 5

Optional

Creating an outline document

In this optional exercise, you'll create the outline document shown below using the Harvard Outline template that ships with FrameMaker.

> ### Ecology
>
> David Fisher
>
> I.   **Natural Products**
>
>   A.   **Tropical Rain Forests**
>
>   1.   South America
>
>   2.   Asia
>
>   B.   **North American Wetlands**
>
>   1.   Canada
>
>   2.   United States
>
>   C.   **Gulf Coast Fisheries**
>
> II.   **Impact Assessment**
>
>   A.   **Overview of Concerns**
>
>   B.   **Contemporary Techniques**

1. From the File menu, choose **New** (in UNIX, in the main FrameMaker window, click **NEW**), then click **Explore Standard Templates**.

   The Standard Templates window appears.

2. If the outlines are not visible in the list, click **More** to display additional templates.

More button ———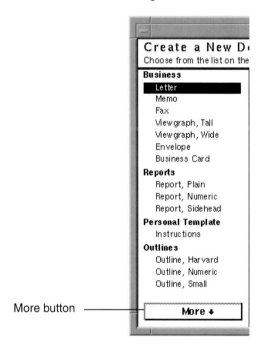

3. Under Outlines, make sure **Outlines, Harvard** is selected.

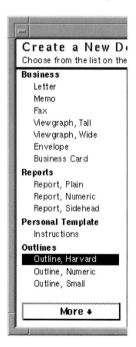

4. Click **Create**.

A blank page appears. The the first blank line is automatically tagged with the Title paragraph format.

> **Elaboration:** When you click Show Sample in the Standard Templates window, the document that appears contains sample text. The paragraph formats in the document have been applied to the sample text to give you an idea of how they should be used. When you click Create instead of Show Sample, a blank document appears. This document contains the same paragraph formats as the sample document, but it is empty so you can enter your own text into the document.

5. Use the Save As dialog box to save the document in the `Class` directory or folder with the new filename: `outline`.

6. Type: `Ecology`

7. Press **Return**.

   The next paragraph is automatically tagged with the Author format.

8. Type your name.

9. Press **Return**.

   The next paragraph format is automatically tagged 1Level, and a Roman numeral one appears at the beginning of the paragraph.

10. Type: `Natural Products`

11. Press **Return**.

12. From the Paragraph Catalog, apply the **2Level** format to the paragraph.

    The paragraph is indented and a capital letter "A" appears at the beginning.

13. Type: `Tropical Rain Forests`

14. Press **Return**.

15. Apply the **3Level** format to the paragraph.

The paragraph is indented further and the number one appears at the beginning.

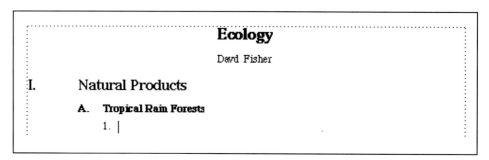

16. Type: South America

17. Press **Return**.

18. Type: Asia

19. Press **Return**.

20. Enter the rest of the text as shown below, applying the appropriate paragraph formats as necessary.

> **Ecology**
>
> David Fisher
>
> I.   Natural Products
>
>   A.   Tropical Rain Forests
>   1. South America
>   2. Asia
>
>   B.   North American Wetlands
>   1. Canada
>   2. United States
>
>   C.   Gulf Coast Fisheries
>
> II.   Impact Assessment
>
>   A.   Overview of Concerns
>
>   B.   Contemporary Techniques

21. Save the file, and close the document.

Review

Test your understanding of the concepts and procedures covered in this module by answering the following review questions. You may check your answers with those listed below.

Question 1: What does the building block < =0> do?

Question 2: What does the building block < > do?

Question 3: When might you need a series label?

Answer 1: It resets the counter to zero without displaying an autonumber.

Answer 2: It suppresses the display of a counter.

Answer 3: When your document contains more than one independently numbered list.

For more information

For more information about autonumbering, see:

Chapter 4 of *Using FrameMaker*

. . . .

PART III

Graphics, Frames, and

Page Types

Graphics

13

Approximate time to complete: 2 hours

Introduction

In this module, you'll become familiar with drawing objects by using the Tools palette and modifying the objects you draw by using the graphics commands.

Module Objectives

In this module, you'll learn how to

- Draw rectangles, ovals, lines, and other objects
- Edit drawings by using Cut, Copy, Paste, Delete, and Undo
- Resize objects
- Position objects by moving, aligning, and distributing them
- Use visible grid lines, the invisible snap grid, and gravity
- Fill objects and change their pen patterns
- Set line widths, line styles, and arrows and other line ends
- Create text frames and text lines
- Use the Smart Selection and Object Selection tools
- Group, stack, flip, and rotate objects
- Smooth, unsmooth, reshape, and join objects
- Copy, paste, and edit clip art

FrameMaker Model

Graphics created using FrameMaker's drawing tools and imported graphics are *objects*.

Drawing Objects

Using FrameMaker drawing tools, you can draw objects such as lines, rectangles, and circles anywhere on a page. Objects you draw on a page don't move as you edit text and are called *page-anchored objects*. If you want graphic objects to move with the surrounding text, you must place them in anchored frames. Anchored frames are *text-anchored objects*—a topic that will be covered in a later module.

Before you draw or edit objects on a page, it is helpful to delete the text frame. That way you can draw directly on the page, not on the text frame.

Exercise 1

Guided Tour

Rectangles, squares, rounded rectangles, ovals, and circles

In this exercise, you'll draw rectangles, rounded-corner rectangles, and ovals. Then you'll use Shift to modify the action of the drawing tools to draw squares, rounded squares, and circles.

1. Create a new **Portrait** document:

   a. Open the dialog box.

Macintosh	From the File menu, choose **New**.
Windows	From the File menu, choose **New**.
UNIX	In the main FrameMaker window, click **NEW**.

   b. Click **Portrait**.

2. Use the Save As dialog box to save the document in the `Class` directory or folder with the filename `draw`.

3. Use your mouse to display the Graphics menu, and make sure **Snap** is turned off.

   You will learn more about this option later in this module.

4. In the upper-right corner of the document window, click the **Tools** button.

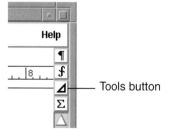
Tools button

The Tools palette appears.

Tip: You can also choose Tools from the Graphics menu to display the Tools palette.

Macintosh

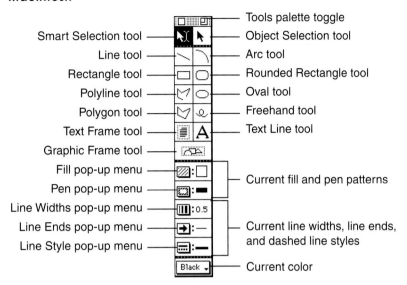

Smart Selection tool	Tools palette toggle
Line tool	Object Selection tool
Rectangle tool	Arc tool
Polyline tool	Rounded Rectangle tool
Polygon tool	Oval tool
Text Frame tool	Freehand tool
Graphic Frame tool	Text Line tool
Fill pop-up menu	
Pen pop-up menu	Current fill and pen patterns
Line Widths pop-up menu	
Line Ends pop-up menu	Current line widths, line ends, and dashed line styles
Line Style pop-up menu	
	Current color

Windows

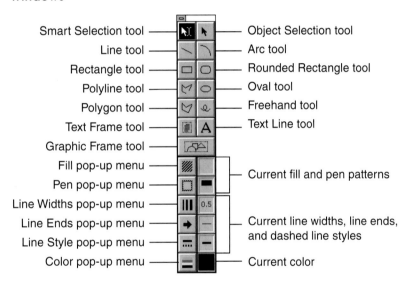

Smart Selection tool	Object Selection tool
Line tool	Arc tool
Rectangle tool	Rounded Rectangle tool
Polyline tool	Oval tool
Polygon tool	Freehand tool
Text Frame tool	Text Line tool
Graphic Frame tool	
Fill pop-up menu	Current fill and pen patterns
Pen pop-up menu	
Line Widths pop-up menu	
Line Ends pop-up menu	Current line widths, line ends, and dashed line styles
Line Style pop-up menu	
Color pop-up menu	Current color

UNIX

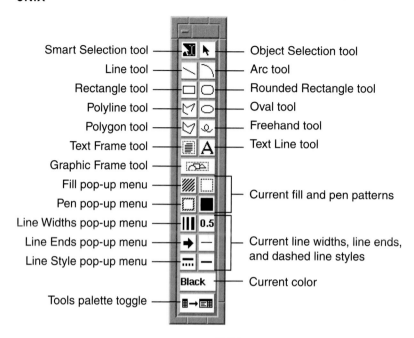

5. Click the **Object Selection tool** (↖).

   The Object Selection tool is covered in detail later in this module.

6. Click anywhere in the text frame to select it.

   The text frame is selected, and handles appear on its borders.

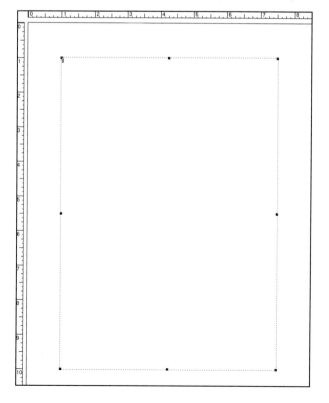

7. Press **Delete** or **Backspace**.

    The text frame is deleted.

8. In the Tools palette, click the **Rectangle tool** (□).

9. Move the pointer over the document window. Notice that the pointer changes to a cross.

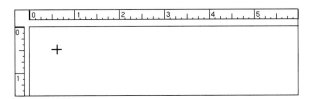

10. Draw a rectangle of any size by holding down the mouse button and dragging diagonally.

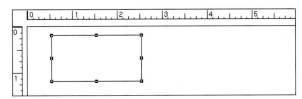

    Once you've finished drawing the rectangle, in the Tools palette, the Smart Selection tool is selected.

11. Click the **Rectangle tool** again.

12. Hold down **Shift** and drag diagonally to draw a perfect square of any size.

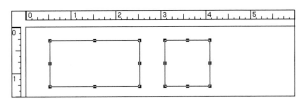

    Note: If you release Shift before releasing the mouse button, you will lose the identical horizontal and vertical dimensions.

13. The Rounded Rectangle tool(▢) and the Oval tool (◯) work the same way as the Rectangle tool. Try creating shapes by using those tools with and without holding down **Shift**.

14. From the Edit menu, choose **Select All on Page** and press **Delete** to delete all selected objects.

Exercise 2

Guided Tour

Drawing lines

In this exercise, you'll draw lines and practice constraining their directions.

1. Hold down **Shift** and click the **Line tool** in the Tools palette.

> **Elaboration:** If you hold down Shift when you click a drawing tool, the drawing tool will remain selected after you finish drawing an object. This allows you to draw as many of the selected objects as you like without having to reselect the drawing tool.

2. Drag diagonally to draw a line of any length.

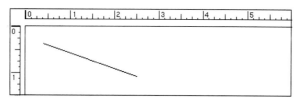

3. Hold down **Shift** and drag horizontally, keeping Shift down until after you release the mouse, to draw a perfectly horizontal line.

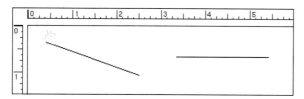

> **Elaboration:** If you hold down Shift as you draw lines, it constrains the tool to draw horizontal, vertical, or 45-degree lines.

4. From the Edit menu, choose **Select All on Page** and press **Delete** to delete the lines.

Editing Drawings with Cut, Copy, Paste, Delete, and Undo

The commands to edit your drawings—Cut, Copy, Paste, Delete (Clear), and Undo—work very much as they do when working with text.

Exercise 3

Guided Tour

Using Cut, Copy, Paste, Delete, and Undo

In this exercise, you'll practice using the editing commands from the Edit menu.

1. Draw a rectangle of any size.

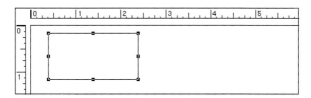

2. From the Edit menu, choose **Copy**.

   The rectangle is copied to the Clipboard.

3. From the Edit menu, choose **Paste**.

   The pasted rectangle appears on top of the existing rectangle.

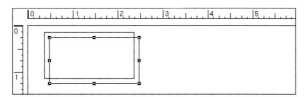

Note: When you paste a graphic, you can't specify where to place it. It is pasted on top of the selected object, slightly offset from it.

4. From the Edit menu, choose **Paste** again.

A third rectangle appears.

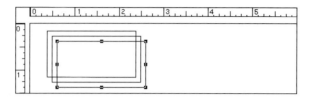

5. From the Edit menu, choose **Undo**.

The Undo command undoes the last action performed. The last rectangle you pasted disappears.

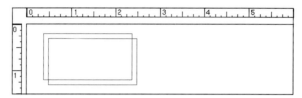

6. Draw a circle of any size.

7. With the circle selected, from the Edit menu, choose **Cut**.

8. Click the border of the second rectangle to select it.

Handles appear on the border of the rectangle.

9. From the Edit menu, choose **Paste**.

The circle is pasted on top of the rectangle. The rectangle is not deleted.

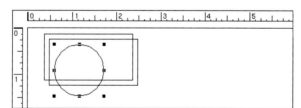

10. From the Edit menu, choose **Select All on Page**, and press **Delete**.

Resizing Objects

You can resize an object in three ways: with the resize handles on the border of the object, with the Object Properties command, and with the Scale command.

Exercise 4

Resizing with handles

In this exercise, you'll practice resizing by dragging resize handles on an object's borders.

1. Draw a rectangle of any size.

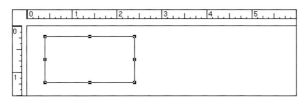

2. With the rectangle selected, move the pointer onto the right side handle and drag it to the right to increase the width of the rectangle.

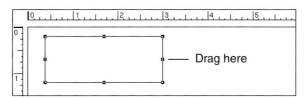

3. Drag the lower-middle handle up to decrease the height of the rectangle.

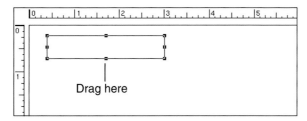

4. Drag the lower-right corner handle down and to the right to increase both the width and the height.

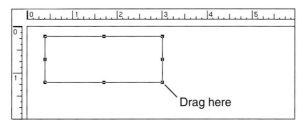

5. Hold down **Shift** and drag the lower-right corner handle up and to the left. This decreases both the width and the height but maintains the rectangle's proportions.

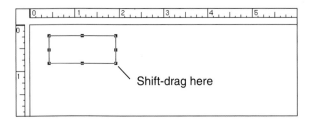

Shift-drag here

6. Leave the rectangle on the page for use in the next exercise.

Exercise 5

Guided Tour

Resizing with the Object Properties and Scale commands

In this exercise, you'll use the Object Properties and Scale commands to resize the rectangle to a percentage of its current size.

1. With the rectangle still selected, from the Graphics menu, choose **Object Properties**.

   The Object Properties dialog box appears.

2. Change the width to **2** and the height to **.5**.

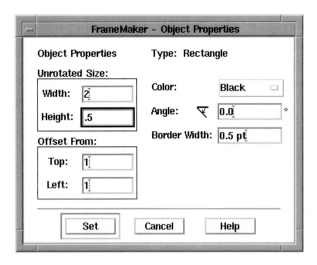

3. Click **Set**.

   The rectangle changes in width and height.

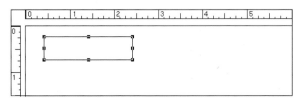

4. With the rectangle still selected, from the Graphics menu, choose **Scale**.

The Scale dialog box appears.

5. Change the contents of the Factor text box to **150**.

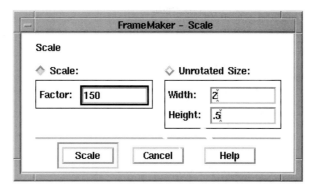

6. Click **Scale**.

The rectangle is now 50% larger, 150% of its original size.

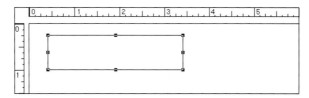

7. Delete the rectangle.

Positioning Objects

You can position objects in several ways:

- Dragging, micropositioning, and setting object properties.
- Aligning horizontally and vertically.
- Distributing horizontally and vertically.

Exercise 6

Guided Tour

Dragging, micropositioning, and setting object properties

In this exercise, you'll move objects by dragging, micropositioning with the arrow keys, and using the Object Properties command.

1. Draw a rectangle of any size.

2. Move the rectangle by dragging its border, but not a handle on the border.

When you release the mouse, the rectangle is in its new position.

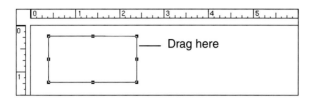

Note: If you dragged a handle instead of a border, you resized the object instead of moving it.

3. With the rectangle still selected, hold down the modifier key for your platform (listed below) and press any arrow key on the keyboard.

Macintosh	Option
Windows	Alt
UNIX	Control

The rectangle moves 1 point in the direction of the arrow.

4. With the rectangle still selected, hold down **Shift** and the modifier key for your platform (listed in the previous step) and press any arrow key.

The rectangle moves 6 points in the direction of the arrow pressed.

5. With the rectangle still selected, from the Graphics menu, choose **Object Properties**.

The Object Properties dialog box appears.

6. Change the Offset From Top to **1**, and the Offset From Left to **1**.

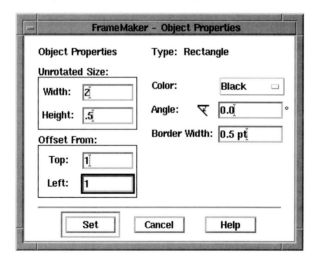

7. Click **Set**.

The rectangle moves so that it is 1 inch from the top of the page and 1 inch from the left of the page.

8. Delete the rectangle.

Selecting objects

FrameMaker allows you to select objects several different ways, as shown in the following example. The way you choose depends on your particular situation.

To select	Do this
A filled object	Point anywhere on object and click
An unfilled object	Point on object's border and click
Multiple objects by using the Shift key	Select first object, then Shift-click to select additional object.
Multiple objects with a selection border	Point outside objects, and drag border to surround the objects completely.

To deselect all the objects on a page, move the pointer over an empty part of page and click. To deselect a single object from several selected objects, Shift-click the object.

Exercise 7

Aligning vertically and horizontally

In this exercise, you'll reposition objects by aligning them with each other. When you align objects, all objects to be aligned must be selected. The last object selected stays where it is, and all other selected objects align with it. If only one object is selected, the object aligns with the page.

1. Draw three rectangles of different sizes, and position them horizontally, similar to the rectangles in the following example.

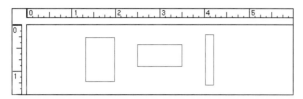

2. Select all three rectangles:

   a. In the Tools palette, make sure the Smart Selection tool ( ) is selected.

   b. Click the border of the left rectangle.

   c. Shift-click the border of the middle rectangle.
   Both rectangles are now selected.

   d. Shift-click the border of the right rectangle.
   All three rectangles are now selected.

3. From the Graphics menu, choose **Align**.
   The Align dialog box appears.

4. In the **Top/Bottom** area, turn on **Tops**, and in the **Left/Right** area, make sure **As Is** is turned on.

5. Click **Align**.

The rectangles align with the top of the rectangle on the right, because it was the last one selected.

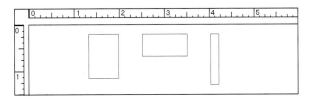

6. From the Graphics menu, choose **Align** again. Change **Top/Bottom** to **T/B Centers**, and leave **Left/Right** set to **As Is**.

7. Click **Align**.

8. Experiment by changing **Top/Bottom** to **As Is** and by changing **Left/Right** to **Left Sides**, **L/R Centers**, and **Right Sides**.

9. Delete all three rectangles.

10. Draw a rectangle and a circle, and position them similarly to those in the following example.

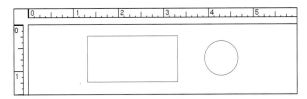

11. Select the rectangle, and Shift-click to select the circle.

12. With both objects selected, from the Graphics menu, choose **Align**.

13. In the Align dialog box, in the **Top/Bottom** area, turn on **T/B Centers**.

14. In the **Left/Right** area, turn on **L/R Centers**.

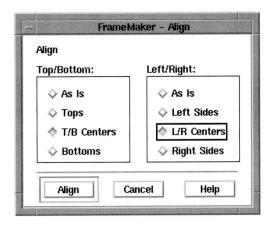

15. Click **Align**.

The rectangle aligns with the center of the circle, and the circle stays where it is because it is the last object selected.

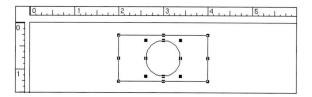

16. Delete the rectangle and the circle.

Tip: You can also use the QuickAccess bar to align objects. If the QuickAccess bar is not visible, from the View menu, choose QuickAccess bar. Click the Page Up/Page Down button until the Graphics Editing page of buttons (shown below) appears. Select the shapes you wish to align, and then click the desired alignment buttons.

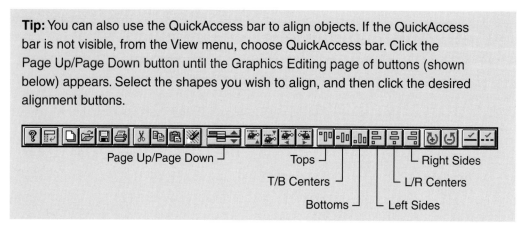

Exercise 8

Guided Tour

Distributing objects horizontally and vertically

The Distribute command is used to even out the spacing between objects. You can distribute objects by precisely specifying the amount of space between the objects (the *edge gap*), or by specifying that the edges or centers of the objects be equidistant.

Horizontal spacing

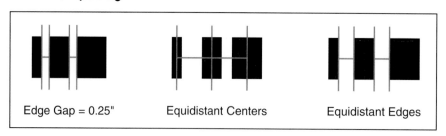

Edge Gap = 0.25"   Equidistant Centers   Equidistant Edges

Vertical spacing

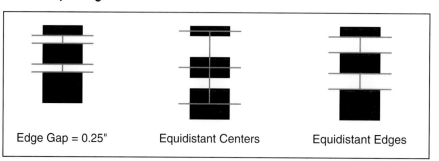

Edge Gap = 0.25"   Equidistant Centers   Equidistant Edges

If you specify that the object centers or the object edges should be equidistant, FrameMaker leaves the left and right objects (or top and bottom objects) where they are and moves the others.

In this exercise, you'll reposition selected objects by distributing them.

1. Draw three rectangles of different sizes, and position them horizontally as in the following example.

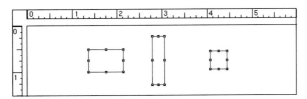

2. Select all three rectangles.

3. From the Graphics menu, choose **Distribute**.

   The Distribute dialog box appears.

4. In the **Horizontal Spacing** area, turn on **Edge Gap**, and change that setting to **.5**.

5. In the **Vertical Spacing** area, make sure **As Is** is turned on.

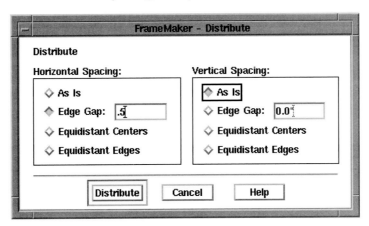

6. Click **Distribute**.

   The rectangles distribute horizontally with an edge gap of .5 inch.

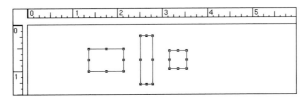

7. Practice distributing by **Equidistant Centers** and **Equidistant Edges**. Notice the different results.

8. Drag the three rectangles, and position them vertically, as in the following example.

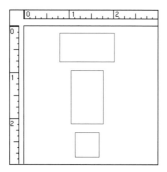

9. Select all three rectangles.

10. From the Graphics menu, choose **Distribute**.

11. Set the Horizontal Spacing to **As Is**, and explore the Vertical Spacing options by entering different values, such as **.5**, **2.0**, and **4.75**, for the Edge Gap.

> **Note:** When you distribute objects horizontally, the leftmost object always remains stationary. When distributing vertically, the topmost object remains stationary.

12. Delete all three rectangles.

Using the Invisible Snap Grid, Visible Grid Lines, and Gravity

Two kinds of grids are available as drawing aids—an invisible snap grid and visible grid lines.

When Snap is turned on, as you draw, move, resize, or reshape objects on the screen, they "snap" to an invisible grid. The snap grid can help you draw objects that are the same size and that are aligned with each other. You can set your own spacing for the snap grid.

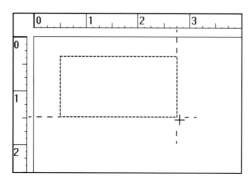

Rectangle being drawn snaps to invisible grid.

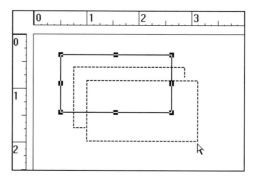

Rectangle being moved snaps to invisible grid.

When Grid Lines is turned on, a visible grid appears on the screen. You can use these nonprinting grid lines as guidelines when you draw or arrange objects. And just as with the snap grid, you can set your own spacing for the visible grid lines.

Visible grid line ———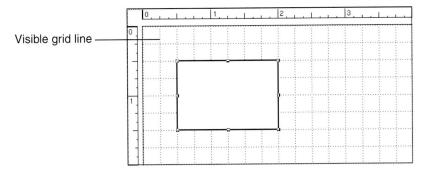

Gravity makes it easier to connect objects precisely. With Gravity turned on, the corner of one object is attracted to the corner of another as you draw, move, or resize other objects. Objects have gravity at their corners, edges, and centers.

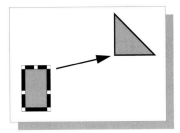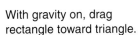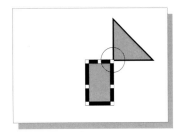

With gravity on, drag rectangle toward triangle.

Corner of rectangle is attracted to corner of triangle.

Exercise 9

Guided Tour

Setting the visible grid lines and the invisible snap grid increments

In this exercise, you will set the spacing of the visible grid lines and the invisible snap grid. The visible grid lines can be turned on or off from the View menu. The invisible snap grid can be turned on or off from the Graphics menu. Both can be turned on or off in the View Options dialog box, where you can also change their settings.

1. From the View menu, choose **Options**.

   The View Options dialog box appears.

2. Turn on **Grid Lines**.

3. From the Grid Lines pop-up menu, choose **1"**.

4. Turn on **Snap**.

5. Change the Grid Spacing to **.5"**.

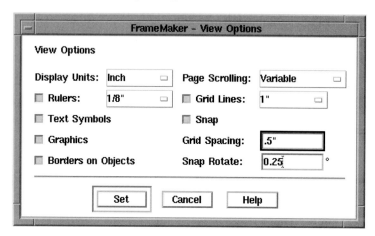

6. Click **Set**.

   The visible grid lines appear as 1-inch squares. Snap is also turned on.

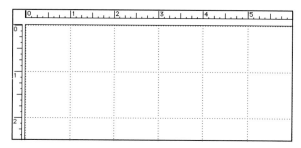

Exercise 10

Guided Tour

Drawing objects by using grid lines, the snap grid, and gravity

In this exercise, you'll practice drawing rectangles with and without the snap grid and with and without gravity.

1. Draw a rectangle of any size.

   Because Snap is turned on and set to .5", the rectangle jumps to ½-inch increments as you draw.

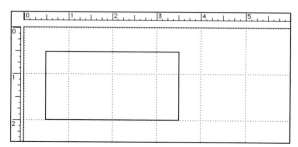

2. From the Graphics menu, choose **Snap** to turn it off.

3. Draw another rectangle of any size.

   Because Snap is turned off, you can draw a rectangle of any size.

4. From the Graphics menu, choose **Gravity** to turn it on.

5. Draw a diagonal line from anywhere outside the rectangle to any corner of the first rectangle. Because Gravity is turned on, as the pointer nears the corner of the rectangle, the pointer gravitates to the corner.

6. Delete all objects on the page.

7. From the View menu, choose **Grid Lines** to turn them off.

8. From the Graphics menu, choose **Gravity** to turn it off.

Filling Objects and Changing Their Pen Patterns

You can change the pattern inside an object (its *fill pattern*), or the border of the object (its *pen pattern*), by selecting from the Fill pop-up menu or the Pen pop-up menu. You can choose these properties before you draw an object, or you can select an existing object and change its properties.

Exercise 11

Guided Tour

Changing the fill pattern

The first eight fill patterns on the Fill pop-up menu range from black to white, with six intermediate shades of gray. To make an object transparent so that objects behind it show through, choose None from the Fill pop-up menu.

In this exercise, you'll practice changing fill patterns by selecting from the Fill pop-up menu on the Tools palette.

1. Draw a rectangle of any size.

2. With the rectangle still selected, from the Fill pop-up menu, choose the black fill pattern in the upper-left corner of the pop-up menu.

Click here...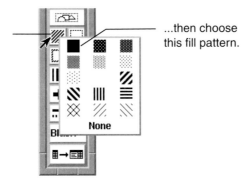

...then choose
this fill pattern.

The rectangle is filled with 100% black.

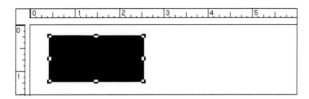

3. Practice using different fill patterns.

4. Reset the fill pattern to **White** (the middle choice).

5. Draw another rectangle, and position it on top of the first rectangle.

   The bottom rectangle does not show through the top rectangle.

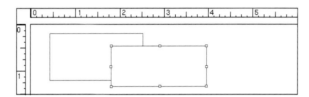

6. Fill the frontmost rectangle with **None**.

   The bottom rectangle shows through the top rectangle.

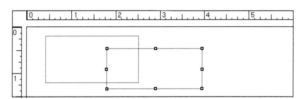

7. Delete the rectangles.

Exercise 12   **Changing the pen pattern**

Guided Tour

The first eight patterns on the Pen pop-up menu range from black to white, with six intermediate shades of gray. If you don't want an object to have a border, choose None.

In this exercise, you'll practice changing pen patterns by selecting from the Pen pop-up menu.

1. Draw a rectangle of any size.

   The rectangle has the same fill pattern (None) that you last selected.

2. With the rectangle still selected, from the Pen pop-up menu, choose a gray pattern.

Click here...

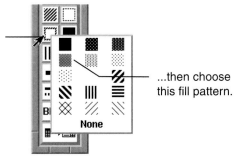

...then choose this fill pattern.

The rectangle's border appears gray.

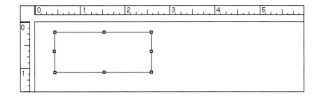

3. Practice using different pen patterns.

4. Change the pen pattern back to black.

5. Delete the rectangle.

Working with Lines

When drawing lines in FrameMaker, you can define

- The thickness of the line (line width)
- The use of arrows and the arrow style
- The cap style for line ends without an arrow
- Whether the lines are solid or dashed, and the dash pattern

Exercise 13   **Changing line widths**

Guided Tour

In this exercise, you'll change the line width of a line and other objects.

1. Draw a horizontal line of any length.

2. With the line still selected, from the Line Widths pop-up menu, choose the last line.

Click here... ——————

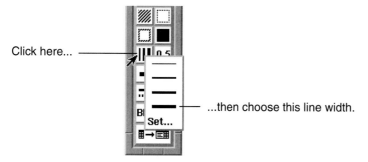

...then choose this line width.

The line is now thicker.

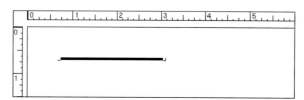

3. From the Line Widths pop-up menu, choose a different line width, and see what happens.

4. From the Line Widths pop-up menu, choose **Set**.

The Line Width Options dialog box appears.

5. Change the value in the fourth text box to **15 pt**.

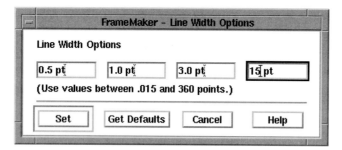

6. Click **Set**.

Notice that the line width does not change.

> **Elaboration:** The changes you make using options dialog boxes, such as the Line Width Options dialog, affect only the choices that appear in the corresponding pop-up menu in the Tools palette; the appearance of any selected objects will not be altered. The new setting will be applied when you select it from a pop-up menu or when you draw a new object.

7. With the line still selected, from the Line Widths pop-up menu, choose the last line.

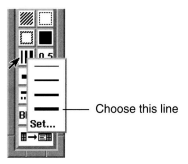

Choose this line

The line is now 15 points thick.

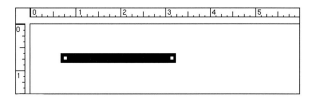

8. Draw a rectangle of any size.

Notice its border is also 15 points thick.

Note: You can change the line width (border) of any object.

9. Delete all objects on the page.

Exercise 14

Guided Tour

Setting line ends (including arrows) and line cap styles

In this exercise, you'll change the line ends by adding arrows, changing the arrow style, and changing the cap style of a line without an arrow.

1. Draw a horizontal line of any length.

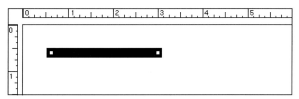

2. From the Line Ends pop-up menu, choose the **second** of the four horizontal lines.

Click here...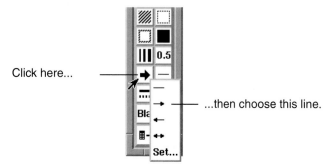

...then choose this line.

An arrowhead appears on the right end.

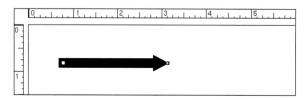

3. Choose other line ends, and see how they look.

4. When you finish, choose the second line end (with the arrowhead pointing right).

5. From the Line Ends pop-up menu, choose **Set**.

The Line End Options dialog box appears.

6. In the Arrow Style area, select any arrow style you wish.

7. In the Cap Style area, turn on **Round**.

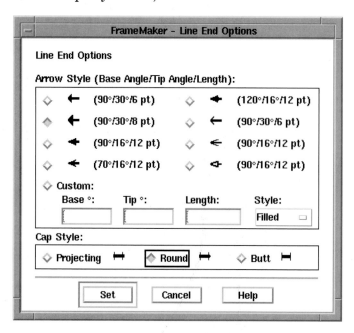

8. Click **Set**.

The appearance of the selected arrow does not change.

9. Draw another line of any length.

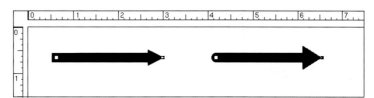

The new line displays the new arrow style and has a rounded cap on the end without an arrow.

10. Delete all objects on the page.

Exercise 15 **Drawing solid lines and dashed lines**

Guided Tour

In this exercise, you'll practice drawing solid lines and dashed lines, and you'll change the dashed line style.

1. Draw a line of any length that is 3 points thick and has no arrowheads.

2. Make sure the line is still selected, and from the Line Styles pop-up menu, choose the **dashed line**.

Click here...

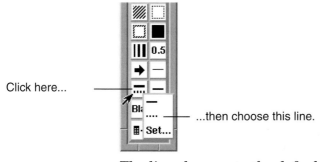

...then choose this line.

The line changes to the default dashed line style.

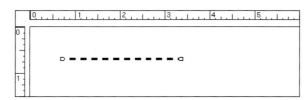

3. From the Line Styles pop-up menu, choose **Set**.

The Dashed Line Options dialog box appears.

4. Turn on the **Dash-Dot-Dot** style.

5. Click **Set**.

   The current line does not change. The changes in the Dashed Line Options dialog box will affect the next line you draw.

6. Draw another line of any length.

   The new line displays the new dashed line style.

7. Select the first line you drew.

8. From the Line Styles pop-up menu, choose the **dashed line**.

   The line displays the new dashed line style.

9. Change the line style back to the solid line, and change the line width back to 1 pt.

10. Delete all objects on the page.

Using Text Lines, Text Frames, and Selection Tools

You can add single lines of text (text lines) or text frames to a graphic. Use text lines for one-line callouts. Use text frames for multiline callouts, paragraphs of text, or any other text that must wrap automatically from line to line.

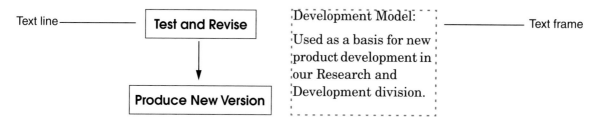

A text line is a single line of text that FrameMaker treats independently from other text. Text lines grow or shrink in length as you edit them, but they don't wrap to the next line. If you press Return when typing a text line, the insertion point moves right below the current text line, where you can type another, totally separate, text line. The two text lines are separate objects but can be grouped together.

Text lines can be formatted with character formats from the Character Catalog, by applying properties from the Character Designer, or by choosing from the Font, Size, and Style submenus of the Format menu.

Text frames can contain paragraphs of text, which wrap from line to line. Text in a text frame can be formatted by using the Paragraph Catalog and Paragraph Designer as well as the Character Catalog, Character Designer, and Format menu.

Exercise 16

Guided Tour

Adding and formatting a text line

In this exercise, you will add a text line and format the text line by applying a character format, as well as a font, size, and style from the Format menu.

1. Draw a rectangle about 2 inches wide and 1 inch high, with a solid 1-point border and a white fill pattern.

2. Click the **Text Line tool** (A).

3. Click in the middle of the rectangle. An insertion point appears.

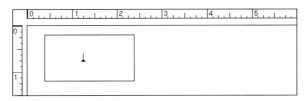

4. Type: FrameMaker

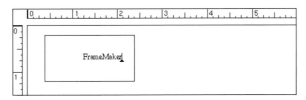

Your word (a text line) appears off center in the rectangle and uses the font properties associated with the last text you clicked.

> **Note:** The last line you clicked affects only the appearance of the next text *line*, not text typed in a text *frame*.

5. Click the **Object Selection tool** (▶).

6. Click anywhere on the text line.

   Handles appear around it.

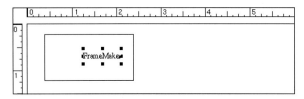

7. From the Format menu, choose **Font>Courier**.

8. From the Format menu, choose **Size>14**.

9. From the Format menu, choose **Style>Bold**.

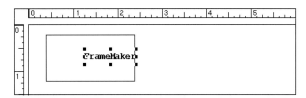

10. With the text line still selected, use the Character Catalog to apply the **Emphasis** character tag.

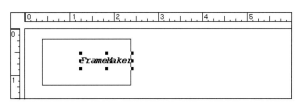

11. With the text line still selected, Shift-click the rectangle.

    Both objects are selected, with the rectangle selected last.

12. From the Graphics menu, choose **Align**.

    The Align dialog box appears.

13. Turn on **T/B Centers** and **L/R Centers**.

14. Click **Align**.

    The text line aligns to the center of the rectangle.

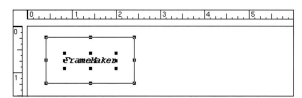

15. Leave the text line and the rectangle on the page for use in a later exercise.

Exercise 17   Drawing a text frame and formatting its text

In this exercise, you will draw a text frame, add paragraphs of text in the text frame, and format the text by using formats from the Paragraph Catalog.

1. Click the **Text Frame tool** (▤).

2. Drag diagonally on the page, creating a text frame approximately 2 inches by 2 inches.

    When you release the mouse, the Create New Text Frame dialog box appears.

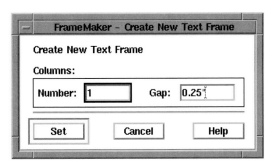

3. Click **Set**.

    The text frame appears, with handles indicating that it is selected.

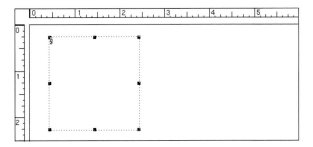

4. Double-click in the text frame to put an insertion point in it.

    The paragraph format is Body.

5. Type:

    Our company has branch offices located in the following
    European cities:

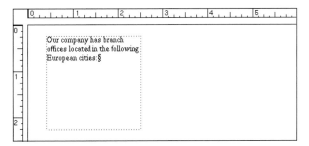

6. Press **Return**, and type the city names as follows.

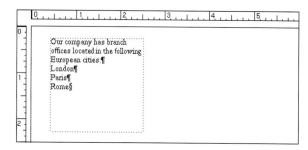

7. Highlight the three city names, and apply the **Bulleted** paragraph tag.

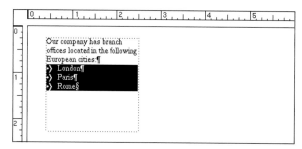

8. Leave the text frame on the page for use in the next exercise.

The Smart Selection tool and the Object Selection tool

FrameMaker provides two tools that you can use to select text and objects—the Smart Selection tool (![I-beam arrow icon]) and the Object Selection tool (![arrow icon]). Normally the Smart Selection tool is active.

In general, use the Smart Selection tool as you work. When the Smart Selection tool is active, the pointer changes shape as you move it.

■ Over a text frame or text line, the pointer is an I-beam, indicating that a click will place an insertion point in text for typing or for selecting text.

■ Over objects, the pointer is a hollow arrow, indicating that a click will select an object (such as a rectangle or circle).

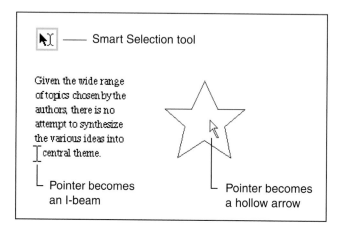

Use the Object Selection tool when you're working with text lines and text frames as objects—for example, when you want to move a text line or resize a text frame. When the Object Selection tool is active, you can select only objects. When you click in text, you select the entire text line or text frame as an object instead of putting an insertion point in the text.

Exercise 18　**Using the Smart Selection tool and the Object Selection tool**

Guided Tour

In this exercise, you'll practice using the Smart Selection tool and the Object Selection tool to select text and objects.

1. Make sure the **Smart Selection tool** is selected.

2. Click the rectangle around the word "FrameMaker."

   Handles appear, indicating that the rectangle is selected.

3. Click the word "FrameMaker."

   An insertion point appears, indicating that you can edit your text.

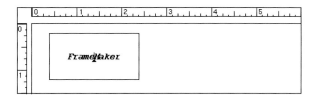

4. Click in the text frame that contains the paragraphs you typed in the previous exercise.

5. Click the **Object Selection tool**.

6. Click the rectangle around the word "FrameMaker" again.

7. Click the word "FrameMaker."

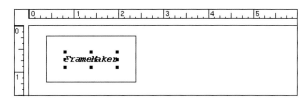

The text line has handles, indicating that it is selected as an object. You cannot type in it, but you can reposition it or apply character formats to it.

8. Click the text frame.

The text frame has handles, indicating that it is selected as an object. You cannot type in it, but you can reposition or resize it.

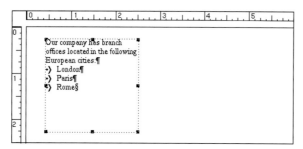

The Object Selection tool selects everything as an object. If you click in a text line or text frame, you select the text line or text frame as an object.

9. Click the **Smart Selection tool**.

10. Click the text line.

The text line now displays an insertion point, indicating that you can edit your text.

11. With the Smart Selection tool active, **Control**-click (on the Macintosh, **Option**-click) in the text line.

The text line has handles, indicating that it is selected as an object.

12. With the Smart Selection tool active, **Control**-click (on the Macintosh, **Option**-click) the text frame.

The text frame has handles, indicating that it is selected as an object. (In Windows, the text line remains selected as well.).

> **Tip:** When a text frame or a text line displays handles and the Smart Selection toll is active, you can double-click the text to get an insertion point.

13. Delete all objects on the page.

Grouping and Ungrouping Objects

You can group objects together to form a single object. When objects are grouped together, you can move, resize, flip, or align them as a single object.

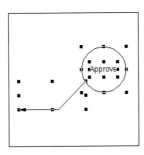 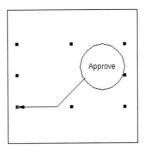

Each object has its own
set of handles.

Grouped objects have
one set of handles.

You can combine a group of objects with other objects to form an even larger group. You can also ungroup objects that have been grouped.

Exercise 19

Guided Tour

Grouping and ungrouping objects

In this exercise, you'll practice grouping and ungrouping objects.

1. Draw a rectangle, an oval, and a line.

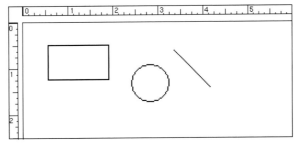

2. Click each object individually.

   Each object has its own handles as you click it.

3. From the Edit menu, choose **Select All on Page**.

   All objects on the page are selected, each with its own handles.

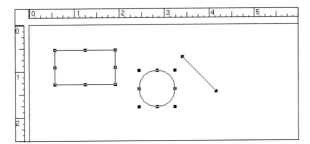

4. From the Graphics menu, choose **Group**.

   One set of handles appears around the objects.

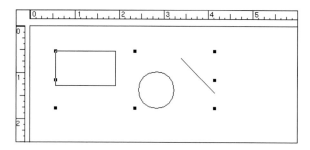

5. Practice resizing and moving the grouped object.

6. From the Graphics menu, choose **Ungroup**.

   Each object has its own handles again.

7. Delete all objects on the page.

Stacking Objects

When you draw or paste an object, FrameMaker places it in front of all other objects on the page. If the object is filled, it obscures objects in back of it. You can control how objects overlap by putting them in front of or in back of other objects.

Exercise 20   **Using the Bring to Front and Send to Back commands**

Guided Tour

In this exercise, you'll practice using the Bring to Front and Send to Back commands.

1. Draw a rectangle filled with black and then an oval filled with white.

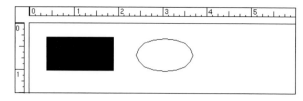

2. Move the oval so it partially overlaps the rectangle.

   Because the oval has a fill pattern, the rectangle behind it is partially covered.

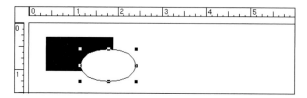

3. With the oval selected, from the Graphics menu, choose **Send to Back**.

   The oval moves behind the rectangle.

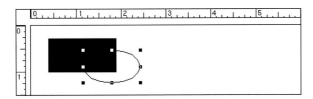

4. With the oval still selected, from the Graphics menu, choose **Bring to Front**.

   The oval moves in front of the rectangle.

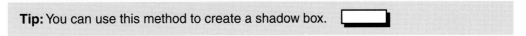

Tip: You can use this method to create a shadow box.

5. Delete all objects on the page.

Flipping and Rotating Objects

You can create a mirror image of an object by flipping it up and down or left and right.

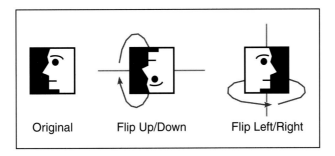

Original   Flip Up/Down   Flip Left/Right

You can rotate all objects (except equations and graphic frames) any number of degrees. Equations and graphic frames rotate in 90-degree increments. All objects except equations and text lines rotate around their centers. Equations and text lines rotate around the alignment points in their lower-left corners.

Most objects rotate
around their centers.

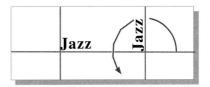

Text objects and equations rotate
around their alignment points.

Exercise 21

Guided Tour

Flipping objects horizontally and vertically, and rotating them

In this exercise, you'll practice flipping objects. You will also practice rotating objects by specifying the degree of rotation and by dragging with the mouse.

1. Using the **Freehand tool**, draw half of a heart, as in the following example.

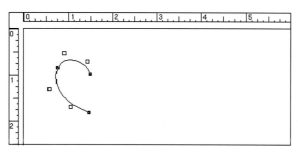

2. With the object selected, from the Edit menu, choose **Copy**.

3. From the Edit menu, choose **Paste**.

   The copy is pasted on top of the original.

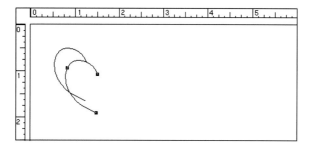

4. With the copy selected, from the Graphics menu, choose **Flip Left/Right**.

5. Move the objects together so they form a heart.

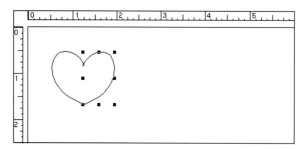

> **Tip:** If you have trouble moving the objects together, make sure Snap is turned off.

6. Select both halves.

7. From the Graphics menu, choose **Group**.

   The heart is one object.

8. From the Graphics menu, choose **Flip Up/Down**.

   The heart is upside down.

   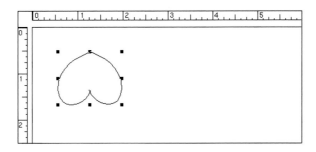

9. With the heart selected, from the Graphics menu, choose **Rotate**.

   The Rotate Selected Objects dialog box appears.

10. Change the Rotate By setting to **45**.

11. In the Direction area, turn on **Clockwise**.

    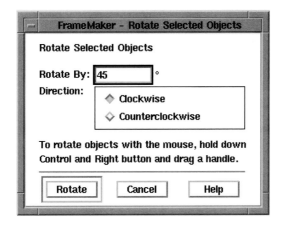

12. Click **Rotate**.

    The heart rotates clockwise by 45 degrees.

    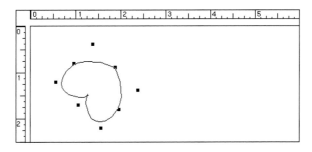

13. With the heart still selected, hold down **Control** and, using the **right** mouse button (on the Macintosh, hold down **Command**; in Windows, hold down **Alt**), drag a handle in the direction you want to rotate the heart.

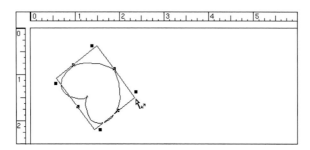

When you release the mouse, the heart is rotated.

14. Delete the heart.

Using FrameMaker Clip Art and Imported Graphics

FrameMaker provides clip art that you can copy and paste into a document. The graphics commands that are used with objects are also used with clip art. You can align, distribute, rotate, scale, flip, group, ungroup, and change the properties of clip art.

Exercise 22   **Copying and editing clip art**

Guided Tour

In this exercise, you'll copy clip art from FrameMaker's clip art files and paste it into your document, where you will edit it.

1. From the FrameMaker list of sample documents, open the clip art document **People**.

   a. Display the FrameMaker list of sample documents:

Macintosh	From the [?] menu, choose **Samples & Clip Art**.
Windows	From the Help menu, choose **Samples & Clip Art**.
UNIX	From a document Help menu, choose **Samples & Clip Art**.

   The FrameMaker samples window appears.

   b. Click **Clip art** to see the list of clip art files.

   c. Double-click **People**.

   The People clip art document appears.

2. Click to select the boy graphic on page 1.

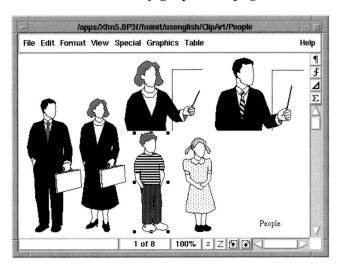

3. From the Edit menu of People, choose **Copy**.

4. Go to your document, and from the Edit menu, choose **Paste**.

5. Ungroup the boy graphic. This graphic uses multiple levels of grouping, so you'll need to ungroup more than once to select the individual objects that make up the graphic.

6. Practice resizing, filling, rotating, and using the other graphics commands you have learned on the elements of the graphic.

| **Exercise 23** | **Importing a graphic** |

Guided Tour

In this exercise, you'll use the FrameMaker online tutorial to learn about importing a graphic.

1. From the Help menu, choose **Tutorial**.

   A dialog box similar to the following appears.

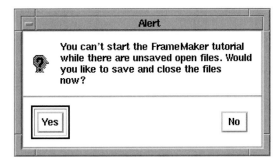

2. Click **Yes**.

Another dialog box appears.

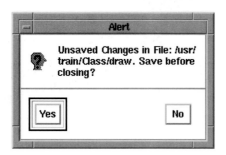

3. Click **No**.

   The Tutorial window appears.

4. Click **Lessons**.

   The Lessons window appears.

5. Click **Creating Graphics**.

   The Creating Graphics window appears.

6. Click **Importing a Graphic**.

7. Complete the lesson on importing a graphic.

8. When you have finished the lesson and the topic at the top of the window reads "Positioning a Graphic," click **Topics**.

9. Click **Exit**, and then click **Yes** to exit the FrameMaker tutorial.

Optional Exercises

The following exercises enable you to enhance your FrameMaker skills and to explore additional FrameMaker features. Some steps are intentionally brief so that they require more independent thought on your part.

Exercise 24

Optional

Drawing with the Arc, Freehand, Polyline, and Polygon tools

In this optional exercise, you'll become familiar with the Arc tool, the Polyline tool, the Polygon tool, and the Freehand tool.

1. Create a new **Portrait** document, and delete its text frame.

2. Click the **Arc tool** (⬔), and practice drawing arcs with and without holding down **Shift**.

3. Click the **Freehand tool** (⬔) and practice drawing various free-form shapes.

4. Use the **Polyline tool** (⬔) to draw the following shape:

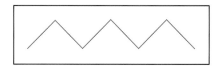

   a. Click the **Polyline tool**.

   b. Click at the starting point of the shape.

   c. Click at the intermediate points of the shape.

   d. Double-click on the final point of the polyline to finish drawing.

Starting point ———   — Double-click here to finish drawing.

Selection handles appear on the polyline.

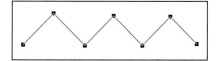

5. Use the **Polygon tool** ( ) to draw the following shape:

a. Click the **Polygon tool**.

b. Click at the starting point of the shape.

c. Click at each intermediate point of the shape.

d. Click twice on the final point of the polygon to finish drawing.

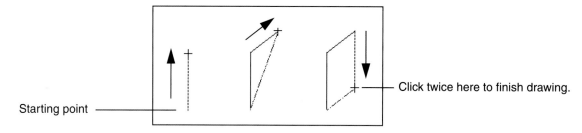

Starting point   Click twice here to finish drawing.

Selection handles appear on the polygon.

6. Delete all the shapes on the page.

Exercise 25   **Joining separate objects**

Optional

When you create symmetrical shapes, rather than draw the entire shape all at once, it is often easier to create half the shape, copy it, flip it, and then join the two halves into a single object that you can fill. In this optional exercise, you'll practice joining separate objects to create an arrow.

1. From the Graphics menu, turn on **Snap**.

2. From the View menu, turn on **Grid Lines**.

3. Click the Polyline tool, and draw half an arrow.

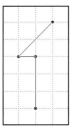

4. Copy the half arrow, and paste it.

Another copy of the half arrow appears on the page.

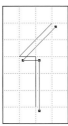

5. From the Graphics menu, choose **Flip Left/Right**.

The second copy of the half arrow appears flipped.

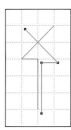

6. From the Graphics menu, turn on **Gravity**.

Turning on Gravity will help you join the tips of the half arrows precisely.

7. Drag the second half arrow so its tip touches the tip of the first half arrow.

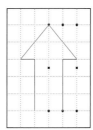

Although the two shapes now appear as a single shape, they will not fill properly, as you'll see in the next two steps.

8. Select both halves of the arrow.

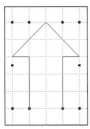

9. In the Tools palette, from the Fill pop-up menu, choose the black fill pattern.
The two halves of the arrow are filled individually.

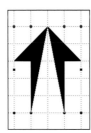

10. From the Graphics menu, choose **Join**.

The two arrow halves are now a single object, and the entire shape appears filled with black.

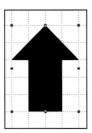

Note: There is no way to unjoin the objects except to choose the Undo command immediately.

11. Turn off **Grid Lines**, **Gravity**, and **Snap**.

12. Delete the arrow.

Exercise 26   Changing the number of sides of an object

In this optional exercise, you'll change a rectangle into a triangle, and a square into an octagon.

1. Draw a rectangle of any size and change its fill pattern to white.

2. With the rectangle selected, from the Graphics menu, choose **Set # Sides**.

   The Set Number of Sides dialog box appears.

3. Make sure Number of Sides is set to 3.

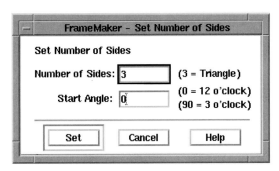

4. Click **Set**.

   The rectangle becomes a triangle.

5. Use **Shift** and the **Rectangle tool** to draw a square.

6. With the square selected, from the Graphics menu, choose **Set # Sides**.

   The Set Number of Sides dialog box appears.

7. Change the Number of Sides setting to **8**.

8. Click **Set**.

   The square becomes an octagon.

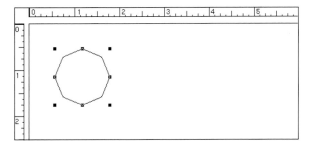

9. Delete the octagon and the triangle.

Exercise 27   Smoothing, unsmoothing, and reshaping an object

Optional

In this optional exercise, you'll practice smoothing, unsmoothing, and reshaping a polyline.

1. Draw a polyline with four line segments:

   a. Click the **Polyline tool** (⬕).

   b. Draw the polyline in the following example. (Double-click to finish drawing the polyline.)

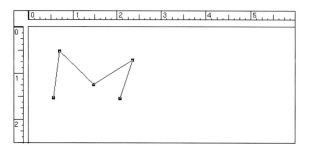

2. With the polyline selected, from the Graphics menu, choose **Smooth**.

   The angles of the polyline are now smooth curves, and reshape handles (solid) and control points (hollow) appear.

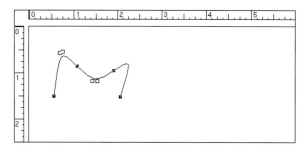

3. Drag any reshape handle or control point to reshape the object.

4. Deselect the object.

5. Select the object again.

   Notice the object has different handles around its border.

6. From the Graphics menu, choose **Reshape**.

   The reshape handles and control points reappear.

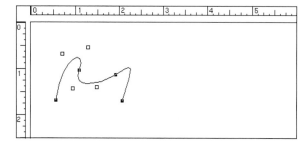

7. From the Graphics menu, choose **Unsmooth**.

The smooth curves change to straight line segments.

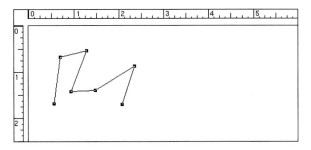

8. Delete the polyline.

Exercise 28

Optional

Creating an organization chart

In this optional exercise, you'll use the skills learned in this module to create the organization chart in the following example. The abbreviated steps following the illustration should help you get started.

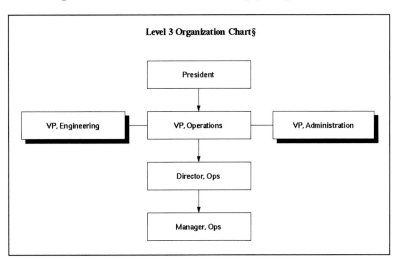

1. Save the document in the Class directory or folder as orgchrt.

2. Create one of the rectangles with text and an arrow:

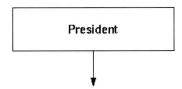

a. Draw a rectangle with a 1-point border and a white fill pattern.

b. Add a text line to the rectangle, and format the text line by using the commands from the Format menu (or create a character format, and add it to the Character Catalog).

    c. Align the text line in the center of the rectangle, and group the text line and the rectangle together.

    d. Draw an arrow aligned to the bottom center of the text line and the rectangle.

    e. Group the arrow with the text line and rectangle.

    f. Position the group toward the top and middle of the page.

3. Copy the group, and paste it three times.

4. Align the left/right centers of the rectangles.

5. Distribute the groups vertically with a vertical edge gap of zero (leaving the horizontal setting As Is). The groups will be distributed down the page.

6. Ungroup the arrow from the bottom rectangle, and delete it.

7. Change the text in the additional rectangles.

8. Use the graphics commands learned in this module to finish the organization chart.

9. Save the file, and close the document.

Review   Test your understanding of the concepts and procedures covered in this module by answering the following review questions. You can check your answers with those listed after the questions.

Question 1:   How do you draw a straight line? A perfect circle?

Question 2:   What are three ways to resize an object? Which method allows you to reposition an object at the same time as you resize it?

Question 3:   When you are aligning objects, with which object will the others align?

Question 4:   How does the snap grid differ from the visible grid lines?

Question 5:   How does a text line differ from a text frame?

Question 6:   When should you use the Object Selection tool instead of the Smart Selection tool?

_____

Answer 1:   Hold down Shift while drawing the objects.

Answer 2:   Dragging a resize handle on the border of the object, using the Object Properties command, and using the Scale command. The Object Properties command allows you to resize and reposition an object at the same time.

Answer 3:   The last object selected.

Answer 4:   The snap grid is invisible. When you move or resize objects on the page manually, they "snap" to line up with the snap grid. The visible grid lines are vertical and horizontal lines you can use to help you draw, position, and resize objects.

Answer 5:   A text frame can contain paragraphs, but a text line can contain only a single line of text.

Answer 6:   You should use the Object Selection tool when you're working with text lines and text frames as objects, such as when you want to move a text line or resize a text frame.

For more information

For more information about drawing tools and graphics commands, see:

Chapters 13 and 14 of *Using FrameMaker*

Graphic Frames and Text Runaround

Approximate time to complete: 30 minutes

Introduction

In this module, you'll become familiar with using graphic frames and text runaround properties. These FrameMaker features are helpful for placing text and graphics in close proximity on a page.

Module Objectives

In this module, you'll learn how to

- Identify a graphic frame
- Know when to use a graphic frame
- Use a graphic frame to crop the edges of a graphic
- Adjust text runaround properties
- Create a new graphic frame
- Use a nonbordered object to mask an area of a graphic

FrameMaker Model

Graphic frames are *objects* that contain other objects—graphics, equations, and text. Text runaround properties are properties of graphic objects.

Graphics and Graphic Frames

A graphic is often placed in a graphic frame so that the graphic can be cropped. To crop a graphic, you reduce the size of the graphic frame so it hides parts of the graphic.

Uncropped graphic

Cropped graphic

Exercise 1

Guided Tour

Identifying a graphic frame

In this exercise, you'll identify a graphic frame and its function in a document.

1. From the FrameMaker list of sample documents, open the **Report** sample:

   a. Display the FrameMaker list of sample documents:

Macintosh	From the ⚇ menu, choose **Samples & Clip Art**.
Windows	From the Help menu, choose **Samples & Clip Art**.
UNIX	From a document Help menu, choose **Samples & Clip Art**. (If there are no open documents, click **NEW**, then **Portrait**, first.)

   The FrameMaker samples window appears.

   b. In the FrameMaker samples list, click **Report**.

   The sample report appears.

2. Use the Save As dialog box to save the document in the `Class` directory or folder with the new filename `gframe`.

3. From the View menu, turn on **Borders**, **Text Symbols**, and **Rulers**.

4. Go to **page 4** in the document.

   The graphic on the page is placed in a graphic frame.

5. Select the border of the frame:

   a. Place the pointer near the edge of the graphic until it turns into a hollow arrow.

   b. Click the border.

   Handles appear on the frame surrounding the graphic.

6. From the Graphics menu, choose **Object Properties**.

   The Object Properties dialog box appears.

   FrameMaker identifies the object type as a graphic frame.

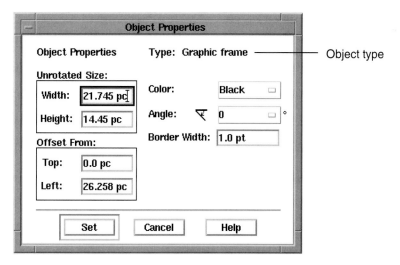

> **Note:** If FrameMaker identifies the object type as an Imported Graphic, not a graphic frame, you have selected the graphic inside the frame, not the frame itself. Try clicking the border of the surrounding frame again.

7. Click **Cancel**.

8. Move your pointer to the middle of the graphic, and click to select the graphic.

   No handles appear to indicate that the graphic is selected, because the graphic is larger than the graphic frame.

9. Hold down the mouse button and drag the graphic toward the lower-left corner of the frame.

When you release the mouse, you may have to wait for the screen to redraw the graphic.

Dragging the graphic moves it within the frame. Notice that the frame crops off the graphic.

10. Drag the graphic out of the frame.

Tip: The location of the pointer arrow when you release your mouse button determines whether a picture will be on the inside or outside of a frame. If the arrow is inside the frame, the picture will be inside. If the arrow is outside the frame, the picture will be outside.

You can see that the graphic is much larger than the frame.

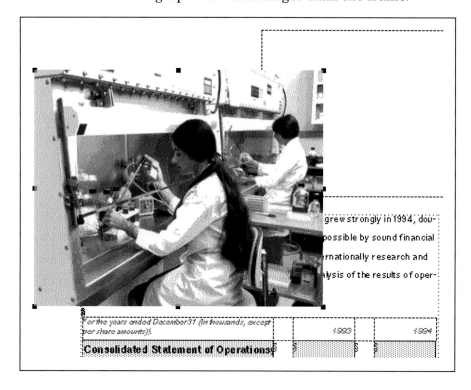

11. Drag the graphic back into the frame.

> **Elaboration:** Both graphics and graphic frames are page-anchored objects that can be positioned anywhere on a page and do not move as you edit text.

Exercise 2

Guided Tour

Cropping with a graphic frame

When the size of a graphic is too large, you can use a graphic frame to crop the graphic to show only a portion of the graphic.

In this exercise, you'll create a new graphic frame and use it to crop the woman graphic used in the previous exercise.

1. From the FrameMaker list of sample documents, open the clip art document named **People**:

   a. Display the FrameMaker list of sample documents.

Macintosh	From the [?] menu, choose **Samples & Clip Art**.
Windows	From the Help menu, choose **Samples & Clip Art**.
UNIX	From the document Help menu, choose **Samples & Clip Art.**

   b. In the FrameMaker samples window, click **Clip art** to see the list of clip art files.

   c. In the clip art list, double-click **People**.

   The People clip art document appears.

2. On page 1, select the woman graphic, and from the Edit menu in `People`, choose **Copy**.

3. Go to your original document, and go to **page 2**.

4. Click in a white area outside the text to make sure you have no insertion point, and from the Edit menu, choose **Paste**.

   The graphic appears in the center of the page.

5. If the Tools palette is not already visible, click the **Tools** button to display it.

6. Click the **Graphic Frame tool**.

Graphic Frame ———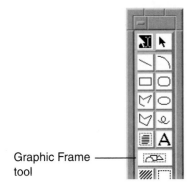
tool

7. Drag to create a graphic frame in the left margin, as in the following example.

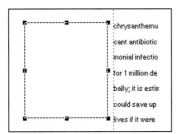

8. Drag the woman graphic into the graphic frame so only her head and upper body are visible.

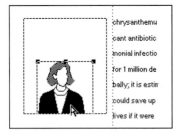

9. Click the edge of the graphic frame to select it, and resize it to frame the cropped woman graphic more closely.

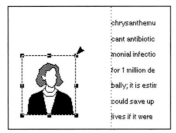

Text Runaround

Page-anchored graphics stay in place as text is added or deleted in a document. Text runaround properties enable you to determine how the text flows around the graphic—whether it flows around the graphic's rectangular boundary or follows the contours of the graphic.

Rectangular boundary around graphic.

Text following contours of graphic.

Graphics also can be placed in text-anchored frames. With text-anchored frames, the graphic moves with the text. Text-anchored frames are covered in the next module.

Exercise 3

Exploring runaround properties

Guided Tour

In this exercise, you'll explore the various text runaround properties.

1. From the FrameMaker list of sample documents, open the clip art document named **Dingbats**.

   a. Display the FrameMaker list of sample documents:

Macintosh	From the [?] menu, choose **Samples & Clip Art**.
Windows	From the Help menu, choose **Samples & Clip Art**.
UNIX	From the document Help menu, choose **Samples & Clip Art**.

   b. In the FrameMaker samples window, click **Clip art** to see the list of clip art files.

   c. In the clip art list, double-click **Dingbats**.

   The Dingbats clip art document appears.

   d. Go to **page 5**.

2. Select the chart in the following example, and from the Edit menu in `Dingbats`, choose **Copy**.

3. Go to your original document, make sure you're on page 2, and then click in a white area outside the text to make sure you have no insertion point.

4. From the Edit menu, choose **Paste**.

   The graphic appears in your document.

   > **Elaboration:** If you have an insertion point in the document when you paste a graphic, it is pasted into an anchored frame that will move when the text moves. If you have no insertion point when you paste, the graphic will not appear in a frame.

5. Drag the graphic so that it touches the left side of the lower-left column on page 2, as in the following example.

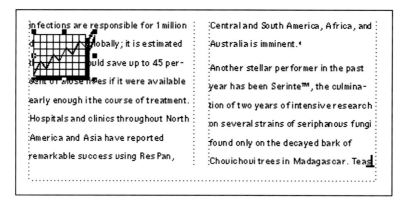

   Notice that the text in the column is hidden behind the graphic.

6. With the pasted graphic still selected, from the Graphics menu, choose **Runaround Properties**.

The Runaround Properties dialog box appears.

7. Turn on **Run around Bounding Box**.

8. Click **Set**.

9. The text runaround property causes the text to go around, not behind the graphic.

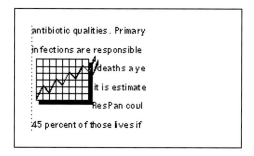

10. Drag the graphic toward the right side of the *same* column.

    The text runs around the left side of the graphic.

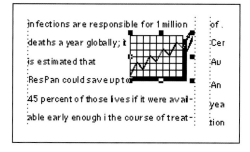

11. Drag the graphic to the middle of both columns and notice what happens to the text. The text runs around both sides of the graphic.

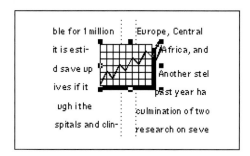

Exercise 4 Using runaround properties with rounded objects

Guided Tour

You have seen how text runs around the bounding box (or square edge) of a graphic. In this exercise, you'll add runaround properties to a graphic with rounded contours.

1. Move the woman graphic on page 2 out of the graphic frame so it overlaps the left side of the first column.

2. With the graphic still selected, from the Graphics menu, choose **Runaround Properties**.

3. In the Runaround Properties dialog box, turn on **Run around Contour**.

4. Click **Set**.

The text runs around the contour of the woman.

5. Create a 10-point gap between the woman graphic and the surrounding text:

   a. With the graphic still selected, from the Graphics menu, choose **Runaround Properties**.

   b. In the Runaround Properties dialog box, change the Gap setting to **10 pt**.

   c. Click **Set**.

   A gap appears between the woman and the text.

Exercise 5

Guided Tour

Working with page-anchored objects

Graphic frames and graphics placed directly onto a page are *page-anchored* objects. Page-anchored objects do not move with text, but rather remain where you position them on a page.

In this exercise, you'll see what happens when text surrounding a page-anchored graphic is modified.

1. Drag the chart to the lower-right corner of the lower-right column so that only one line of text appears below the graphic.

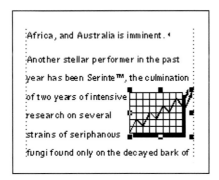

2. Put the insertion point at the end of the paragraph just above the chart.

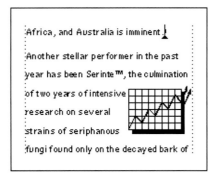

3. Type: `ReSpan is currently available only in the`
   `United States, Canada, and Mexico.`

   The graphic stays put while the text around it rewraps to accommodate the new words.

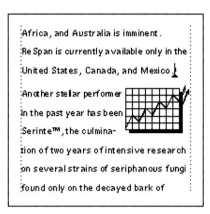

4. Save the file, and keep the document open if you intend to complete the optional exercise in this module. Otherwise, close this and any other open documents.

Optional Exercise

The following exercise enables you to enhance your FrameMaker skills and to explore additional FrameMaker features. Some steps are intentionally brief so that they require more independent thought on your part.

Exercise 6

Optional

Masking

When the size of a graphic is too large, you can crop the edges of the graphic to show only a portion of it. Masking occurs on areas that are not on the edges of a graphic. For example, masking would block out an area in the middle of a graphic. To mask an area, draw a nonbordered object (such as a rectangle) and place it on top of the area to be masked.

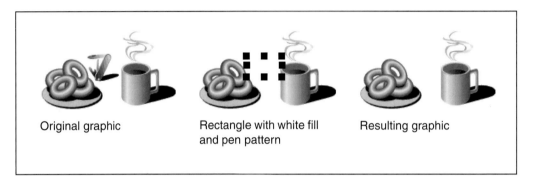

Original graphic   Rectangle with white fill   Resulting graphic
                     and pen pattern

In this optional exercise, you'll draw a nonbordered object to mask an area in the middle of the graphic.

1. Go to **page 3.**

In the graphic below, bubbles appear in the neck of the test tube.

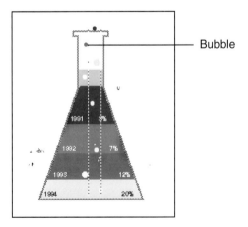

Bubble

2. Draw a nonbordered object to mask one of the bubbles:

   a. Select the graphic frame surrounding the graphic.

   b. From the Zoom pop-up menu, choose **200%**.

   c. Draw a small rectangle over one of the bubbles in the neck of the test tube.

   d. Change the fill color to match the area to be masked. (In this instance, the fill is white.)

3. Change the pen pattern to **None** so that the line disappears around the rectangle.

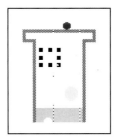

4. If necessary, reposition the small rectangle over the area to be masked.

5. Click off the rectangle to deselect the handles.
   The area of the graphic is now masked.

6. Save the file, and close the document. Also close any other open documents.

Review   Test your understanding of the concepts and procedures covered in this module by answering the following review questions. You can check your answers with those listed after the questions.

Question 1: How can you tell if a graphic is in a graphic frame?

Question 2: How do you crop a graphic?

Question 3: How does the Run around Bounding Box setting differ from the Run around Contour setting?

Question 4: What happens when text is added to a document that includes page-anchored graphics?

Question 5: How do you mask unwanted portions of a graphic?

Answer 1: When Borders are turned on, the graphic is surrounded by a dotted border. Also, when you choose Object Properties from the Graphics menu, the object type is Graphic frame.

Answer 2: Place a graphic inside a graphic frame that is smaller than the graphic.

Answer 3: When the Run around Bounding Box setting is turned on, text follows the graphic's bounding box, which is indicated by the selection handles that surround the graphic. When Run around Contour is turned on, the text follows the contour of the graphic itself.

Answer 4: The text moves. The graphics do not.

Answer 5: Draw a nonbordered object that is the same color as the background over the unwanted area.

For more information

For more information about graphic frames, see:

Chapter 13 of *Using FrameMaker*

Anchored Frames

Approximate time to complete: 1 hour 15 minutes

Introduction

In this module, you'll become familiar with anchored frames. When you create an illustration that is related to specific text, you can put the illustration in an anchored frame— a graphic frame that is anchored to the text. Then, when you edit the text, the frame and its contents move along with the text automatically.

Module Objectives

In this module, you'll learn how to

- Create anchored frames and position them inside the text column

- Place graphics in anchored frames

- Align the anchored frame and its contents

- Resize, copy, paste, and delete anchored frames

- Use Cropped and Floating features

- Control space above and below an anchored frame with a separate paragraph format for anchoring the frame

- Position anchored frames outside the text column and text frame and at the insertion point

FrameMaker Model

Anchored frames, like graphic frames, are *objects* that contain other objects— graphics, equations, and text.

Working with Anchored Frames

An anchored frame can contain graphics you draw, clip art you copy from another document, imported graphics, and text. When you anchor a graphic frame to a specific text passage, FrameMaker inserts an anchor symbol at the insertion point in the text. The anchored frame—and everything in it — moves with the anchor symbol, so you don't have to reposition graphics when you edit the document.

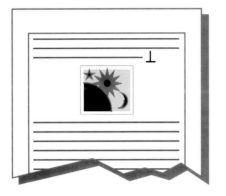

Before inserting text.

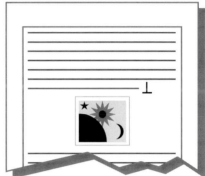

Anchored frame moves down when text is added above it.

When you create an anchored frame, you specify its size and where you want the frame to appear in relation to the anchor symbol.

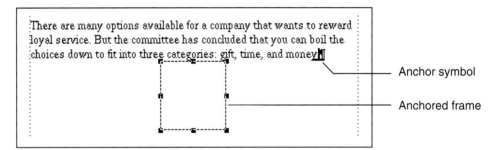

You can use an anchored frame for small graphics that appear in line with paragraph text or for art that appears between columns or in the page margin. You can also use an anchored frame for an illustration in a column of text—below the line containing the anchor symbol, at the top of the column, or at the bottom.

Anchoring positions

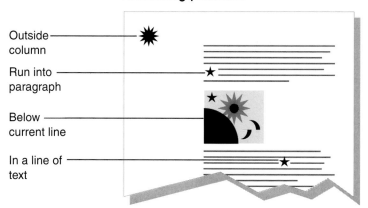

Outside column

Run into paragraph

Below current line

In a line of text

Exercise 1   Creating an anchored frame

Guided Tour

In this exercise, you'll create an anchored frame and paste a graphic into the frame, and then you'll edit the surrounding text to see the frame (and its contents) move with the text.

1. From the FrameMaker list of sample documents, open the **Report** sample:

    a. Display the FrameMaker list of sample documents.

Macintosh	From the 🄿 menu, choose **Samples & Clip Art**.
Windows	From the Help menu, choose **Samples & Clip Art**.
UNIX	From a document Help menu, choose **Samples & Clip Art**. (If there are no open documents, click **NEW**, then **Portrait**, first.)

    The FrameMaker samples window appears.

    b. In the FrameMaker samples list, click **Report**.

    The sample report appears.

2. Use the Save As dialog box to save the document in the `Class` directory or folder with the new filename `anchor`.

3. From the View menu, turn on **Borders**, **Text Symbols** and **Rulers**.

4. Go to **page 2**.

5. In the second column, put the insertion point after the word "imminent."

6. From the Special menu, choose **Anchored Frame**.

   The Anchored Frame dialog box appears.

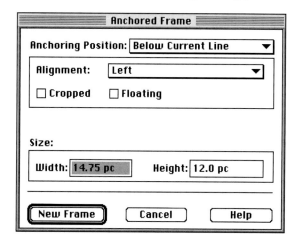

7. Make sure **Below Current Line** is selected from the Anchoring Position pop-up menu.

8. From the Alignment pop-up menu, choose **Center**.

9. Change the Width setting to **1.5 in**.

10. Change the Height setting to **1.5 in**.

> **Elaboration:** Although the display units of this document are set to picas (pc), those units can be overridden by typing the abbreviation of other units in the Width and Height text boxes.

11. Click **New Frame**.

A 1.5-inch by 1.5-inch anchored frame appears centered below the line with the insertion point. An anchor symbol appears at the insertion point.

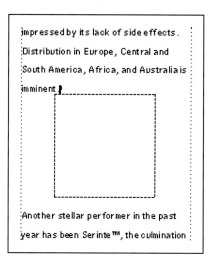

12. From **page 1** of the `Symbols` sample document, copy the baby clip art:

a. Display the FrameMaker list of sample documents.

Macintosh	From the ⟦?⟧ menu, choose **Samples & Clip Art**.
Windows	From the Help menu, choose **Samples & Clip Art**.
UNIX	From the document Help menu, choose **Samples & Clip Art**.

b. In the FrameMaker samples window, click **Clip art** to see the list of clip art files.

c. Double-click **Symbols**.

The Symbols clip art document appears.

d. Click to select the baby graphic in the middle of the first line on **page 1** of `Symbols`.

e. From the Edit menu in `Symbols`, choose **Copy**.

13. In your document, make sure the anchored frame is selected, and from the Edit menu of your document, choose **Paste**.

   Because the frame was selected, the graphic is pasted in the center of the selected frame.

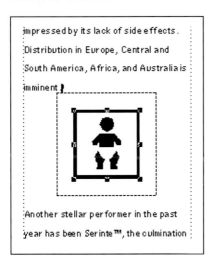

14. In the paragraph above the anchored frame, select the text "Central and South America, Africa," and press **Delete**.

   Notice that the anchored frame and its contents move up the page. As you edit the text, anchored frames and their contents move with the text flow.

Exercise 2

Guided Tour

Realigning an anchored frame and its contents

In this exercise, you'll change the alignment properties of the anchored frame so that the frame aligns to the left side of the column, not the center.

1. In your document, click the border of the anchored frame, not the graphic, to select the anchored frame.

   Handles appear on the border of the frame.

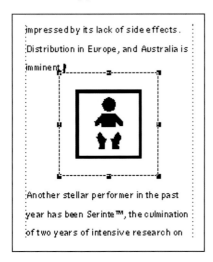

2. From the Special menu, choose **Anchored Frame**.

   The Anchored Frame dialog box appears. Because you selected the existing frame in your document before choosing Anchored Frame from the Special menu, the dialog box reflects the properties of the current frame.

3. From the Alignment pop-up menu, choose **Left**.

4. Click **Edit Frame**.

   The anchored frame aligns to the left side of the text column.

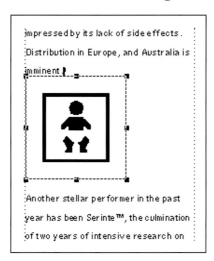

5. Click the graphic, not the frame, to select the graphic.

   Handles appear on the border of the graphic.

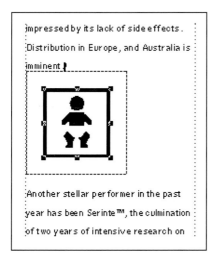

6. From the Graphics menu, choose **Align**.

   The Align dialog box appears.

7. In the **Top/Bottom** area, turn on **As Is**.

8. In the **Left/Right** area, turn on **Left Sides**.

9. Click **Align**.

Because the graphic is in a frame, the graphic aligns to the left side of the frame, not the left side of the entire page or some other selected object.

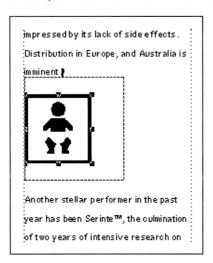

Exercise 3   Resizing and copying an anchored frame

In this exercise, you'll change the size of the anchored frame, both manually and by using the Anchored Frame command.

1. In your document, click the border of the anchored frame, not the graphic, to select the anchored frame.

Handles appear on the border of the frame.

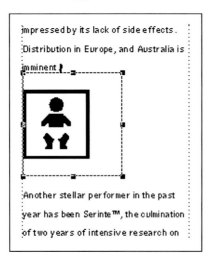

2. From the Special menu, choose **Anchored Frame**.

The Anchored Frame dialog box appears. Because you selected the existing frame in your document before choosing Anchored Frame from the Special menu, the dialog box reflects the properties of the current frame.

3. Change the Width setting to **7.5 pc**.

4. Change the Height setting to **7.5 pc**.

5. Click **Edit Frame**.

   The anchored frame gets smaller.

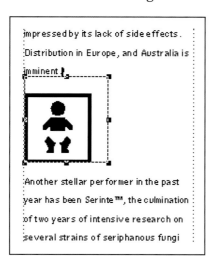

6. Drag the right resize handle (the one in the middle of the right side) to the right to make the frame as wide as the text column.

7. Drag the bottom resize handle (the one in the middle of the bottom) downward to make the frame a little taller.

   Your document should look similar to this.

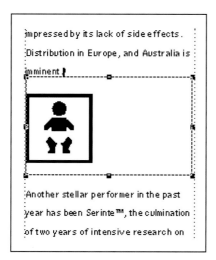

Elaboration: You can resize the frame with the resize handles, but you cannot move a frame anchored in the text column. (Try dragging the edge of the frame in your document and see what happens.) You must use the Anchored Frame command (Special menu) to reposition a frame anchored in the text column.

8. With the anchored frame still selected, from the Edit menu, choose **Copy**.

9. Put the insertion point at the end of the first paragraph at the top of the page (page 2).

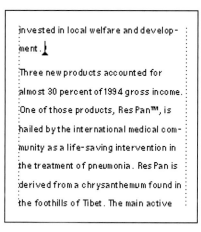

10. From the Edit menu, choose **Paste**.

    The anchored frame, along with its contents, is pasted below the line containing the insertion point. The first anchored frame you inserted moves to page 3.

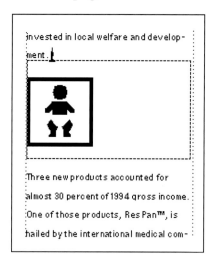

Elaboration: Because anchored frames are text-anchored objects, you must put the insertion point in the document text to paste the anchored frame. This is unlike page-anchored objects, which don't require having a specific location on a page.

11. On page 2, click the border of the anchored frame, not the graphic, to select the anchored frame.

12. Press **Delete**.

    The frame and its contents disappear, and the original frame returns to the bottom of page 2.

Exercise 4

Cropping and floating

You can prevent a wide frame from extending beyond the edge of the column of text by *cropping* the frame.

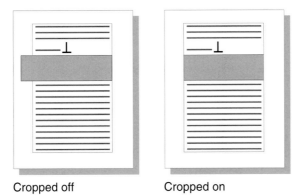

Cropped off   Cropped on

If the frame and its anchor symbol won't fit in the same column, you can let the frame *float* to the next column that can hold it, while the anchor symbol remains in the previous column.

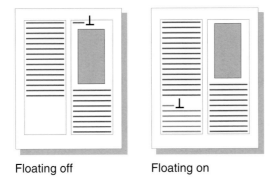

Floating off   Floating on

In this exercise, you'll work with both cropping and floating features to position an anchored frame in a document.

1. On page 2, click the border of the anchored frame to select it.

2. From the Special menu, choose **Anchored Frame**.

   The Anchored Frame dialog box appears.

3. Change the Alignment to **Center**, and turn on **Cropped**.

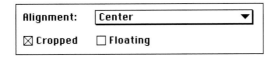

4. Click **Edit Frame**.

5. Drag the right resize handle (the one in the middle of the right side) until the anchored frame extends to the edge of the page.

Notice that the anchored frame and any of its contents that extend beyond the width of the text column are cropped off by the text column. Also notice that because the alignment of the frame is centered, equal amounts of the frame extend beyond the left and right sides of the column.

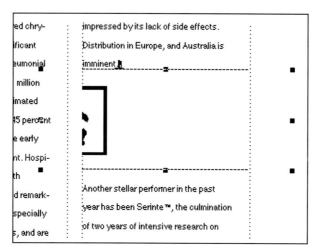

6. With the anchored frame still selected, from the Special menu, choose **Anchored Frame**.

7. In the Anchored Frame dialog box, turn off **Cropped**.

8. Click **Edit Frame**.

    The anchored frame moves to the top of the next page and is no longer cropped off by the text column.

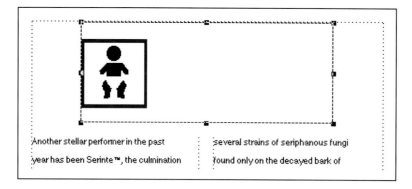

Elaboration: When you make an anchored frame with Cropped turned off wider than a single column, the frame straddles both columns. In this case, there is not enough space at the bottom of the page after the frame's anchor symbol for the straddle. As a result, the frame straddles the columns at the top of the following page.

9. Use the right resize handle to resize the anchored frame so it is wider than the text frame.

   The anchored frame and its contents extend into the margins of the page.

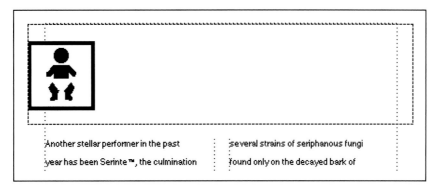

Another stellar performer in the past   several strains of seriphanous fungi

year has been Serinte™, the culmination   found only on the decayed bark of

Elaboration: When an anchored frame is wider than both the text columns together (wider than the entire text frame), the frame overlays the text frame and extends into the margins of the page.

10. Resize the anchored frame to the width of the graphic.

    The anchored frame and its contents return to page 2.

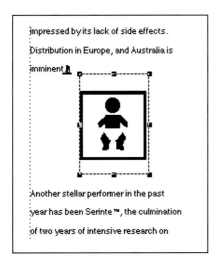

impressed by its lack of side effects.

Distribution in Europe, and Australia is

imminent.

Another stellar performer in the past

year has been Serinte™, the culmination

of two years of intensive research on

11. Add five lines of text in the paragraph before the graphic to see what happens when the frame is too large to fit in the column:

a. Select the five lines of text in the left column as in the following example.

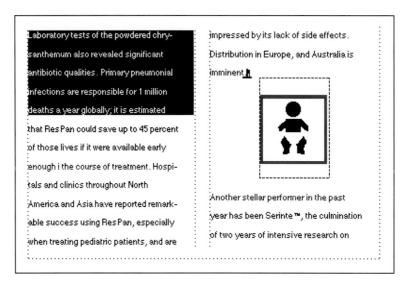

b. From the Edit menu, choose **Copy**.

c. Put the insertion point at the beginning of the selected text, and from the Edit menu, choose **Paste**.

The graphic no longer appears on the page, and a significant amount of white space appears at the bottom of the text columns.

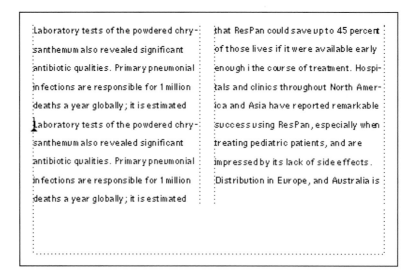

> **Elaboration:** When floating is turned off, the anchored frame must stay with its anchor symbol. So if the frame and its anchor symbol cannot fit in the column, they move to the top of the next column where they fit, and white space remains at the bottom of the column where they did not fit. In the example above, white space appears at the bottoms of both text columns, since FrameMaker is balancing the two text columns.

12. Turn on **Floating** for the anchored frame:

    a. Go to **page 3**.

    b. Click the border of the frame to select it.

    c. From the Special menu, choose **Anchored Frame**.

    d. In the Anchored Frame dialog box, turn on **Floating**.

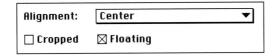

    e. Click **Edit Frame**.

13. Go to **page 2**.

    Notice that the white space is backfilled by text that would normally appear after the frame.

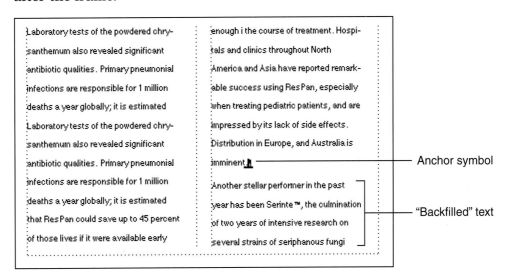

14. Delete the five lines of text you pasted in earlier.

The frame returns to page 2 and is no longer floating, although the option is turned on in case you edit the text and the frame needs to float again.

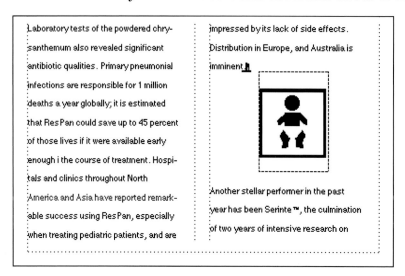

Exercise 5   Creating an anchored frame by pasting a graphic

Guided Tour

Rather than having to decide exactly how large to make the anchored frame before pasting the graphic, you can have FrameMaker create the anchored frame for you, sized to fit your graphic.

1. Click to select the baby graphic, not the anchored frame.

2. From the Edit menu, choose **Copy**.

3. Click the border of the anchored frame, and press **Delete** to delete the frame and its contents.

4. Make sure the insertion point appears after the word "imminent."

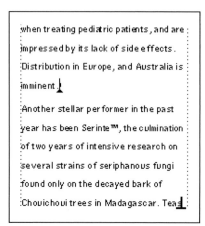

5. From the Edit menu, choose **Paste**.

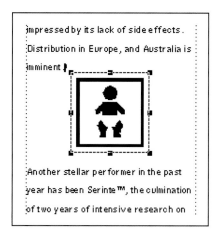

The graphic appears below the line with the insertion point in an anchored frame, centered in the text column and sized to fit the graphic.

Exercise 6

Guided Tour

Controlling space above and below anchored frames

The spacing above and below an anchored frame is controlled by the paragraph that contains the anchor symbol. That being the case, the easiest way to control an anchored frame's spacing is to create a special paragraph format just for holding anchored frames. The paragraph should use the smallest possible point size to minimize its impact on total spacing measurements, and it should contain no text—just the frame's anchor symbol. In this exercise, you'll create just such a paragraph.

Frame anchored to empty paragraph.

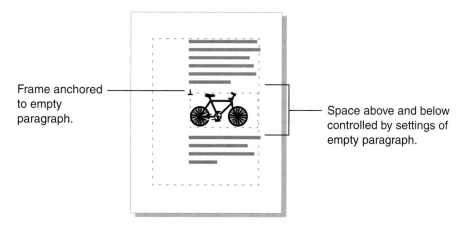

Space above and below controlled by settings of empty paragraph.

1. Put the insertion point after the word "imminent" and the period ending the sentence, but just to the left of the anchor symbol for the frame.

This is easier to do if you zoom to 200%.

2. Press **Return**.

The anchor symbol and insertion point move to the next paragraph, empty except for the anchor symbol and the frame below the current line. The anchor symbol is set against the left edge of the text column and may be difficult to see.

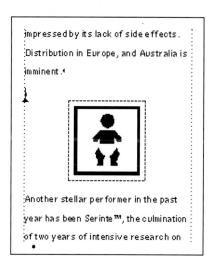

Notice that you are in a Body paragraph. Next, you'll create a new paragraph format specifically for controlling how much space appears above and below the frame.

3. Create a new paragraph format called **Picture** with a default font size of **2 pt**, Space Above set to **0 pt** and Space Below set to **12 pt**:

a. From the Format menu, choose **Paragraphs>Designer**.

The Paragraph Designer appears.

b. In the Paragraph Designer, from the Commands pop-up menu, choose **New Format**.

The New Format dialog box appears.

c. In the Tag text box, type: Picture

d. Make sure **Store in Catalog** and **Apply to Selection** are turned on.

e. Click **Create**.

f. From the Properties pop-up menu, choose **Default Font**.

g. Change the Size setting to **2**.

h. Click **Update All**.

The anchor symbol gets very small. Just 4 points of space is being used by the line anchoring the frame.

i. From the Properties pop-up menu, choose **Basic**.

j. Change the Space Above setting to **0 pt**.

k. Change the Space Below setting to **12 pt**.

l. Click **Update All**, and turn off the borders.

   The space above and below the frame appears equal. By using this new paragraph format to anchor frames, the spacing will be controlled when you include anchored frames in a document.

4. Save the file, and close the document.

Positioning Anchored Frames in the Margin

Anchored frames can also be positioned in the margins so that as you edit the text in the document, the anchored frames (and their contents) move with the text. When you position an anchored frame using the Outside Column setting or the Outside Text Frame setting, you can choose from several locations:

- Left or right side

- On the side closer to or farther from the page edge

- On the side closer to or farther from the binding in a double-sided layout

Exercise 7

Project

Using the Outside Text Column property

In this exercise, you'll add an anchored frame outside the text column in the sample report that uses side heads.

1. From the FrameMaker list of standard templates, open a copy of the **Report, Sidehead** template with sample text:

   a. Open the New dialog box.

      | **Macintosh** | From the File menu, choose **New**. |
      | **Windows** | From the File menu, choose **New**. |
      | **UNIX** | In the main FrameMaker window, click **NEW**. |

   b. At the bottom of the dialog box, click **Explore Standard Templates**.

   c. In the list of templates, click **Report, Sidehead**.

   d. Click **Show Sample**.

2. Use the Save As dialog box to save the document in the Class directory or folder with the new filename margin.

3. Put the insertion point at the beginning of the heading that says, "The Quake Came Wednesday Morning."

4. From the Special menu, choose **Anchored Frame**.

5. In the Anchored Frame dialog box, specify the following settings.

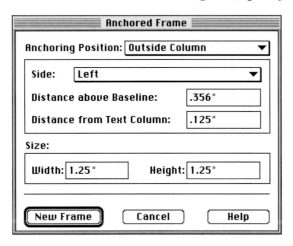

6. Click **New Frame**.

   The frame appears outside the text column on the left side, at a slight distance away from the text column and above the baseline of text where it is anchored. (Text Symbols are currently off, so you cannot see the anchor symbol.)

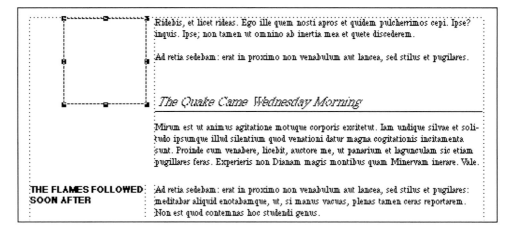

7. Using the border of the frame but not the handle, drag the frame to the position shown in the following example.

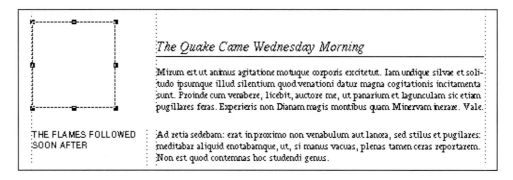

Frames anchored outside the text column (or text frame) can be dragged vertically and horizontally for repositioning. If you drag a frame vertically, you change its Distance above Baseline. If you drag a frame horizontally, you change its Distance from Text Column (or Text Frame).

8. From **page 4** of the `Symbols` sample document, copy the fire clip art, and paste it into the anchored frame.

The Quake Came Wednesday Morning

Mirum est ut animus agitatione motuque corporis excitetur. Iam undique silvae et solitudo ipsumque illud silentium quod venationi datur magna cogitationis incitamenta sunt. Proinde cum venabere, licebit, auctore me, ut panarium et lagunculam sic etiam pugillares feras. Experieris non Dianam magis montibus quam Minervam inerrare. Vale.

THE FLAMES FOLLOWED SOON AFTER

Ad retia sedebam: erat in proximo non venabulum aut lancea, sed stilus et pugillares: meditabar aliquid enotabamque, ut, si manus vacuas, plenas tamen ceras reportarem. Non est quod contemnas hoc studendi genus.

a. Display the FrameMaker list of sample documents:

Macintosh	From the **[?]** menu, choose **Samples & Clip Art.**
Windows	From the Help menu, choose **Samples & Clip Art.**
UNIX	From the document Help menu, choose **Samples & Clip Art.**

b. In the FrameMaker samples window, click **Clip art** to see the list of clip art files.

c. Double-click **Symbols**.

d. Go to **page 4** of `Symbols` and select the fire graphic.

e. From the Edit menu in `Symbols`, choose **Copy**.

f. In your document, select the border of the frame you just inserted.

g. From the Edit menu, choose **Paste**.

   Because the frame was selected, the graphic is pasted in the center of the selected frame.

9. Using the resize handles of the frame, resize the frame to hide the art's border.

10. From the View menu, turn off **Borders** to see the final result.

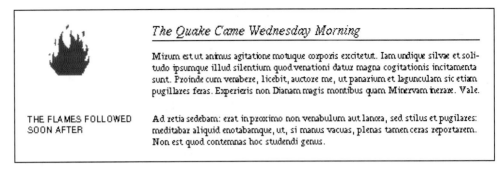

11. Turn on borders before continuing.

Using Run Into Paragraph

You can position an anchored frame at the beginning of a paragraph, with the paragraph text running around the frame—for example, to set a small graphic or drop cap (a larger initial letter) at the beginning of the paragraph.

When you run text around an anchored frame, you can choose from several locations: on the left or right side of the column, or on the side closest to or farthest from the binding in a double-sided layout. The anchored frame is aligned vertically with the top edge of the text in the paragraph.

Anchored frame aligned vertically with top edge of text.

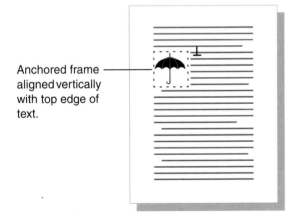

Exercise 8

Using the Run Into Paragraph property

In this exercise, you'll create a drop cap to appear at the start of a paragraph.

1. Go to **page 2**.

2. At the beginning of the paragraph to the right of the side head "THE FIRST DAY," delete the letter "N" from the text "Non est quod...".

3. From the Special menu, choose **Anchored Frame**.

4. In the Anchored Frame dialog box, specify the following settings.

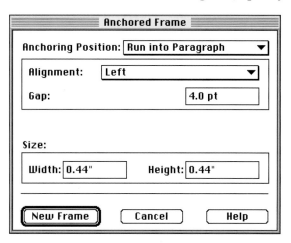

5. Click **New Frame**.

   The frame appears running into the paragraph.

   > on est quod contemnas hoc studendi genus. Mirum est ut animus agitatione
   > motuque corporis excitetur. Iam undique silvae et solitudo ipsumque illud
   > silentium quod venationi datur magna cogitationis incitamenta sunt. Proinde
   > cum venabere, licebit, auctore me, ut panarium et lagunculam sic etiam pugillares feras.
   > Experieris non Dianam magis montibus quam Minervam inerare. Vale.

6. Create the letter "N" shown in the example below.

   > **N** on est quod contemnas hoc studendi genus. Mirum est ut animus agitatione
   > motuque corporis excitetur. Iam undique silvae et solitudo ipsumque illud
   > silentium quod venationi datur magna cogitationis incitamenta sunt. Proinde
   > cum venabere, licebit, auctore me, ut panarium et lagunculam sic etiam pugillares feras.
   > Experieris non Dianam magis montibus quam Minervam inerare. Vale.

   a. On the upper-right side of the document window, click the **Tools** button to display the Tools palette:

   b. In the Tools palette, select the **Text Line tool** (A) and click in the left side of the anchored frame.

   c. Type: N

    d. Select the letter "N" you just typed.

    e. From the Format menu, select **Size>Other**.
The Font Size dialog box appears.

    f. Change the Size setting to **42 pt**.

    g. Click **Set**.

    h. With the letter selected, from the Format menu, choose **Style>Bold**.

    i. **Control-click** (on the Macintosh, **Option-click**) to select the letter as an object.

    j. From the Graphics menu, choose **Align**.

    k. Turn on **T/B Centers** and **L/R Centers**.

    l. Click **Align**.

7. Turn off the borders to see the final result.

8. Save the file, avvnd close the document.

Optional Exercise

The following exercise enables you to enhance your FrameMaker skills and to explore additional FrameMaker features. Some steps are intentionally brief so that they require more independent thought on your part.

Exercise 9

Optional

Positioning a graphic within a line

A frame anchored at the insertion point is most often used to include very small graphics in a line of text. In this optional exercise, you'll add an anchored frame at the insertion point in the book chapter, `response.doc`.

> asked them to satisfy. They especially emphasize the relationship of health hazard levels of pollution to Impact Assessment Study ⊕ as a subject demanding more exploration. They also

1. Open the **response.doc** sample file:

   a. Display the FrameMaker list of sample documents.

Macintosh	From the [?] menu, choose **Samples & Clip Art**.
Windows	From the Help menu, choose **Samples & Clip Art**.
UNIX	From a document Help menu, choose **Samples & Clip Art**. (If there are no open documents, click **NEW**, then **Portrait**, first.)

   b. Click **Book**.

   c. Double-click **response.doc**.

2. Use the Save As dialog box to save the document in the `Class` directory or folder with the new filename `inline`.

3. From the FrameMaker list of sample documents, copy the World icon from **page 8** of the clip art document named `Icons`.

4. In the `inline` document, go to **page 32**.

5. Under the heading "3.8 Ecological Damage," put the insertion point after the words "Impact Assessment Study."

> **3.8 Ecological Damage**
>
> They call for the use of contemporary ecological techniques and complex models. Ecologists will have to fill gaps both on the applied and basic research level to meet the needs society has asked them to satisfy. They especially emphasize the relationship of health hazard levels of pollution to Impact Assessment Study as a

6. From the Edit menu, choose **Paste**.

7. The World icon is pasted inside an anchored frame below the insertion point.

8. Select the graphic, and use the Scale command (Graphics menu) to change both the width and height of the World icon to **14 pt**.

9. Use the Align command (Graphics menu) to make the reduced icon appear in the top-left corner of the anchored frame.

10. Select the anchored frame, use the Anchored Frame command to specify the following settings, and click **Edit Frame**.

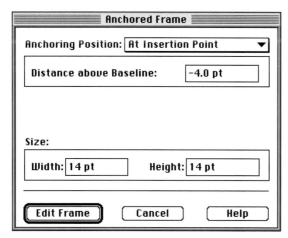

The anchored frame appears anchored at the insertion point, slightly below the baseline of the text, and smaller.

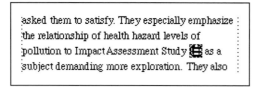

11. Type a space before or after the anchored frame, as necessary.

12. Save the file, and close the document. Also close any other open windows at this time.

Review   Test your understanding of the concepts and procedures covered in this module by answering the following review questions. You can check your answers with those listed after the questions.

Question 1:   How do you add an anchored frame to a document?

Question 2:   How do you change the size or position of an existing anchored frame?

Question 3:   When a single graphic is selected within an anchored frame, how does the Align command affect that graphic?

Question 4:   When Floating is off, what happens if an anchored frame doesn't have enough space in the column and so moves to the next column? What happens when Floating is on?

Question 5:   When Cropped is off, what happens if an anchored frame is wider than the column in which it is anchored? What happens when Cropped is on?

Answer 1:   Put the insertion point in a text column or table cell (not in a text line), then from the Special menu, choose Anchored Frame. In the Anchored Frame dialog box, specify the location of the frame and its size. Click New Frame.

Answer 2:   Select the frame, and from the Special menu, choose Anchored Frame. Modify settings in the dialog box, and click Edit Frame. You can also change the size by dragging one or more handles, and you can drag frames that are anchored in the margin to reposition them.

Answer 3:   The Align command aligns the graphic with relation to the anchored frame.

Answer 4:   When Floating is off, there is white space left at the bottom of the column from which the frame was moved. When Floating is on, the text "backfills" the white space left at the bottom of the column from which the frame was moved. When Floating is on, the frame and the anchor symbol can end up in different text columns.

Answer 5:   When Cropped is off, the anchored frame and its contents can extend beyond the borders of the text column. When Cropped is on, the anchored frame and its contents are cut off by the borders of the text column in which the frame is anchored.

For more information

For more information about anchored frames, see:

Chapter 15 of *Using FrameMaker*

Master Pages

. . . .

Approximate time to complete: 45 minutes

Introduction

In this module, you'll become familiar with master pages in FrameMaker documents. Master pages control page layout characteristics such as placement and size of text frames, header and footer information, and background graphics.

Module Objectives

In this module, you'll learn how to

- Identify items on a master page

- Use graphics on master pages

- Set up headers and footers on a master page by using background text frames

- Use a template text frame on a master page

- Change a single-sided document into a double-sided document creating alternating page layouts

- Create a new custom master page

- Apply a custom master page to a body page

- Import page layouts from one document into another document

FrameMaker Model

Master *pages* contain background text and graphics and text frame templates—text frames that are automatically copied to body pages to standardize the page layout.

Background Graphics and Text on Master Pages

Master pages are one of three types of pages in a FrameMaker document. Master pages determine the basic layout of corresponding body pages. You do most of your work on *body pages*—they are the pages you normally think of as the pages in the document. (The third type of pages, *reference pages*, are covered in the next module.)

Master pages contain two types of objects:

- Background text and graphics.

  Every time FrameMaker displays a body page, it displays background text (text lines and text frames with no flow tag) and graphics from the corresponding master page. On body pages, background objects are visible, but not editable. Some examples of background objects are headers, footers, logos, and lines.

- Template text frames.

  FrameMaker creates text frames on body pages by copying template text frames from the corresponding master pages. Template text frames have flow tags, which make them the foreground on the body pages. You type text into the template text frames on the body pages.

Background text and graphics ———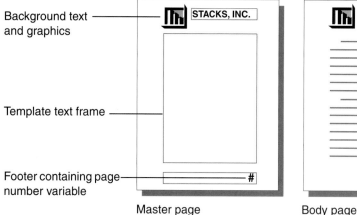

Template text frame ———

Footer containing page number variable ———

Master page   Body page

Exercise 1 Viewing master pages

Guided Tour

In this exercise, you'll become familiar with the various object types on a master page.

1. From the FrameMaker list of sample documents, open the **Letter** sample:

   a. Display the FrameMaker list of sample documents.

Macintosh	From the [?] menu, choose **Samples & Clip Art**.
Windows	From the Help menu, choose **Samples & Clip Art**.
UNIX	From a document Help menu, choose **Samples & Clip Art**. (If there are no open documents, click **NEW**, then **Portrait** first.)

   b. In the FrameMaker samples list, click **Letter**.

      The sample letter appears.

2. Use the Save As dialog box to save the document in the `Class` directory or folder with the new filename `viewltr`.

3. Turn on **Borders** and **Text Symbols**.

   Notice the following page layout items in the letter:

- Company logo (bicycle graphic)

- Company name (Zephyr Bicycles Limited)

- Date

- Body of the letter

- Company address (at bottom of page)

4. From the View menu, choose **Master Pages**.

   The master page corresponding to the first body page appears.

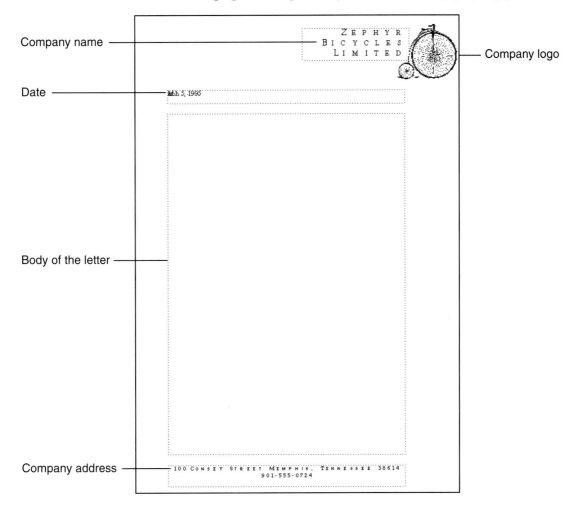

5. In the status bar, notice the name of the master page.

Name of master ——— First (2 of 2) *   100%   z Z

This master page is named First, and it is the second of two master pages in this document.

6. Click the **Previous Page** button.

In the status bar, notice the name of the master page.

Right (1 of 2) *   100%   z Z

This master page is named Right. It is the first of the two master pages in the document and is automatically applied to all body pages. The master page named First is a custom master page. It has been manually applied to the first body page of the document.

> **Tip:** To determine which master page a body page is using, go to the body page and from the View menu, choose Master Pages. FrameMaker will take you to the master page that the body page is using.

7. Click the **Next Page** button.

You have returned to the master page named First.

First (2 of 2) *   100%   z Z

Notice that a bicycle graphic appears in the upper-right corner. This *background graphic* is page-anchored on the master page and appears in exactly the same place on the first body page of the letter.

8. Put the insertion point in the text frame containing the company name, and look in the status bar.

There is no flow tag in this text frame. It is a *background* or *untagged text frame*. Just like background graphics, it will appear exactly as it appears here, on all body pages that use this master page.

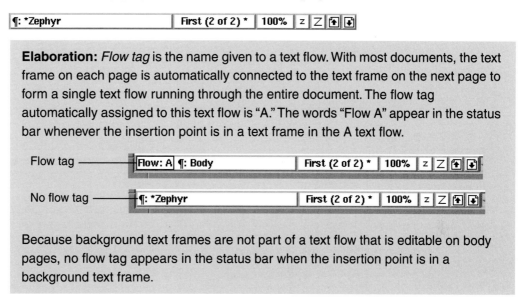

Elaboration: *Flow tag* is the name given to a text flow. With most documents, the text frame on each page is automatically connected to the text frame on the next page to form a single text flow running through the entire document. The flow tag automatically assigned to this text flow is "A." The words "Flow A" appear in the status bar whenever the insertion point is in a text frame in the A text flow.

Flow tag ——
No flow tag ——

Because background text frames are not part of a text flow that is editable on body pages, no flow tag appears in the status bar when the insertion point is in a background text frame.

9. Put the insertion point in the text frame containing the date and then in the text frame containing the company address at the bottom of the page.

   Notice that neither text frame has a flow tag. They are also background text frames.

10. Put the insertion point in the large text frame called the *template text frame*.

    Notice that it has a flow tag, Flow A.

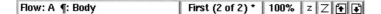

Note: When a text frame has a flow tag on the master page, it will have a flow tag on the body page, and you will be able to type in it on the body page. When a text frame does not have a flow tag on the master page, the contents of the text frame will appear as background information on the body page, visible but not editable. The only place you can edit the untagged text frame is on the master page.

11. From the View menu, choose **Body Pages**.

    Body page 1 appears.

12. Click the bicycle logo, and try to select it.

You are not able to select the bicycle logo, because it is a background object coming from the master page.

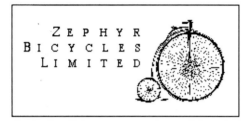

13. Try to select the company name, date, or company address.

    Background text and graphics are visible on body pages, but not editable here.

14. Put the insertion point at the end of the last paragraph in the letter, and type enough text (any text will do) so the closing of the letter moves to the top of a new page.

> The new bicycles went into production last month and are currently in stock. We can start shipping immediately via express air freight. Please let me know if you have any questions or need more information. ASDFKJ A;SFKJ SA;DKFJ AS;DFK JALKF JASD;FLK JF KJASDF KJAS;D KFJAS ;DKF JASD;KF JA;DF KJF;KJF; KJF KJASD;F KJASD;FK JASDFKJ A;DF KJASD;F KJASF KJASD;F KJASD;KF JASD; KFJA; K F;KDFL;DF J;LFJ AKFJA ;KFJASD;F KASDF;L KJASD;F KJ KJF ;KADF; LKASDF ;LDF; LKASJDF ;LDF ;F J;A JF;AJF ;ASKF JAS;DLKFJ SAD;KF JAKF JALKF JAS;DKF JASFJ AKF JASFK JAS;DFJK A;SDKFJ A;SDJKF AS;DLKF JAS;DFLKJ ALKFJ ASL KJAS;DL KFJA;SDKF JA;SDFK JALKF JAS-LKF JAK JA;SDKFJ ASD¶

> 100 CONSEY STREET MEMPHIS, TENNESSEE 38614
> 901-555-0724

Text frames with flow tags on master pages appear as foreground on corresponding body pages. You can change the contents of text frames on the body pages.

15. Go to **page 2**.

    Notice that the layout of page 2 is different from the layout of page 1.

16. From the View menu, choose **Master Pages**.

    The Right master page appears because this body page uses the Right master page.

17. Save the file, and close the document.

Exercise 2

Guided Tour

Using background text frames and graphics on master pages

In this exercise, you'll add background text and graphics to a master page.

1. Create a new **Portrait** document.

2. Use the Save As dialog box to save the document in the `Class` directory or folder with the new filename `lettrhd`

3. From the View menu, choose **Master Pages**.

   The master page named Right appears. It is the first and only master page in the document. The document is single sided, which means that all body pages use the same master page and have the same layout.

   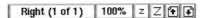

4. From **page 6** of the `Icons` clip art file, copy the links graphic:

   a. From the Help menu, choose **Samples & Clip Art**.

   b. Click **Clip art**.

   c. Double-click **Icons**.

   d. Go to **page 6**.

   e. Select the links graphic, and from the Edit menu, choose **Copy**.

5. In your document, click *outside* all text frames so you do *not* have an insertion point.

6. From the Edit menu, choose **Paste**.

   The graphic is pasted in the middle of the Right master page.

   Note: If you had an insertion point in the text frame, the graphic would have been pasted in an anchored frame.

7. Using the Object Properties command, reposition the graphic with an Offset From Top of **.25"** and Offset From Left of **7"**:

   a. With the graphic still selected, from the Graphics menu, choose **Object Properties**.

   The Object Properties dialog box appears.

b. Change the Offset From Top setting to **.25"**.

c. Change the Offset From Left setting to **7"**.

d. Click **Set**.

The graphic moves to the upper-right corner of the page.

8. Click in the header text frame at the top of the page, and type:

`County Chain Link Fence Co.`

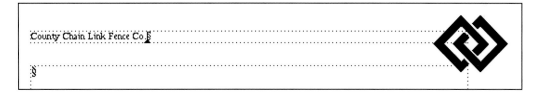

Notice that the default paragraph format being used is Header.

9. Open the Paragraph Catalog, and apply the **Title** paragraph format to the text.

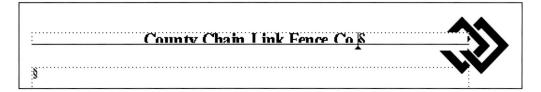

The text appears cut off, because the text frame is not tall enough to display all of the text.

10. Using the Object Properties command, resize the text frame to a height of **.2"**:

a. **Control-click** (on the Macintosh, **Option-click**) the text frame to select it as an object.

b. From the Graphics menu, choose **Object Properties**.

The Object Properties dialog box appears.

c. Change the Height setting to **.2"**.

d. Click **Set**.

The header text frame resizes to fit the text.

11. Click in the footer text frame at the bottom of the page.

    Notice that the default paragraph format is Footer and that the Footer format has tabs.

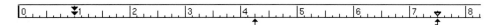

12. Type: 1234 South Main Street, Columbia, SC 29510

13. Press **Tab** twice.

    The insertion point moves to the right-aligned tab.

14. Type: Page

15. Press the **Space bar**.

16. From the Format menu, choose **Headers & Footers>Insert Page #**.

    The page number variable (#) appears in the footer. (You will see the actual page number when you go back to the body pages.)

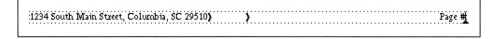

17. From the View menu, choose **Body Pages**.

    Body page 1 appears.

18. Put your insertion point in the text frame, and press and hold down **Return** until you have created a total of five body pages.

    Five body pages will help you see the layout changes you will be making.

19. Page through the document, and notice that the layout is the same on every page. Each page has a page number in the lower-right corner.

Exercise 3

Guided Tour

Modifying template text frames on master pages

In this exercise, you'll adjust the size of the template text frame on the master page.

1. From the View menu, choose **Master Pages**.

   The Right master page appears.

2. **Control-click** (on the Macintosh, **Option-click**) the template text frame to select it as an object.

   Handles appear on the borders of the text frame.

3. From the Graphics menu, choose **Snap** to turn it on.

4. Resize the frame so its right edge is at the 6½-inch mark on the ruler at the top.

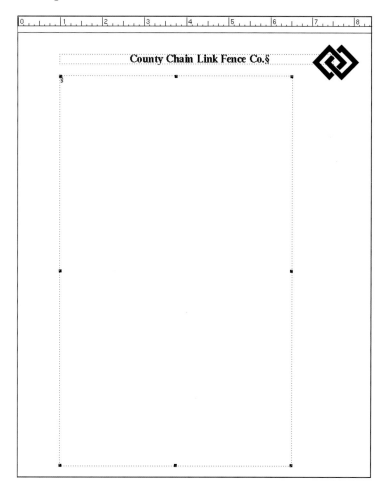

5. From the View menu, choose **Body Pages**.

   The body page you last viewed appears.

6. Page through the document to verify that the modified text frame appears on every page.

Single-Sided and Double-Sided Documents

A document in which all the body pages have a similar layout is referred to as *single-sided*. Single-sided documents use one master page called Right.

Body pages of a single-sided document

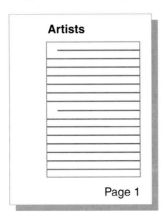 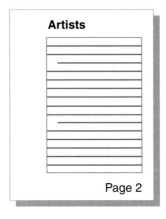 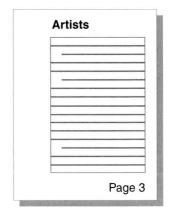

A document can also have body pages with alternating page layouts. For example, headers and footers can be left-aligned on left-facing pages and right-aligned on right-facing pages.

A document with alternating page layouts on even and odd pages is referred to as a *double-sided* document. Double-sided documents have two master pages, usually named Left and Right. As you add body pages in your document, FrameMaker automatically applies one master page to all even-numbered body pages, and the other master page to all odd-numbered body pages.

Body pages of a double-sided document

 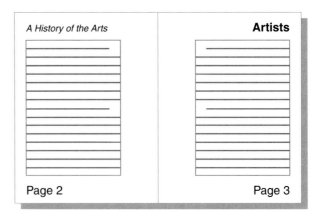

Exercise 4

Project

Changing from a single-sided to a double-sided document

In this exercise, you'll change the `lettrhd` document to a double-sided document, which adds a master page named Left. The Left master page will be automatically applied to the even-numbered pages in the document.

1. From the View menu, choose **Master Pages**.

   The Right master page appears.

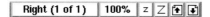

2. From the Format menu, choose **Page Layout>Page Size**.

   The Page Size dialog box appears.

3. In the Pagination area, turn on **Double-Sided**.

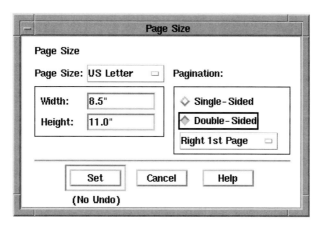

4. Click **Set**.

   Notice that you now have two master pages in this document and that the Left master page is currently displayed.

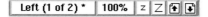

   When you changed the document to double-sided, a Left master page was added. Notice that the positions of the graphic and text frames on this page mirror those of the Right master page.

5. Reverse the positions of the text in the footer so that the page number appears on the left and the address appears on the right:

   a. On the Left master page, click the footer in front of the word "Page."

   > 1234 South Main Street, Columbia, SC 29510》   》   Page #

   b. Press **Backspace** or **Delete** two times to delete the two tabs.

   > 1234 South Main Street, Columbia, SC 29510Page #§

   c. Select the word "Page" and the page number variable (#), but not the end of flow symbol (§).

   > 1234 South Main Street, Columbia, SC 29510Page #§

   d. From the Edit menu, choose **Cut**.

   e. At the beginning of the footer text frame, click in front of the address.

   > 1234 South Main Street, Columbia, SC 29510§

   f. From the Edit menu, choose **Paste**.

   The page number is pasted in front of the address.

   > Page #1234 South Main Street, Columbia, SC 29510§

   g. Press **Tab** twice.

   The address moves to the right.

   > Page #》   》   1234 South Main Street, Columbia, SC 29510

6. From the View menu, choose **Body Pages**.

   The body page you last viewed appears.

7. Page through the document to notice the layout alternating from page to page.

Custom Master Pages

The Right and Left master pages are applied automatically to the corresponding body pages. You can create custom master pages for the first page, a landscape page, or a page that contains only graphics. Custom master pages are not automatically applied to body pages— you have to apply them manually.

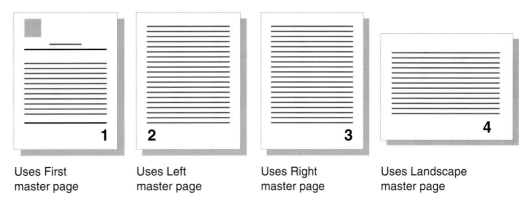

Uses First
master page

Uses Left
master page

Uses Right
master page

Uses Landscape
master page

Exercise 5

Project

Creating and applying custom master pages

In this exercise, you'll create a custom master page named First. This master page will be based on the Right master page, and then be modified. You will then apply the custom master page to the first body page.

1. From the View menu, choose **Master Pages**.

   The master pages appear.

2. From the Special menu, choose **Add Master Page**.

   The Add Master Page dialog box appears.

3. In the name text box, type: First

4. Make sure **Copy from Master Page** is turned on, and from the Copy from Master Page pop-up menu, choose **Right**.

5. Click **Add**.

The First master page is created.

| First (3 of 3) * | 100% | z | Z | ⬆ | ⬇ |

6. Resize the template text frame so that the top of it is at the 3-inch mark on the left ruler.

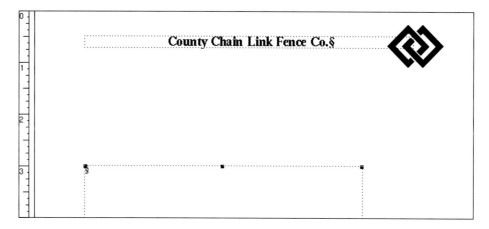

7. Move the header text frame so that the top of it is 2.5 inches from the top of the page:

   a. **Control-click** (on the Macintosh, **Option-click**) the header text frame to select it as an object.

   b. From the Graphics menu, choose **Object Properties**.

   c. In the Customize Text Frame dialog box, change the Offset From Top setting to **2.5"**.

   d. Click **Set**.

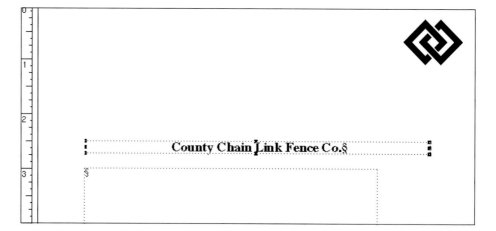

8. Scale the graphic by **200%**, align it and the page's **L/R Centers**, and position it with an Offset From Top of **.5"**:

a. Select the graphic.

b. From the Graphics menu, choose **Scale**.

    The Scale dialog box appears.

c. Change the Factor setting to **200%**.

d. Click **Scale**.

    The graphic is twice its previous size.

e. With the graphic still selected, from the Graphics menu, choose **Align**.

f. In the Align dialog box, in the Top/Bottom area, make sure **As Is** is turned on, and in the Left/Right area, turn on **L/R Centers**.

g. Click **Align**.

    Since no other object was selected, the graphic aligns with the L/R Center of the page.

h. With the graphic still selected, from the Graphics menu, choose **Object Properties**.

i. In the Object Properties dialog box, change the Offset From Top setting to **.5"**.

j. Click **Set**.

9. Click an empty area of the page to deselect the graphic.

    Next, you'll apply the First master page to the first body page.

10. From the View menu, choose **Body Pages**.

    The body page you last viewed appears.

11. If you are not already there, go to **page 1**.

12. From the Format menu, choose **Page Layout>Master Page Usage**.

    The Master Page Usage dialog box appears.

13. In the Use Master Page area, turn on **Custom** and choose **First** from the Custom pop-up menu.

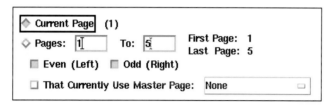

14. In the Apply To area, make sure **Current Page (1)** is turned on.

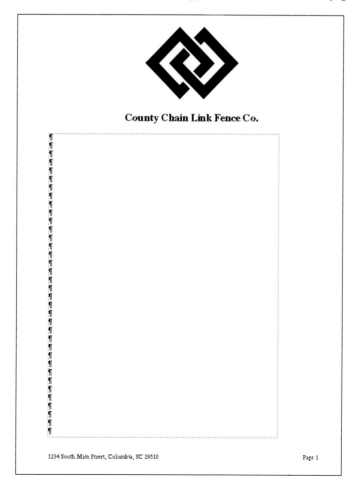

Note: The (1) is the body page number you are on. If you were on body page 3, you would see Current Page (3).

15. Click **Apply**.

The First master page is applied to the first body page.

16. Zoom to 25%.

Notice the layout of your pages.

17. Zoom back to 100%.

Exercise 6 Adjusting master pages

In this exercise, you'll adjust each of the three master pages (Left, Right, and First) by adding a line between the footer and the template text frame.

1. From the View menu, choose **Master Pages**.

2. Go to the **Left** master page.

3. Draw a 3-point line, and position it between the footer and the template text frame:

   a. In the Tools palette, click the **Line tool**.

   b. Draw a horizontal line of any length, anywhere on the page.

   c. With the line still selected, from the Graphics menu, choose **Object Properties**.
   The Object Properties dialog box appears.

   d. Change the Width setting to **6.5"**.

   e. Change the Height setting to **0"**.

   f. Change the Offset From Top setting to **10.25"**.

   g. Change the Offset From Left setting to **1"**.

h. Change the Line Width setting to **3 pt**.

i. Click **Set**.

The line appears above the footer text frame.

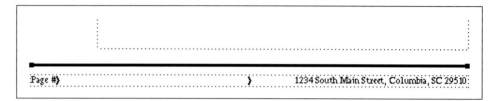

4. Copy the line you just drew to the Right and First master pages:

a. With the line still selected, from the Edit menu, choose **Copy**.

b. Click the **Next Page** button to go to the Right master page.

c. From the Edit menu, choose **Paste**.

The line is pasted on the Right master page in the same position it was on the Left master page.

d. Click the **Next Page** button to go to the First master page.

e. From the Edit menu, choose **Paste**.

The line is pasted above the footer.

5. From the View menu, choose **Body Pages**.

The body page you last viewed appears.

6. Page through the document to see the horizontal line above the footer on all pages.

7. Save the file, and keep the document open if you intend to complete the optional exercise in this module. Otherwise, close all documents that are open at this time.

Optional Exercise

The following exercise enables you to enhance your FrameMaker skills and to explore additional FrameMaker features. Some steps are intentionally brief so that they require more independent thought on your part.

Exercise 7

Optional

Importing page layouts into another document

In this optional exercise, you'll import into another file the three-master-page layout created in this module.

1. From the FrameMaker list of sample documents, open the **Letter** sample.

2. Use the Save As dialog box to save the document in the `Class` directory or folder with the filename `pglay`.

3. From the File menu, choose **Import>Formats**.

4. From the Import from Document pop-up menu, choose **letterhd**.

5. Turn off all import options *except* **Page Layouts**.

6. Click **Import**.

   The letter changes to display the First master page from the `letterhd` document.

7. From the View menu, choose **Master Pages**.

8. Page through the master pages.

   Notice that the original First, Left and Right master pages have been replaced by the imported page layouts from the `letterhd` document.

9. Save the file, and close the document. Also close all other documents that are open at this time.

Review   Test your understanding of the concepts and procedures covered in this module by answering the following review questions. You may check your answers with those listed after the questions.

Question 1:   How can you tell which text frames on a master page are background text.

Question 2:   If you make a change on a master page, what do you need to do to apply that change to corresponding body pages?

Question 3:   How do you add a new master page?

Question 4:   How do you make a document double sided? What happens to the master pages when you do?

Question 5:   How do you apply a custom master page to a particular body page in the document?

Answer 1:   On a master page, put the insertion point in the text frame and look at the tag area of the status bar. If there is no flow tag, then it is a background text frame. In addition, on body pages, the borders of background text frames don't display.

Answer 2:   Nothing. Changes on the master page are applied automatically to corresponding body pages.

Answer 3:   Go to the master pages, and from the Special menu, choose Add Master Page. To start with a layout from an existing master page, make a selection from the Copy from Master Page pop-up menu.

Answer 4:   To make a document double sided, from the Format menu, choose Page Layout>Page Size and turn on Double-Sided. When you do this, a new Left master page, which is a mirror image of the Right master page, is added to the document.

Answer 5:   Go to the body page to which you want to apply the master page, and from the Format menu, choose Pages>Master Page Usage. In the dialog box, choose the name of the custom master page you want to apply from the Custom Master Page pop-up menu. Click Set.

For more information

For more information about master pages, see:

Chapter 19 of *Using FrameMaker*

Reference Pages

Approximate time to complete: 30 minutes

Introduction

In this module, you'll become familiar with FrameMaker reference pages. Reference pages are great places to store graphics that you designate to appear automatically with specified paragraph formats.

Module Objectives

In this module, you'll learn how to

- Identify Frame Above/Below paragraph properties

- Add a graphic to a reference page

- Include a reference frame as part of a paragraph format

- Import reference page formats to another document

FrameMaker Model

Reference *pages* commonly contain boilerplate graphics or graphics that can be associated with a paragraph format via the Frame Above/Below paragraph property.

Using Reference Page Graphics on a Body Page

A reference page can store graphic images you reference from a body page, allowing you to use one set of graphics consistently throughout a document. Typically, you'll use these graphics to put a line above or below a paragraph, such as a heading, or to put a line between body text and footnotes.

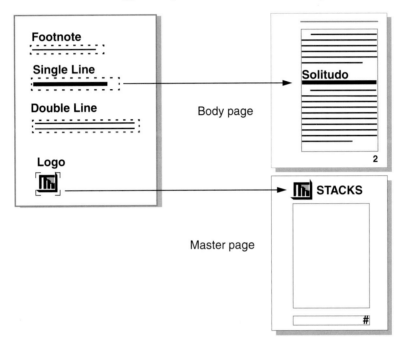

Every new FrameMaker document has a reference page, called Reference, with some reference frames already created. Some templates have additional reference pages. You can add your own graphics to the existing Reference page or add more reference pages to hold graphics.

Exercise 1

Guided Tour

Applying a paragraph format that uses reference frames

In this exercise, you'll become familiar with a paragraph format that includes reference page graphics.

1. From the FrameMaker list of sample documents, open the book chapter **resource.doc**:

    a. Display the FrameMaker list of sample documents.

Macintosh	From the 🗩 menu, choose **Samples & Clip Art**.
Windows	From the Help menu, choose **Samples & Clip Art**.
UNIX	From a document Help menu, choose **Samples & Clip Art**. (If there are no open documents, click **NEW**, then **Portrait**, first.)

    b. In the FrameMaker samples window, click **Book**.

    c. Double-click **resource.doc**.

2. Use the Save As dialog box to save the document in the `Class` directory or folder with the new filename `refpgs`.

3. From the View menu, turn on **Borders**.

4. Put the insertion point in the second paragraph under section 1.1, which begins "Amazing as it may seem. . ."

   Notice that the status bar indicates that this is a Body paragraph.

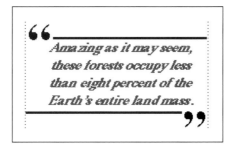

5. Apply the **Pullquote** paragraph format from the Paragraph Catalog.

   The Pullquote paragraph format makes large quotation marks and thick lines appear above and below the paragraph. The lines and quotation marks are stored on a reference page.

Exercise 2

Guided Tour

Identifying art referenced by Above/Below paragraph properties

In this exercise, you'll see how the Advanced properties of the Pullquote paragraph format are used to refer to art on a reference page. Then you'll view the reference page objects that are used in the Pullquote paragraph format.

1. Make sure the insertion point still appears in the Pullquote paragraph.

2. From the Format menu, choose **Paragraphs>Designer**.

3. In the Paragraph Designer, from the Properties pop-up menu, choose **Advanced**.

The Paragraph Designer displays the Advanced properties for the current Pullquote paragraph.

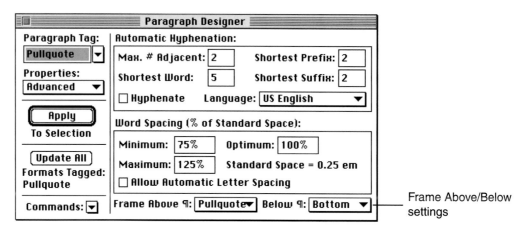

Frame Above/Below settings

Notice the Frame Above and Below settings. Two pieces of art are referenced: One is named Pullquote, the other is named Bottom.

4. From the View menu, choose **Reference Pages**.

The reference pages appear.

Notice the name of the reference page in the middle of the status bar. This is the first and only reference page in this document.

Reference (1 of 1)	100%

The graphics for the Pullquote paragraph appear on the reference page.

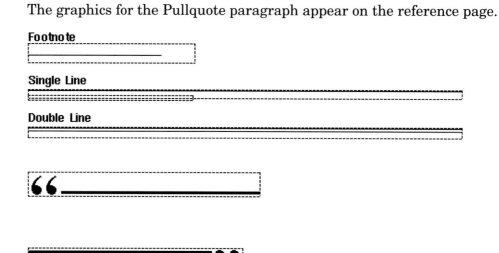

> **Elaboration:** The three graphics at the top of the reference page include a name to identify the art; however, no names appear above the Pullquote and Bottom art. Placing a name above art on a reference page is optional.

5. Click to select the reference frame around the line with the left quotation marks.

   The name of the reference frame appears in the status bar.

   Frame: Pullquote *   100%

6. From the Graphics menu, choose **Object Properties**.

   The Object Properties dialog box appears, identifying the object type as a Graphic Frame with the name Pullquote.

   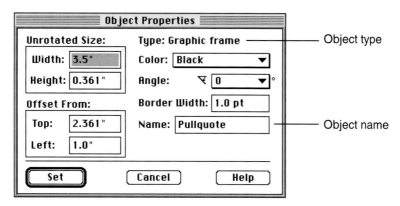

7. Click **Cancel**.

Exercise 3

Guided Tour

Adding a graphic on a reference page

In this exercise, you'll draw your own reference frame and put a thick line inside it.

1. Draw a frame of any size with the name `Section Art`:

   a. In the Tools palette, click the **Graphic Frame tool**.

   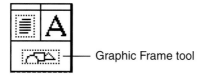
   — Graphic Frame tool

   b. Draw a frame of any size toward the bottom of the page.

      When you release the mouse, you will not see the reference frame, but the Frame Name dialog box appears.

   c. In the Name text box, type: `Section Art`

   d. Click **Set**.

Now the reference frame you drew appears.

Elaboration: The name you type in the Frame Name dialog box is the same name that appears in the Frame Above/Frame Below pop-up menus in the Advanced properties of the Paragraph Designer.

2. Resize the frame to a width of 3.25 inches and height of .3 inches, and reposition the frame so it appears offset 4.5 inches from the top and 1.0 inches from the left of the page:

   a. With the frame still selected, from the Graphics menu, choose **Object Properties**.

   b. Change the Width setting to **3.25"**.

   c. Change the Height setting to **.3"**.

   d. Change the Offset From Top setting to **4.5"**.

   e. Change the Offset From Left setting to **1.0"**.

   f. Click **Set**.

3. Draw a line five points thick with a length of 3.25 inches aligned to the left of the frame:

   a. In the Tools palette, click the **Line tool**.

   b. Draw a horizontal line of any length in the reference frame you already drew.

   c. With the line still selected, from the Graphics menu, choose **Object Properties**.

   d. Change the Width setting to **3.25"**.

   e. Change the Height setting to **0"**.

Note: If you drew a perfectly horizontal line, the height is already 0 inches. Changing this value to 0 inches will straighten a crooked line.

f. Change the Offset From Top setting to **.15"**.

g. Change the Offset From Left setting to **0"**.

This will align the line to the left edge of the reference frame.

h. If you're using a color monitor, from the Color pop-up menu, choose **Blue**.

i. Change the Line Width setting to **5 pt**.

j. Click **Set**.

The five-point thick line aligns to the left of the reference frame.

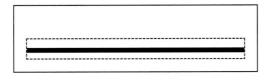

4. Create a text line above the frame that contains the name of the reference frame:

a. Put the insertion point in any existing label on the page.

In the next few steps, when you type the name of the reference frame you drew, the text will have the same font properties as the text frame the insertion point was in just prior to typing.

b. In the Tools palette, click the **Text Line tool** (**A**).

c. Click above the frame you drew to get an insertion point.

d. Type: Section Art

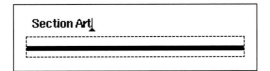

Exercise 4

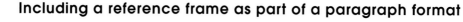

Including a reference frame as part of a paragraph format

In this exercise, you'll include the newly created graphic in a paragraph format and then view the results in the document.

1. From the View menu, choose **Body Pages**.

2. Click the Section paragraph, "1.1 Tropical Rain Forests."

3. From the Format menu, choose **Paragraphs>Designer**.

4. In the Paragraph Designer, in the Advanced properties, from the Frame Above pop-up menu, choose **Section Art**.

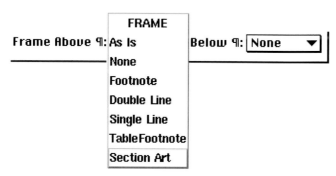

5. Click **Update All**.

   The reference frame containing the five-point thick line appears above the Section paragraph.

   > **1.1   Tropical Rain Forests**
   >
   > At least a quarter of all pharmaceutical products are derived from tropical rain forests. An even more impressive statistic, when you consider that less than one percent of all Amazon plants have been intensively examined for their medicinal properties.

6. Page through the document, and notice that the reference frame appears above all the Section paragraphs.

7. Save the file, and keep the document open if you intend to complete the optional exercise in this module. Otherwise, close all documents that are currently open.

Optional Exercise

The following exercise enables you to enhance your FrameMaker skills and to explore additional FrameMaker features. Some steps are intentionally brief so that they require more independent thought on your part.

Exercise 5

Optional

Importing reference page formats into another document

In this optional exercise, you'll import the Pullquote paragraph format into another document in two phases. You'll do it this way to see the importance of importing both paragraph formats and reference pages when your paragraph formats use reference frames.

1. Open the **response.doc** sample file:

   a. Display the FrameMaker list of sample documents.

Macintosh	From the [?] menu, choose **Samples & Clip Art**.
Windows	From the Help menu, choose **Samples & Clip Art**.
UNIX	From a document Help menu, choose **Samples & Clip Art**. (If there are no open documents, click **NEW**, then **Portrait**, first.)

   b. Click **Book**.

   c. Double-click **response.doc**.

2. Use the Save As dialog box to save the document in the `Class` directory or folder with the new filename `pullqt`.

3. From the File menu, choose **Import>Formats**.

4. From the Import From Document pop-up menu, choose **refpgs**.

5. Turn off all import options *except* **Paragraph Formats**.

6. Click **Import**.

   If you have a color monitor, notice that the Section paragraph on this page, "3.1 Water Pollution," changed to red, but the 5-point thick line did not appear above the heading.

7. To make the line appear above the Section paragraph, reimport formats from `refpgs`, as in the steps above, and include the **Reference Pages** when importing.

8. Save the file, and close the document. Also close all other documents that are currently open.

> **Note:** When you import reference pages into a document, any page that has the same name as the imported page is replaced by the imported page. Any page that does not have the same name is added to the existing references pages.

Review   Test your understanding of the concepts and procedures covered in this module by answering the following review questions. You can check your answers with those listed after the questions.

Question 1: How do you display a reference page?

Question 2: How do you prepare a graphic element for use in paragraph formatting?

Question 3: How do you add a graphic element to a paragraph format?

Question 4: When importing paragraph formats into a document, why is it important to import *both* paragraph formats and reference pages?

Answer 1: From the View menu, choose Reference Pages.

Answer 2: Go to the document's reference page. Use the Graphic Frame tool to draw a frame on the page, and name the frame. Create your graphic inside the frame. If desired, you can also use the Text Line tool to label the frame.

Answer 3: In the Paragraph Designer, display the Advanced properties. From the Frame Above/Below pop-up menus, choose the name of a graphic element on the reference page, and update all.

Answer 4: If you import only paragraph formats, any graphic elements used in the paragraph formats will not appear, because the graphics are not on the reference pages.

For more information

For more information about using Reference Pages, see:

■ Chapter 19 of *Using FrameMaker*

For more information about reference frames, see:

■ Chapter 11 of *Using FrameMaker*

. . . .

PART IV

Tables, Variables, and

Conditional Text

Working with Tables

Approximate time to complete: 1 hour

Introduction

In this module, you'll become familiar with inserting and modifying tables. FrameMaker supplies you with two default table formats, which can be used as they are or modified to accommodate the text and graphics placed into the table.

Module Objectives

In this module, you'll learn how to

- Insert a table in a document
- Add and delete text in the cells
- Select cells, rows, columns, and the entire table
- Add, delete, copy, and paste rows and columns
- Resize table columns
- Use the Table Designer to change the ruling and shading pattern

FrameMaker Model

Tables are text-anchored *objects.* They are organized matrices with each cell containing one or more paragraphs for text or text-anchored objects, or both.

Using Tables

A table organizes information, placing it into cells that are arranged in rows and columns.

Table 1: Title

A FrameMaker table is anchored to text in a text frame and moves with the text as you edit the document.

A FrameMaker table has one or more body rows and columns, and an optional title, heading rows, and footing rows. The smallest table contains just one body cell (the intersection of one row and one column); the largest is limited only by the computer's memory.

	Monday	Tuesday	Wednesday	Thursday	Friday
Team A: Days	111	121	131	122	132
Team B: Days	132	123	111	121	112
Team C: Nights	111	121	123	122	132

Technical Support Calls — Wrong numbers and misdirected calls are not included in the count.

A table title can appear above or below the table, and the title can include an autonumber as part of its paragraph format.

Individual cells can contain one or more paragraphs, using the same or different paragraph formats. Text in table cells uses paragraph and character formats in the same way as text outside the table.

A *table format* is like a paragraph or character format. The table format specifies properties such as the table's alignment in the text column (left, center, right), space above and below the entire table, rulings separating rows and columns, shading on rows or columns, and so on.

FrameMaker templates come with two default table formats: Format A and Format B. You can use the default formats as they are, modify them, or create formats of your own. Table formats are covered in detail in a later module.

In the exercises in this module, you'll create a phone log similar to the one in the following example.

Table 1: Technical Support Calls

	Monday	Tuesday	Wednesday	Thursday	Friday	Saturday
Team A: Days	111	121	131	122	132	122
Team B: Days	132	123	111	121	112	121
Team C: Nights	111	121	123	122	132	122
Total	354	365	365	365	376	365

Exercise 1

Guided Tour

Inserting a table into a document

In this exercise, you'll insert a standard table into a document, use some default settings, and change a setting.

1. Create a new **Landscape** document:

   a. Open the New dialog box.

Macintosh	From the File menu, choose **New**.
Windows	From the File menu, choose **New**.
UNIX	In the main FrameMaker window, click **NEW**.

   b. Click **Landscape**.

2. Use the Save As dialog box to save the document in the `Class` directory or folder with the new filename `log`.

3. From the Table menu, choose **Insert Table**.

   The Insert Table dialog box appears with Format A selected. The default number of columns, body rows, heading rows, and footing rows appear in the four text boxes.

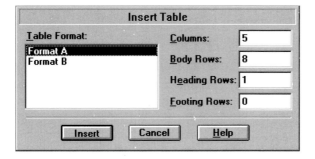

4. Change the settings to **6 Columns** and **4 Body Rows**.

Columns:	6
Body Rows:	4
Heading Rows:	1
Footing Rows:	0

The table will have 6 columns, 4 body rows, 1 heading row, and no footing row. Whenever you add a table, you can change these numbers.

5. Click **Insert**.

The table appears.

Table 1: §

§	§	§	§	§	§
§	§	§	§	§	§
§	§	§	§	§	§
§	§	§	§	§	§
§	§	§	§	§	§

A table anchor symbol (⊥) appears in the empty Body paragraph at the top of the page at the location of the insertion point. The table anchor symbol is difficult to see because it is next to the left edge of the text frame.

Table anchor ——— symbol

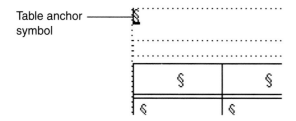

Elaboration: The anchor symbol appears because the table is anchored to the text where the insertion point is located when the table is inserted into the document.

The insertion point is in the table title text frame linked to the top of the table.

§	§	§	§	§	§
§	§	§	§	§	§
§	§	§	§	§	§
§	§	§	§	§	§

Table 1: § — Insertion point

Notice that the default paragraph format for the table title is TableTitle.

6. With the insertion point still in the table title, type: Technical Support Calls

§	§	§	§	§	§
§	§	§	§	§	§
§	§	§	§	§	§
§	§	§	§	§	§
§	§	§	§	§	§

Table 1: Technical Support Calls§

Exercise 2   Adding and deleting text in a table

Guided Tour

As you type text in a cell, FrameMaker resizes the cell (and the row) automatically to fit the text.

In this exercise, you'll add text to the table.

1. Put the insertion point in the second cell of the heading row.

Notice that the default paragraph format for the cell is CellHeading.

2. Type: Monday

§	Monday§	§	§	§	§

3. Press the **Tab** key.

   The insertion point appears in the third cell in the heading row.

   > **Elaboration:** When you press the Tab key, FrameMaker moves you to the next cell and selects the contents of that cell. (If you want to type a tab character in the table cell, press Esc Tab.)

4. Type: `Tuesday`

5. In the remaining heading cells, continue pressing **Tab** and typing the names of the days of the week:

   `Wednesday    Thursday    Friday`

§	Monday§	Tuesday§	Wednesday§	Thursday§	Friday§

6. Press **Tab** to highlight the first cell in the first body row.

§	Monday§	Tuesday§	Wednesday!	Thursday§	Friday§
§	§	§	§	§	§

7. Type: `Team A: Days`

   The cell expands vertically to fit the text.

§	Monday§	Tuesday§	Wednesday§	Thursday§	Friday§
Team A: Days§	§	§	§	§	§

8. Type the remaining text as in the following example. (The exact numbers are not important.)

Table 1: Technical Support Calls§					
§	Monday§	Tuesday§	Wednesday§	Thursday§	Friday§
Team A: Days§	111§	121§	131§	122§	132§
Team B: Days§	132§	123§	111§	121§	112§
Team C: Nights§	111§	121§	123§	122§	132§
Team D: Nights§	117§	125§	113§	112§	121§

Selecting and deselecting in a table

You select text (and graphics) in table cells the same way you do elsewhere in the document. You can then copy, cut, delete, and paste text and graphics in the table.

When you select one or more table cells, the entire cell area is highlighted. Resize handles appear on the right side of the selection, and the type of cell (heading, body, or footing) appears in the Tag area of the status bar.

To	Do this
Select a single cell	Control-click (on the Macintosh, Option-click) the cell, or drag across the cell's border and back into the cell.
Select multiple cells	Drag across all the cells you want to select.
Extend the selection	With a cell selected, Shift-click the last cell you want in the selection.
Select a row	Hold down Control (on the Macintosh, hold down Option), point on a column (vertical) border in the row, and double-click.
Select a column	Hold down Control (on the Macintosh, hold down Option), point on a row (horizontal) border in the column, and double-click.
Select the entire table	Select any cell (rather than the text in a cell) and then choose Select All of Table from the Edit menu, or Control-triple-click (on the Macintosh, Option-triple-click) a cell.

Exercise 3

Guided Tour

Selecting and deselecting text, cells, rows, and columns

In this exercise, you'll become familiar with selecting and deselecting in a table.

1. In the first cell of the first body row, **double-click** to select the word "Team."

Team A: Days§	111§	121§	131§	122§	132§

2. **Triple-click** to select the entire paragraph in the same cell.

Team A: Days§	111§	121§	131§	122§	132§

3. **Control-click** (on the Macintosh, **Option-click**) anywhere in the same cell to select the entire cell as an object.

Team A: Days§	111§	121§	131§	122§	132§

A resize handle appears on the right side of the cell. Resizing is covered in detail later in this module.

4. Drag across the first body row (from left to right, or right to left) to select the entire row.

§	Monday§	Tuesday§	Wednesday§	Thursday§	Friday§
Team A: Days§	111§	121§	131§	122§	132§
Team B: Days§	132§	123§	111§	121§	112§
Team C: Nights§	111§	121§	123§	122§	132§
Team D: Nights§	117§	125§	113§	112§	121§

Note: You also can select a row by Control-double-clicking (on the Macintosh, Option-double-clicking) any of the vertical lines within the row.

5. Drag through the first column (from top to bottom or from bottom to top) to select the entire column.

§	Monday§	Tuesday§	Wednesday§	Thursday§	Friday§
Team A: Days§	111§	121§	131§	122§	132§
Team B: Days§	132§	123§	111§	121§	112§
Team C: Nights§	111§	121§	123§	122§	132§
Team D: Nights§	117§	125§	113§	112§	121§

Note: You also can select a column by Control-double-clicking (on the Macintosh, Option-double-clicking) any of the horizontal lines within the column.

6. Hold down the **Control** key (on the Macintosh, the **Option** key) and **triple-click** anywhere in the table to select the entire table, including the table title.

Make sure not to move the pointer while you are clicking.

The entire table is selected.

Table 1: Technical Support Calls§					
§	Monday§	Tuesday§	Wednesday§	Thursday§	Friday§
Team A: Days§	111§	121§	131§	122§	132§
Team B: Days§	132§	123§	111§	121§	112§
Team C: Nights§	111§	121§	123§	122§	132§
Team D: Nights§	117§	125§	113§	112§	121§

Note: You also can select the entire table by selecting one cell and, from the Edit menu, choosing Select All of Table. (You'll see Select All in Flow if a cell is not selected.)

7. **Control-click** (on the Macintosh, **Option-click**) the "Team A: Days" cell.

Team A: Days§	111§	121§	131§	122§	132§

A resize handle appears on the right side of the cell. This indicates that the entire cell, not just the text in the cell, is selected.

8. **Shift-click** the "Team D: Nights" cell.

Table 1: Technical Support Calls§					
§	Monday§	Tuesday§	Wednesday§	Thursday§	Friday§
Team A: Days§	111§	121§	131§	122§	132§
Team B: Days§	132§	123§	111§	121§	112§
Team C: Nights§	111§	121§	123§	122§	132§
Team D: Nights§	117§	125§	113§	112§	121§

The selection is extended to the "Team D: Nights" cell.

Adjusting Tables

You can make adjustments to a table to reorganize it or to help present your information more clearly. Such adjustments include

- Resizing columns
- Adding and deleting rows and columns
- Copying and pasting columns
- Changing the text alignment in a cell
- Applying table formats
- Changing the ruling and shading pattern

Exercise 4

Guided Tour

Manually resizing columns

You can manually resize a column horizontally—make it narrower or wider—by selecting it and dragging a resize handle on the right border of selected cells. You can do this by selecting a single cell in the column, the entire column, or several columns.

In this exercise, you'll manually resize the far-left column so that the text does not wrap.

1. Drag to select the far-left column.

§	Monday§	Tuesday§	Wednesday§	Thursday§	Friday§
Team A: Days§	111§	121§	131§	122§	132§
Team B: Days§	132§	123§	111§	121§	112§
Team C: Nights§	111§	121§	123§	122§	132§
Team D: Nights§	117§	125§	113§	112§	121§

2. Drag any handle approximately ³/₈ inch to the right, making the column wider so all the text in each cell fits on a single line.

Table 1: Technical Support Calls§					
§	Monday§	Tuesday§	Wednesday§	Thursday§	Friday§
Team A: Days§	111§	121§	131§	122§	132§
Team B: Days§	132§	123§	111§	121§	112§
Team C: Nights§	111§	121§	123§	122§	132§
Team D: Nights§	117§	125§	113§	112§	121§

Exercise 5

Adding and deleting rows and columns

When you select entire rows or columns and try to delete or cut them, FrameMaker asks you to specify whether you want to remove just the contents of the cells or the cells themselves. (Cells can be removed from the table only if you select the entire row or column.)

In this exercise, you'll add and delete rows and columns in the table.

1. Put the insertion point in any cell in the last row of the table.

Table 1: Technical Support Calls§					
§	Monday§	Tuesday§	Wednesday§	Thursday§	Friday§
Team A: Days§	111§	121§	131§	122§	132§
Team B: Days§	132§	123§	111§	121§	112§
Team C: Nights§	111§	121§	123§	122§	132§
Team D: Nights§	117§	125§	113§	112§	121§

2. From the Table menu, choose **Add Rows or Columns**.

    The Add Rows or Columns dialog box appears.

3. Change the settings to match the following.

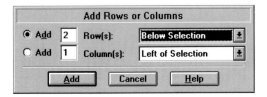

4. Click **Add**.

    Two rows are added below the last row of your table, and the insertion point is positioned in the first cell of the first added row.

§	Monday§	Tuesday§	Wednesday§	Thursday§	Friday§
Team A: Days§	111§	121§	131§	122§	132§
Team B: Days§	132§	123§	111§	121§	112§
Team C: Nights§	111§	121§	123§	122§	132§
Team D: Nights§	117§	125§	113§	112§	121§
§	§	§	§	§	§
§	§	§	§	§	§

5. Put the insertion point anywhere in the last row, and press **Control-Return**.

An additional row is added to your table.

§	Monday§	Tuesday§	Wednesday§	Thursday§	Friday§
Team A: Days§	111§	121§	131§	122§	132§
Team B: Days§	132§	123§	111§	121§	112§
Team C: Nights§	111§	121§	123§	122§	132§
Team D: Nights§	117§	125§	113§	112§	121§
§	§	§	§	§	§
§	§	§	§	§	§
§	§	§	§	§	§

Elaboration: Control-Return is a keyboard shortcut for adding rows to a table.

6. Add one column on the right side of the table:

   a. Put the insertion point anywhere in the far-right column.

§	Monday§	Tuesday§	Wednesday§	Thursday§	Friday§
Team A: Days§	111§	121§	131§	122§	132§
Team B: Days§	132§	123§	111§	121§	112§
Team C: Nights§	111§	121§	123§	122§	132§
Team D: Nights§	117§	125§	113§	112§	121§
§	§	§	§	§	§
§	§	§	§	§	§
§	§	§	§	§	§

   b. From the Table menu, choose **Add Rows or Columns**.

   c. In the Add Rows or Columns dialog box, change the settings to add one column to the **Right of Selection**.

   d. Click **Add**.

   The table looks like the following example.

§	Monday§	Tuesday§	Wednesday§	Thursday§	Friday§	§
Team A: Days§	111§	121§	131§	122§	132§	§
Team B: Days§	132§	123§	111§	121§	112§	§
Team C: Nights§	111§	121§	123§	122§	132§	§
Team D: Nights§	117§	125§	113§	112§	121§	§
§	§	§	§	§	§	§
§	§	§	§	§	§	§
§	§	§	§	§	§	§

7. Delete the last three rows to remove them from the table:

   a. Drag to select the last three rows.

§	Monday§	Tuesday§	Wednesday§	Thursday§	Friday§	§
Team A: Days§	111§	121§	131§	122§	132§	§
Team B: Days§	132§	123§	111§	121§	112§	§
Team C: Nights§	111§	121§	123§	122§	132§	§
Team D: Nights§	117§	125§	113§	112§	121§	§
§	§	§	§	§	§	§
§	§	§	§	§	§	§
§	§	§	§	§	§	§

   b. Press **Delete**.

   c. In the Clear Table Cells dialog box, turn on **Remove Cells from Table**.

   d. Click **Clear**.

   The rows are deleted from the table.

§	Monday§	Tuesday§	Wednesday§	Thursday§	Friday§	§
Team A: Days§	111§	121§	131§	122§	132§	§
Team B: Days§	132§	123§	111§	121§	112§	§
Team C: Nights§	111§	121§	123§	122§	132§	§
Team D: Nights§	117§	125§	113§	112§	121§	§

8. Drag to select the entire "Team D" row.

§	Monday§	Tuesday§	Wednesday§	Thursday§	Friday§	§
Team A: Days§	111§	121§	131§	122§	132§	§
Team B: Days§	132§	123§	111§	121§	112§	§
Team C: Nights§	111§	121§	123§	122§	132§	§
Team D: Nights§	117§	125§	113§	112§	121§	§

9. Press **Delete**.

   The Clear Table Cells dialog box appears.

10. Turn on **Leave Cells Empty**.

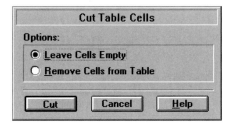

11. Click **Clear.**

The text is deleted from the cells, and the number of rows in the table remains the same.

§	Monday§	Tuesday§	Wednesday§	Thursday§	Friday§	§
Team A: Days§	111§	121§	131§	122§	132§	§
Team B: Days§	132§	123§	111§	121§	112§	§
Team C: Nights§	111§	121§	123§	122§	132§	§
§	§	§	§	§	§	§

Exercise 6

Guided Tour

Copying and pasting columns

In this exercise, you'll copy and paste a column in the table.

1. In the last row of the table, type the text as follows. (The exact numbers are not important.)

Total§	354§	365§	365§	365§	376§	§

2. Drag to select the entire "Thursday" column.

§	Monday§	Tuesday§	Wednesday§	Thursday§	Friday§	§
Team A: Days§	111§	121§	131§	122§	132§	§
Team B: Days§	132§	123§	111§	121§	112§	§
Team C: Nights§	111§	121§	123§	122§	132§	§
Total§	354§	365§	365§	365§	376§	§

3. From the Edit menu, choose **Copy.**

The column and its contents are copied to the Clipboard.

4. Put the insertion point anywhere in the empty rightmost column.

§	Monday§	Tuesday§	Wednesday§	Thursday§	Friday§	§
Team A: Days§	111§	121§	131§	122§	132§	§
Team B: Days§	132§	123§	111§	121§	112§	§
Team C: Nights§	111§	121§	123§	122§	132§	§
Total§	354§	365§	365§	365§	376§	§

5. From the Edit menu, choose **Paste.**

The Paste Columns dialog box appears.

You have the option of pasting the "Thursday" column to the left or the right, or to replace the current column. Because the "Saturday" numbers are identical to the "Thursday" numbers you're pasting, you'll replace the current column.

6. Turn on **Replace Current Columns**.

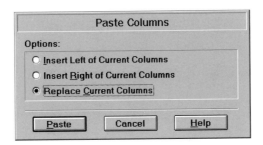

7. Click **Paste**.

The "Thursday" column replaces the empty column.

§	Monday§	Tuesday§	Wednesday§	Thursday§	Friday§	Thursday§
Team A: Days§	111§	121§	131§	122§	132§	122§
Team B: Days§	132§	123§	111§	121§	112§	121§
Team C: Nights§	111§	121§	123§	122§	132§	122§
Total§	354§	365§	365§	365§	376§	365§

8. In the heading cell of the rightmost column, delete "Thursday" and type:
   `Saturday`

§	Monday§	Tuesday§	Wednesday§	Thursday§	Friday§	Saturday§
Team A: Days§	111§	121§	131§	122§	132§	122§
Team B: Days§	132§	123§	111§	121§	112§	121§
Team C: Nights§	111§	121§	123§	122§	132§	122§
Total§	354§	365§	365§	365§	376§	365§

Exercise 7

Project

Changing text alignment in a cell

In this exercise, you'll make all the numbers center aligned in their cells.

1. Drag to select the cells with numbers in them.

§	Monday§	Tuesday§	Wednesday§	Thursday§	Friday§	Saturday§
Team A: Days§	111§	121§	131§	122§	132§	122§
Team B: Days§	132§	123§	111§	121§	112§	121§
Team C: Nights§	111§	121§	123§	122§	132§	122§
Total§	354§	365§	365§	365§	376§	365§

2. From the Alignment pop-up menu in the formatting bar, choose **Center**.

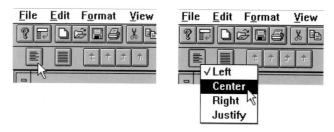

The text in the cells is now centered.

§	Monday§	Tuesday§	Wednesday§	Thursday§	Friday§	Saturday§
Team A: Days§	111§	121§	131§	122§	132§	122§
Team B: Days§	132§	123§	111§	121§	112§	121§
Team C: Nights§	111§	121§	123§	122§	132§	122§
Total§	354§	365§	365§	365§	376§	365§

Exercise 8 Applying table formats

Guided Tour

You can change the appearance or position of a table by applying a table format to it. In this exercise, you'll apply a different table format to your table by using the Table Designer.

1. From the View menu, turn off **Borders** and **Text Symbols**.

2. Put the insertion point in the table.

3. From the Table menu, choose **Table Designer**.

   The Table Designer appears.

4. From the Table Tag pop-up menu in the upper-left corner, choose **Format B**.

Table tag pop-up menu

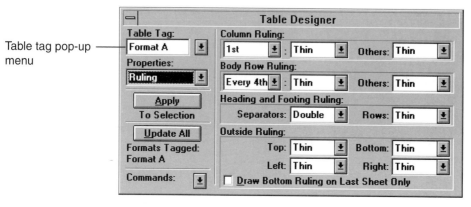

5. Click **Apply**.

The table is now center aligned, and its ruling pattern has changed.

Table 1: Technical Support Calls

	Monday	Tuesday	Wednesday	Thursday	Friday	Saturday
Team A: Days	111	121	131	122	132	122
Team B: Days	132	123	111	121	112	121
Team C: Nights	111	121	123	122	132	122
Total	354	365	365	365	376	365

6. Reapply the Format A table format:

   a. In the Table Designer, from the Table Tag pop-up menu in the upper-left corner, choose **Format A**.

   b. Click **Apply**.

      The table returns to its previous format.

Table 1: Technical Support Calls

	Monday	Tuesday	Wednesday	Thursday	Friday	Saturday
Team A: Days	111	121	131	122	132	122
Team B: Days	132	123	111	121	112	121
Team C: Nights	111	121	123	122	132	122
Total	354	365	365	365	376	365

Note: Unlike paragraph and character formats, which have catalogs separate from the Paragraph Designer and the Character Designer, a catalog of table formats can be found only in the Table Designer.

Exercise 9

Project

Changing the ruling pattern

The ruling pattern of the table is specified in the Ruling properties of the Table Designer. In this exercise, you'll use the Table Designer to change your table's regular ruling pattern so it appears as follows.

Table 1: Technical Support Calls

	Monday	Tuesday	Wednesday	Thursday	Friday	Saturday
Team A: Days	111	121	131	122	132	122
Team B: Days	132	123	111	121	112	121
Team C: Nights	111	121	123	122	132	122
Total	354	365	365	365	376	365

1. Make sure the insertion point appears somewhere in the table.

2. In the Table Designer, from the Properties pop-up menu, choose **Ruling**. The Ruling properties for the table appear in the Table Designer.

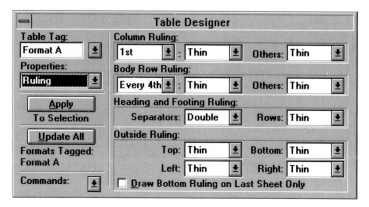

3. Change the Column Ruling settings to match the following.

4. Click **Apply**.

   A thick rule appears to the right of the first column. The ruling is removed from the rest of the columns.

Table 1: Technical Support Calls

	Monday	Tuesday	Wednesday	Thursday	Friday	Saturday
Team A: Days	111	121	131	122	132	122
Team B: Days	132	123	111	121	112	121
Team C: Nights	111	121	123	122	132	122
Total	354	365	365	365	376	365

5. Change the Body Row Ruling settings to match the following.

6. Click **Apply**.

A medium rule appears after the second body row. The other body rows have very thin rules.

Table 1: Technical Support Calls

	Monday	Tuesday	Wednesday	Thursday	Friday	Saturday
Team A: Days	111	121	131	122	132	122
Team B: Days	132	123	111	121	112	121
Team C: Nights	111	121	123	122	132	122
Total	354	365	365	365	376	365

Note: Thin and Very Thin rulings do not appear different on-screen, but they do when you print the table.

7. In the Heading and Footing Ruling area, from the Separators pop-up menu, choose **Thick**.

8. Click **Apply**.

A thick rule appears below the heading row. If this table had a footing row, a thick rule would also appear above the footing row.

Table 1: Technical Support Calls

	Monday	Tuesday	Wednesday	Thursday	Friday	Saturday
Team A: Days	111	121	131	122	132	122
Team B: Days	132	123	111	121	112	121
Team C: Nights	111	121	123	122	132	122
Total	354	365	365	365	376	365

9. Change all the **Outside Ruling** settings to **Thick**.

10. Click **Apply**.

A thick rule appears around the outside of the table.

Table 1: Technical Support Calls

	Monday	Tuesday	Wednesday	Thursday	Friday	Saturday
Team A: Days	111	121	131	122	132	122
Team B: Days	132	123	111	121	112	121
Team C: Nights	111	121	123	122	132	122
Total	354	365	365	365	376	365

Exercise 10   Changing the shading pattern

Project

You can create a shading pattern to highlight specific rows or columns. A table's shading pattern is specified in the Shading properties of the Table Designer. In this exercise, you'll use the Table Designer to change your table's regular shading pattern so it appears as in the following example.

Table 1: Technical Support Calls

	Monday	Tuesday	Wednesday	Thursday	Friday	Saturday
Team A: Days	111	121	131	122	132	122
Team B: Days	132	123	111	121	112	121
Team C: Nights	111	121	123	122	132	122
Total	354	365	365	365	376	365

1. Make sure the insertion point appears somewhere in the table.

2. In the Table Designer, from the Properties pop-up menu, choose **Shading**.

   The Shading properties for the table appear in the Table Designer.

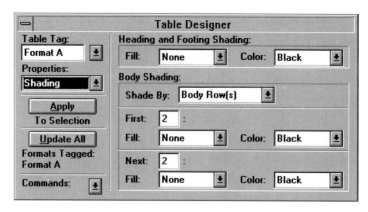

3. In the Body Shading area, from the Shade By pop-up menu, choose **Row(s)**.

4. Change the remaining settings to match the following.

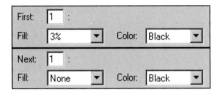

5. Click **Apply**.

   Your table should now appear as follows.

Table 1: Technical Support Calls

	Monday	Tuesday	Wednesday	Thursday	Friday	Saturday
Team A: Days	111	121	131	122	132	122
Team B: Days	132	123	111	121	112	121
Team C: Nights	111	121	123	122	132	122
Total	354	365	365	365	376	365

6. Save the file, and close the document. Also close the Table Designer.

Optional Exercises

The following exercises enable you to enhance your FrameMaker skills and to explore additional FrameMaker features. Some steps are intentionally brief so that they require more independent thought on your part.

Exercise 11

Optional

Anchoring tables to straddle paragraphs

You can make tables straddle columns in two ways: by making the table wider than a column, or by making the paragraph to which the table is anchored straddle columns. In this optional exercise, you'll use both methods of creating table straddles.

1. From the FrameMaker list of sample documents, open the book chapter **resource.doc.**

2. Use the Save As dialog box to save the document in the `Class` directory or folder with the new filename `tblstrdl`.

3. Go to **page 6**.

4. From the View menu, turn on **Borders**.

5. At the top of the right column, put the insertion point at the end of the first full paragraph, after the words "natural systems."

Further study has been indicated as a probable follow-up to this ongoing problem.

Projections in Table 2 were developed directly in response to pressures to quantify impacts on natural systems.

Lack of specific information and hesitancy to project or extrapolate data is easily interpreted as

6. Insert a table with five columns and three body rows, and with one heading row and no footing row using Format B:

   a. From the Table menu, choose **Insert Table**.

      The Insert Table dialog box appears.

   b. In the Table Format scroll list, click **Format B**.

   c. Make sure Columns is set to **5**.

   d. Change Body Rows to **3**.

   e. Click **Insert**.

Since the table is too wide to fit in one column, it straddles both columns.

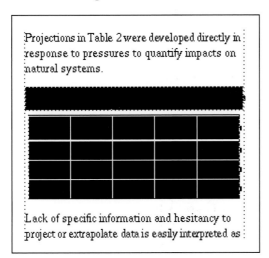

based on social necessity. The wetlands were classified into types, mapped and areal extents determined. Total vegetated wetlands in Wallop

natural systems.

Lack of specific information and hesitancy to project or extrapolate data is easily interpreted as

system cannot be conveyed easily in the context of a Impact Assessment Study. This last question

7. **Control-triple-click** (on the Macintosh, **Option-triple-click**) to select the entire table, and drag a resize handle to reduce the width of the table until it is narrow enough to fit in one column.

Projections in Table 2 were developed directly in response to pressures to quantify impacts on natural systems.

Lack of specific information and hesitancy to project or extrapolate data is easily interpreted as

8. Put the insertion point anywhere in the paragraph just above the table.

Projections in Table 2 were developed directly in response to quantify impacts on natural systems.

9. Straddle the paragraph across all columns:

   a. From the Format menu, choose **Paragraphs>Designer**.

   b. In the Paragraph Designer, from the Properties pop-up menu, choose **Pagination**.

   c. In the Format area, turn on **Across All Columns**.

   d. Click **Apply**.

   Since the paragraph containing the table anchor straddles both columns, the table also straddles the columns.

   behavior, otherwise the judge may set standards based on social necessity. The wetlands were

   follow-up to this ongoing problem.

   Projections in Table 2 were developed directly in response to pressures to quantify impacts on natural systems.

   Lack of specific information and hesitancy to project or extrapolate data is easily interpreted as

   system cannot be conveyed easily in the context of a Impact Assessment Study. This last question

10. Save the file, and close the document. Also close any other windows that are currently open.

Exercise 12 Converting text to a table

In this optional exercise, you'll take text separated by tab characters and convert it to a table.

1. Create a new **Portrait** document.

2. Use the Save As dialog box to save the document in the `Class` directory or folder with the new filename `convert`.

3. Set the tabs of the Body paragraph format to repeat every .75 inches:

   a. In the Paragraph Designer, display the Basic properties.

   b. In the Tab Stops area, click **Edit**.

   c. Change the New Position setting to **.75"**.

   d. Turn on **Repeat Every**, and in the Repeat Every text box, type: `.75"`.

   e. Click **Continue**.

     Tab stops appear every 0.75 inch in the ruler

   f. Click **Update All**.

4. Type a few lines of text, pressing **Tab** between words. For example:

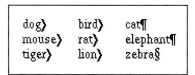

5. Select the text.

6. From the Table menu, choose **Convert to Table**.

   The Convert to Table dialog box appears.

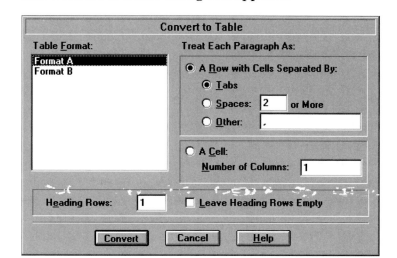

7. In the Treat Each Paragraph As area, make sure **Tabs** is turned on.

   When you convert using this setting, each tab character marks the end of a table cell.

8. Make sure **Format A** is selected, and in the Heading Rows area, turn on **Leave Heading Rows Empty**.

9. Click **Convert**.

   The text appears in a table.

Table 1: §		
§	§	§
dog§	bird§	cat§
mouse§	rat§	elephant§
tiger§	lion§	zebra§

10. Save the file, and close the document.

Review   Test your understanding of the concepts and procedures covered in this module by answering the following review questions. You can check your answers with those listed after the questions.

Question 1:   How do you select a table cell? A block of cells? The entire table?

Question 2:   How do you change the width of table columns?

Question 3:   What happens when you type into a cell more text than there is room for?

Question 4:   What settings do you change on a Format A table to create the ruling pattern shown in the example below?

Table 1:

	1st Qtr	2nd Qtr
Product A	1,200	1,300
Product B	890	950
Product C	1,200	1,400

Question 5:   What shading settings do you change to create the following shading pattern?

Table 1:

	1st Qtr	2nd Qtr
Product A	1,200	1,300
Product B	890	950
Product C	1,200	1,400

Answer 1:   Control-click (on the Macintosh, Option-click) to select a cell. Drag across a block of cells to select them. Control-triple-click (on the Macintosh, Option-triple-click) to select the entire table.

Answer 2:   Select the column or columns to be resized. To resize the columns manually, drag a resize handle.

Answer 3:   The row height automatically increases to accommodate the text.

Answer 4:   In the Column Ruling area, change both line thicknesses to None. In the Body Row Ruling area, make sure both line thicknesses are set to Thin. In the Heading and Footing Ruling area, change the Separators setting to Thick.

Answer 5:   In the Body Shading area, make sure Shading is set to Body Rows. Set First to 1 and its fill to 3%. Set Next to 1 and its fill to None.

For more information

For more information about using tables, see:

Chapter 6 of *Using FrameMaker*

Customizing Tables

Approximate time to complete: 45 minutes

Introduction

In this module, you'll learn several ways to customize the appearance of tables. You can customize tables by specifying where a page will break in a table, changing the height of a row, straddling cells, changing the ruling or shading of a single cell or group of cells, and rotating cells.

Module Objectives

In this module, you'll learn how to

- Specify a page break in a table
- Change row height
- Add a footing row
- Straddle cells
- Set custom ruling and shading
- Rotate cells
- Add graphics to a table
- Create a single-cell table
- Create a calendar by using a table format

FrameMaker Model

Tables are *objects* that can be customized many different ways.

Row and Column Formatting

A table may have so many rows that it continues over more than one page. When this happens, the table title, heading rows, and footing rows, if any, are automatically recreated on every page of the table. To change where the table breaks, you can use the Row Format dialog box to specify manually a different row to start at the top of the page.

The Row Format dialog box can also be used to manually adjust the height of a row. You can set a minimum height limit so that a cell will appear a specified height even when there is not enough text to fill the cell. You can set a maximum height so that the row will not expand, even when all the text does not fit in the cell.

In the previous module, you resized columns by dragging resize handles. Many other options are available to resize columns precisely, using the Resize Columns dialog box.

Exercise 1	Setting page breaks in a table

Guided Tour

In this exercise, you'll see how to set a manual page break in a table.

1. Open the file named `log`, which you created in the previous module and saved in the `Class` directory or folder.

2. From the View menu, turn on **Borders** and **Text Symbols**.

3. Drag to select the third row, "Team C: Nights."

Table 1: Technical Support Calls§						
§	Monday§	Tuesday§	Wednesday§	Thursday§	Friday§	Saturday§
Team A: Days§	111§	121§	131§	122§	132§	122§
Team B: Days§	132§	123§	111§	121§	112§	121§
Team C: Nights§	111§	121§	123§	122§	132§	122§
Total§	354§	365§	365§	365§	376§	36 5§

4. From the Table menu, choose **Row Format**.

   The Row Format dialog box appears.

5. From the Start Row pop-up menu, choose **Top of Page**.

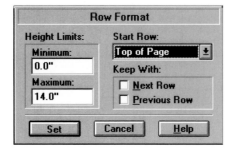

6. Click **Set**.

   The third row appears at the top of the next page, and the table title and heading row are recreated on this additional page of the table.

Table 1: Technical Support Calls§						
§	Monday§	Tuesday§	Wednesday§	Thursday§	Friday§	Saturday§
Team C: Nights§	111§	121§	123§	122§	132§	122§
Total§	354§	365§	365§	365§	376§	36 5§

7. Using the same dialog box, remove the page break:

   a. From the Table menu, choose **Row Format**.

      The Row Format dialog box appears.

   b. From the Start Row pop-up menu, choose **Anywhere**.

   c. Click **Set**.

      The entire table is again on the first page of the document.

Exercise 2

Guided Tour

Changing row height and column width

In this exercise, you will make more adjustments to the table by specifying a row height and column width in dialog boxes.

1. Drag to select the heading row.

§	Monday§	Tuesday§	Wednesday§	Thursday§	Friday§	Saturday§
Team A: Days§	111§	121§	131§	122§	132§	122§
Team B: Days§	132§	123§	111§	121§	112§	121§
Team C: Nights§	111§	121§	123§	122§	132§	122§
Total§	354§	365§	365§	365§	376§	36 5§

2. From the Table menu, choose **Row Format**.

3. In the Row Format dialog box, change the minimum height limit to **0.7"**.

4. Click **Set**.

   The heading row increases in height.

§	Monday§	Tuesday§	Wednesday§	Thursday§	Friday§	Saturday§
Team A: Days§	111§	121§	131§	122§	132§	122§
Team B: Days§	132§	123§	111§	121§	112§	121§
Team C: Nights§	111§	121§	123§	122§	132§	122§
Total§	354§	365§	365§	365§	376§	36 5§

5. Drag to select the first column in the table.

§	Monday§	Tuesday§	Wednesday§	Thursday§	Friday§	Saturday§
Team A: Days§	111§	121§	131§	122§	132§	122§
Team B: Days§	132§	123§	111§	121§	112§	121§
Team C: Nights§	111§	121§	123§	122§	132§	122§
Total§	354§	365§	365§	365§	376§	36 5§

6. Drag the resize handle to the left so the text wraps in the cells.

§	Monday§	Tuesday§	Wednesday§	Thursday§	Friday§	Saturday§
Team A: Days§	111§	121§	131§	122§	132§	122§
Team B: Days§	132§	123§	111§	121§	112§	121§
Team C: Nights§	111§	121§	123§	122§	132§	122§
Total§	354§	365§	365§	365§	376§	36 5§

7. With the column still selected, from the Table menu, choose **Resize Columns**. The Resize Selected Columns dialog box appears.

8. Turn on **To Width of Selected Cells' Contents**.

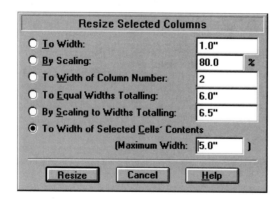

9. Click **Resize**.

The column resizes so it fits the longest selected paragraph.

§	Monday§	Tuesday§	Wednesday§	Thursday§	Friday§	Saturday§
Team A: Days§	111§	121§	131§	122§	132§	122§
Team B: Days§	132§	123§	111§	121§	112§	121§
Team C: Nights§	111§	121§	123§	122§	132§	122§
Total§	354§	365§	365§	365§	376§	36 5§

Tip: You can also use the Resize Columns command to resize columns to a specific numeric width, to scale columns, to make columns the width of another column, to make columns equal widths totalling some number, and to scale columns to widths totalling some number (the width of the text column, perhaps).

Straddling and Rotating

You can select cells, rows, columns, or a block of cells and combine them into a single "straddle" cell that extends across other cells. This cell functions as one cell unless you unstraddle. Any number of adjacent cells of the same type (heading, body, or footing), whether vertical, horizontal, or in blocks, can be combined in a straddle.

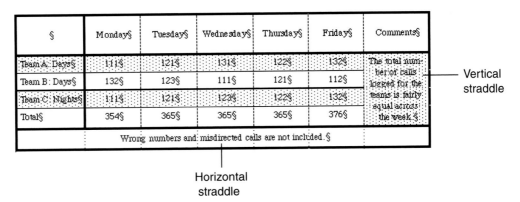

Vertical straddle

Horizontal straddle

You can also rotate cells and their contents in 90-degree increments. Although you can rotate any cell, heading cells are the ones most commonly rotated. When a cell is rotated, its height expands to accommodate the now vertically oriented text.

Table 1: Technical Suppo

Monday	Tuesday	Wednesday
111	121	131

Before rotating

Table 1: Technical Suppo

Monday	Tuesday	Wednesday
111	121	131

After rotating

Exercise 3

Project

Straddling columns and rows

In this exercise, you'll add a footing row and make the footing row a straddle. You'll also straddle part of the rightmost column of the table.

1. Add one footing row to the table:

   a. Put the insertion point anywhere in the table.

   b. From the Table menu, choose **Add Rows or Columns**.

   c. In the Add Rows or Columns dialog box, change the settings to add **1** row, and from the pop-up menu, choose **To Footing**.

   d. Click **Add**.

   A footing row appears at the bottom of the table.

§	Monday§	Tuesday§	Wednesday§	Thursday§	Friday§	Saturday§
Team A: Days§	111§	121§	131§	122§	132§	122§
Team B: Days§	132§	123§	111§	121§	112§	121§
Team C: Nights§	111§	121§	123§	122§	132§	122§
Total§	354§	365§	365§	365§	376§	365§
§	§	§	§	§	§	§

2. Drag to select the entire footing row.

§	Monday§	Tuesday§	Wednesday§	Thursday§	Friday§	Saturday§
Team A: Days§	111§	121§	131§	122§	132§	122§
Team B: Days§	132§	123§	111§	121§	112§	121§
Team C: Nights§	111§	121§	123§	122§	132§	122§
Total§	354§	365§	365§	365§	376§	36 5§
§	§	§	§	§	§	§

3. From the Table menu, choose **Straddle**.

   The ruling line between the first and second cells disappears as the row becomes a straddle cell. (The dotted border lines are still visible, but they do not print.)

§	Monday§	Tuesday§	Wednesday§	Thursday§	Friday§	Saturday§
Team A: Days§	111§	121§	131§	122§	132§	122§
Team B: Days§	132§	123§	111§	121§	112§	121§
Team C: Nights§	111§	121§	123§	122§	132§	122§
Total§	354§	365§	365§	365§	376§	36 5§
§						

4. Put the insertion point in the footing row cell straddle, and type:

   ```
   Wrong numbers and misdirected calls are not included.
   ```

§	Monday§	Tuesday§	Wednesday§	Thursday§	Friday§	Saturday§
Team A: Days§	111§	121§	131§	122§	132§	122§
Team B: Days§	132§	123§	111§	121§	112§	121§
Team C: Nights§	111§	121§	123§	122§	132§	122§
Total§	354§	365§	365§	365§	376§	36 5§
Wrong numbers and misdirected calls are not included.§						

   Next, you'll remove just the contents of the "Saturday" column and change it into a wider "Comments" column with four cells combined in a vertical straddle.

5. Delete the contents of the "Saturday" column:

   a. Select the "Saturday" column.

§	Monday§	Tuesday§	Wednesday§	Thursday§	Friday§	Saturday§
Team A: Days§	111§	121§	131§	122§	132§	122§
Team B: Days§	132§	123§	111§	121§	112§	121§
Team C: Nights§	111§	121§	123§	122§	132§	122§
Total§	354§	365§	365§	365§	376§	36 5§
Wrong numbers and misdirected calls are not included.§						

   b. Press **Delete**.

c. In the Clear Table Cells dialog box, turn on **Leave Cells Empty.**

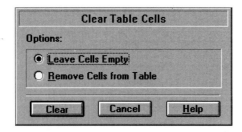

d. Click **Clear.**

6. In the empty heading cell, type: Comments

§	Monday§	Tuesday§	Wednesday§	Thursday§	Friday§	Comments§
Team A: Days§	111§	121§	131§	122§	132§	§
Team B: Days§	132§	123§	111§	121§	112§	§
Team C: Nights§	111§	121§	123§	122§	132§	§
Total§	354§	365§	365§	365§	376§	§
Wrong numbers and misdirected calls are not included.§						

7. Make the four empty cells in the rightmost column a straddle:

a. Drag to select the four empty cells in the rightmost column.

§	Monday§	Tuesday§	Wednesday§	Thursday§	Friday§	Comments§
Team A: Days§	111§	121§	131§	122§	132§	§
Team B: Days§	132§	123§	111§	121§	112§	§
Team C: Nights§	111§	121§	123§	122§	132§	§
Total§	354§	365§	365§	365§	376§	§
Wrong numbers and misdirected calls are not included.§						

b. From the Table menu, choose **Straddle.**

The ruling lines disappear, and all the cells appear shaded as they become a straddle.

§	Monday§	Tuesday§	Wednesday§	Thursday§	Friday§	Comments§
Team A: Days§	111§	121§	131§	122§	132§	§
Team B: Days§	132§	123§	111§	121§	112§	
Team C: Nights§	111§	121§	123§	122§	132§	
Total§	354§	365§	365§	365§	376§	
Wrong numbers and misdirected calls are not included.§						

Elaboration: A straddle takes on the shading settings of the cell in the upper left corner of the straddle.

8. Click in the straddle cell, and type: The total number of calls logged for the teams is fairly equal across the week.

§	Monday§	Tuesday§	Wednesday§	Thursday§	Friday§	Comments§
Team A: Days§	111§	121§	131§	122§	132§	The total number of calls logged for the teams is fairly equal across the week.§
Team B: Days§	132§	123§	111§	121§	112§	
Team C: Nights§	111§	121§	123§	122§	132§	
Total§	354§	365§	365§	365§	376§	
Wrong numbers and misdirected calls are not included.§						

Notice how the straddle cell grows vertically to fit the text, affecting the spacing in the final body row.

9. Use the Resize Columns command to resize the "Comments" column to a width of 1.2 inches:

   a. Drag to select the "Comments" column.

§	Monday§	Tuesday§	Wednesday§	Thursday§	Friday§	Comments§
Team A: Days§	111§	121§	131§	122§	132§	The total number of calls logged for the teams is fairly equal across the week.§
Team B: Days§	132§	123§	111§	121§	112§	
Team C: Nights§	111§	121§	123§	122§	132§	
Total§	354§	365§	365§	365§	376§	
Wrong numbers and misdirected calls are not included.§						

   b. From the Table menu, choose **Resize Columns**.

      In the Resize Selected Columns dialog box, turn on **To Width**, and change that setting to **1.2"**.

   c. Click **Resize**.

      The column widens, and the last body row shrinks in height.

§	Monday§	Tuesday§	Wednesday§	Thursday§	Friday§	Comments§
Team A: Days§	111§	121§	131§	122§	132§	The total number of calls logged for the teams is fairly equal across the week.§
Team B: Days§	132§	123§	111§	121§	112§	
Team C: Nights§	111§	121§	123§	122§	132§	
Total§	354§	365§	365§	365§	376§	
Wrong numbers and misdirected calls are not included.§						

10. From the View menu, turn off **Borders** and to see how the table will look when it is printed.

11. Turn borders and text symbols back on.

Exercise 4

Rotating cells

In this exercise, you'll rotate cells in the table created in earlier exercises.

1. In the heading row, select the "Monday" through "Friday" cells.

§	Monday§	Tuesday§	Wednesday§	Thursday§	Friday§	Comments§
Team A: Days§	111§	121§	131§	122§	132§	The total num-
Team B: Days§	132§	123§	111§	121§	112§	ber of calls logged for the
Team C: Nights§	111§	121§	123§	122§	132§	teams is fairly
Total§	354§	365§	365§	365§	376§	equal across the week.§
Wrong numbers and misdirected calls are not included.§						

2. From the Graphics menu, choose **Rotate**.

   The Rotate Table Cells dialog box appears.

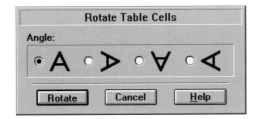

3. Turn on the rightmost option for the rotation angle.

4. Click **Rotate**.

   The cells rotate 90 degrees counterclockwise.

§	Monday§	Tuesday§	Wednesday§	Thursday§	Friday§	Comments§
Team A: Days§	111§	121§	131§	122§	132§	The total num-
Team B: Days§	132§	123§	111§	121§	112§	ber of calls logged for the
Team C: Nights§	111§	121§	123§	122§	132§	teams is fairly
Total§	354§	365§	365§	365§	376§	equal across the week.§
Wrong numbers and misdirected calls are not included.§						

Custom Ruling and Shading

Exercise 5   **Using custom ruling and shading**

Guided Tour

In this exercise, you'll work with ruling and shading properties, and you'll align text in selected cells. With custom ruling and shading, you can call attention to individual cells or groups of cells by shading them or putting ruling around them.

1. Put the insertion point anywhere in the footing row.

§	Monday§	Tuesday§	Wednesday§	Thursday§	Friday§	Comments§
Team A: Days§	111§	121§	131§	122§	132§	The total number of calls logged for the teams is fairly equal across the week.§
Team B: Days§	132§	123§	111§	121§	112§	
Team C: Nights§	111§	121§	123§	122§	132§	
Total§	354§	365§	365§	365§	376§	
Wrong numbers and misdirected calls are not included.§						

2. From the Table menu, choose **Custom Ruling & Shading**.

   The Custom Ruling and Shading dialog box appears.

3. Make sure **Custom Cell Ruling** is turned *off* and **Custom Cell Shading** is turned *on*.

4. From the Fill pop-up menu, choose **3%**.

Custom Cell Ruling

Custom Cell Shading

Fill pop-up menu

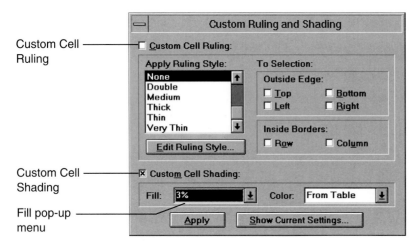

5. Click **Apply**.

The footing row is shaded.

§	Monday§	Tuesday§	Wednesday§	Thursday§	Friday§	Comments§
Team A: Days§	111§	121§	131§	122§	132§	The total num-
Team B: Days§	132§	123§	111§	121§	112§	ber of calls logged for the
Team C: Nights§	111§	121§	123§	122§	132§	teams is fairly
Total§	354§	365§	365§	365§	376§	equal across the week.§
Wrong numbers and misdirected calls are not included.§						

6. Apply a **Double** ruling style to the straddle cell in the rightmost column, and remove the shading:

   a. Click anywhere in the straddle cell in the "Comments" column.

   b. In the Custom Ruling and Shading dialog box, turn *on* **Custom Cell Ruling**.

   c. In the Apply Ruling Style scroll list, click **Double**.

   d. In the To Selection area, make sure **Top, Bottom, Left**, and **Right** are turned on.

   e. Leave the Inside Borders settings unchanged.

   > **Elaboration:** Since the Inside Borders settings apply to the borders between selected cells, they are relevant only when more than one cell is selected.

   f. In the Custom Cell Shading area, from the Fill pop-up menu, choose **None**.

   g. Click **Apply**.

   A double-style ruling appears around the current cell, and the shading has disappeared.

§	Monday§	Tuesday§	Wednesday§	Thursday§	Friday§	Comments§
Team A: Days§	111§	121§	131§	122§	132§	The total num-
Team B: Days§	132§	123§	111§	121§	112§	ber of calls logged for the
Team C: Nights§	111§	121§	123§	122§	132§	teams is fairly
Total§	354§	365§	365§	365§	376§	equal across the week.§
Wrong numbers and misdirected calls are not included.§						

Optional Exercises

The following exercises enable you to enhance your FrameMaker skills and to explore additional FrameMaker features. Some steps are intentionally brief so that they require more independent thought on your part.

Exercise 6

Optional

Adding graphics to a table

In this optional exercise, you'll add clip art to the table.

Table 1: Technical Support Calls

	Monday	Tuesday	Wednesday	Thursday	Friday	Comments
Team A: Days	111	121	131	122	132	The total number of calls logged for the teams is fairly equal across the week.
Team B: Days	132	123	111	121	112	
Team C: Nights	111	121	123	122	132	
Total	354	365	365	365	376	
Wrong numbers and misdirected calls are not included						

1. Open the **OfficeLayout** clip art file:

    a. From the Help menu, choose **Samples & Clip Art**.

    b. In the FrameMaker samples window, click **Clip art** to see the list of clip art files.

    c. Double-click **OfficeLayout**.

2. Copy the telephone graphic from page 1.

3. Paste the graphic into the first cell in the heading row.

> **Note:** As long as you have an insertion point when you paste the graphic, an anchored frame will be created for you.

4. If necessary, adjust the position of the graphic (keeping it within the anchored frame) to center it in the table cell.

5. Turn off borders and text symbols to display the table as it will appear when printed.

6. Save the file, and close the document. Also close any other windows currently open.

Exercise 7

Starting a table at the top of a page

When a short table page breaks awkwardly from one page to the next, you can keep the entire table together by forcing the table to start at the top of the next page. In this optional exercise, you'll create a table that extends across two pages, and you'll change the table format to make the table start at the top of the second page.

1. Put the insertion point at the beginning of the document, and press **Return** until only two of the table's body rows appear at the bottom of the page.

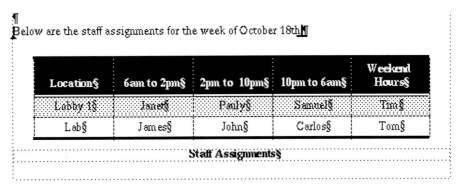

2. Go to **page 2**.

    Notice that some of the table cells appear at the top of this page.

3. Put the insertion point in the table, and in the Table Designer, use the Basic properties to change the Start setting to **Top of Page.**

4. Click **Apply** so that the change is applied only to this table, and not included in the table format's definition.

    The entire table appears on page 2.

5. Save the file, and close the document.

Exercise 8

Creating a calendar table format

In this optional exercise, you'll create a table to use as a calendar.

September 1996

Sun	Mon	Tues	Wed	Thur	Fri	Sat
1	2	3	4	5	6	7
8	9	10	11	12	13	14
15	16	17	18	19	20	21
22	23	24	25	26	27	28
29	30					

1. Create a new **Portrait** document.

2. Use the Save As dialog box to save the document in the `Class` directory or folder with the new filename `calendar`.

3. Insert a Format A table that has seven columns, five body rows, and one heading row.

4. Select the entire table, and resize it to make it the same width as the text frame.

5. Turn off autonumbering in the table title:

   a. Put the insertion point in the table title.

   b. In the Paragraph Designer, display the **Numbering** properties.

   c. Click *twice* in the **Autonumber Format** checkbox to turn it off.

   d. Click **Update All**.

6. Type the month name and the year in the title, and the abbreviated days of the week in the heading row.

7. Use the Paragraph Designer to change the default font of the CellHeading paragraph format to **Bold**.

8. Make the body rows 0.75 inch high.

9. In the Ruling properties, change the Heading and Footing Ruling Separators to **Thin** and **Update All**.

10. In the Shading properties, change the Heading and Footing Shading Fill to **10%** and **Update All**.

11. Select all the cells in the body of the calendar, and use the Paragraph Catalog to apply the **Numbered** paragraph format.

12. Select the cells that should *not* be numbered, and apply the **CellBody** paragraph format.

13. Use the Paragraph Designer to remove the period and tab character (\t) from the autonumber format of the Numbered paragraph format, and **Update All**.

14. Apply custom shading to the unnumbered cells.

15. Apply a thick custom rule around the outside edge of the cell representing the 29th of the month.

16. Save the file, and close the document.

Review   Test your understanding of the concepts and procedures covered in this module by answering the following review questions. You can check your answers with those listed after the questions.

Question 1:   How do you change the height of table rows?

Question 2:   How do you straddle table cells?

Question 3:   How do you rotate a cell or group of cells?

Question 4:   How do you shade a single table cell or group of cells?

Answer 1:   When you type text into a cell, the row height automatically increases to accommodate the text. To increase the row height without adding text, select the cell and use the Row Format command from the Table menu.

Answer 2:   Select the cells, and from the Table menu, choose Straddle.

Answer 3:   Select the cell or cells, and from the Graphics menu, choose Rotate. Select an angle, and click Rotate.

Answer 4:   Select the cell or cells, and from the Table menu, choose Custom Ruling & Shading. Turn off Custom Cell Ruling. Turn on Custom Cell Shading, and select a fill. Click Apply.

For more information

For more information about using tables, see:

Chapter 6 of *Using FrameMaker*

Table Formats

Approximate time to complete: 45 minutes

Introduction

In this module, you'll become familiar with creating table formats. With FrameMaker's table properties, you can create a custom format to be used for one document or as a template for several documents.

Module Objectives

In this module, you'll learn how to

- Create a new table format
- Modify existing table formats
- Set spacing above and below a table, and other Basic properties
- Modify paragraph formats used in a table

FrameMaker Model

Table *formats* specify shading and ruling patterns, and they determine table alignment, position of table autonumbering, and space above and below the table.

Creating and Modifying Table Formats

Table formats are created with the Table Designer. A list of table formats in the Table Catalog can be found only in the Table Tag pop-up menu in the Table Designer—there is no Catalog window for table formats that can be displayed and that remain on your screen, like the Paragraph Catalog or Character Catalog.

In the exercises in this module, you'll create a new table format that is used to post staff assignments for various locations and shifts.

Location§	6am to 2pm§	2pm to 10pm§	10pm to 6am§	Weekend Hours§
Lobby 1§	Janet§	Pauly§	Samuel§	Tim§
Lab§	James§	John§	Carlos§	Tom§
Infirmary§	Jenny§	Craig§	Bill§	Gary§
Gate§	Jack§	Brad§	Torrey§	Larry§

Staff Assignments§

Exercise 1 — Creating the table

Guided Tour

In this exercise, you'll create the table with text that you'll use in the remainder of the module.

1. Create a new **Portrait** document.

2. Use the Save As dialog box to save the document in the Class directory or folder with the new filename assign.

3. At the insertion point, type: Below are the staff assignments for the week of October 18th.

4. Insert a table using Format A that has five columns, four body rows, and one heading row:

   a. Make sure the insertion point is at the end of the text you just typed.

   b. From the Table menu, choose **Insert Table**.
   The Insert Table dialog box appears.

   c. In the Table Format scroll list, click **Format A**.

   d. Make sure Columns is set to **5**.

   e. Change Body Rows to **4**.

   f. Make sure Heading Rows is set to **1** and Footing Rows is set **0**.

g. Click **Insert**.

The table appears in your document.

Below are the staff assignments for the week of October 18th.§

Table 1: §				
§	§	§	§	§
§	§	§	§	§
§	§	§	§	§
§	§	§	§	§
§	§	§	§	§

5. Type some text in the table, as in the following example.

Table 1: Staff Assignments§				
Location§	6am to 2pm§	2pm to 10pm§	10pm to 6am§	Weekend Hours§
Lobby 1§	Janet§	Pauly§	Samuel§	Tim§
Lab§	James§	John§	Carlos§	Tom§
Infirmary§	Jenny§	Craig§	Bill§	Gary§
Gate§	Jack§	Brad§	Torrey§	Larry§

6. Select all the columns in the table, and resize them to a width of 85 points:

a. Drag to select all the columns.

b. From the Table menu, choose **Resize Columns**.
The Resize Selected Columns dialog box appears.

c. Change the To Width setting to **85 pt**.

d. Click **Resize**.
The columns widen.

Table 1: Staff Assignments§				
Location§	6am to 2pm§	2pm to 10pm§	10pm to 6am§	Weekend Hours§
Lobby 1§	Janet§	Pauly§	Samuel§	Tim§
Lab§	James§	John§	Carlos§	Tom§
Infirmary§	Jenny§	Craig§	Bill§	Gary§
Gate§	Jack§	Brad§	Torrey§	Larry§

7. Put the insertion point after the anchor symbol that follows the words "October 18th" above the table, and press **Return**.

> **Tip:** The easiest way to put the insertion point after an anchor symbol is to click just to the left of the anchor symbol and press the right arrow key once.

The insertion point moves below the table.

Below are the staff assignments for the week of October 18th.¶

		Table 1: Staff Assignments§		
Location§	6am to 2pm§	2pm to 10pm§	10pm to 6am§	Weekend Hours§
Lobby 1§	Janet§	Pauly§	Samuel§	Tim§
Lab§	James§	John§	Carlos§	Tom§
Infirmary§	Jenny§	Craig§	Bill§	Gary§
Gate§	Jack§	Brad§	Torrey§	Larry§

Insertion point ——— §

8. Type: `This schedule subject to change without notice.`

Exercise 2

Guided Tour

Creating a new table format

In this exercise, you'll use the Table Designer to create a new table format.

1. Put the insertion point anywhere in the table.

2. From the Table menu, choose **Table Designer**.
   The Table Designer appears.

3. From the Commands pop-up menu in the lower-left corner, choose **New Format**.
   The New Format dialog box appears.

4. In the Tag text box, type: `Staff`

5. Make sure **Store in Catalog** and **Apply to Selection** are turned on.

6. Click **Create**.

The Staff table format is applied to the current table and added to the Table Catalog. The Staff format is displayed in the Table Designer.

Exercise 3

Setting Basic table properties

table properties such as alignment, indents, space above and below the table, default cell margins, and title position are set in the Basic properties of the Table Designer.

In this exercise, you'll specify several Basic table properties for the Staff table format.

1. Make sure you have an insertion point in the table.

2. In the Basic properties of the Table Designer, from the **Alignment** pop-up menu, choose **Center**.

3. Click **Update All**.

The table appears centered between the left and right borders of the text frame.

Below are the staff assignments for the week of October 18th.¶

Table 1: Staff Assignments§

Location§	6am to 2pm§	2pm to 10pm§	10pm to 6am§	Weekend Hours§
Lobby 1§	Janet§	Pauly§	Samuel§	Tim§
Lab§	James§	John§	Carlos§	Tom§
Infirmary§	Jenny§	Craig§	Bill§	Gary§
Gate§	Jack§	Brad§	Torrey§	Larry§

This schedule subject to change without notice.§

Elaboration: When you use Update All, the changes are applied to all tables in the document that have the same table format, as well as to the format stored in the Table Catalog.

4. Change Space Above to **20 pt**.

5. Change Space Below to **20 pt**.

6. Click **Update All**.

More space appears above and below the table.

Below are the staff assignments for the week of October 18th.¶

Table 1: Staff Assignments§				
Location§	6am to 2pm§	2pm to 10pm§	10pm to 6am§	Weekend Hours§
Lobby 1§	Janet§	Pauly§	Samuel§	Tim§
Lab§	James§	John§	Carlos§	Tom§
Infirmary§	Jenny§	Craig§	Bill§	Gary§
Gate§	Jack§	Brad§	Torrey§	Larry§

This schedule subject to change without notice. §

7. From the Title Position pop-up menu, choose **Below Table**.

8. Click **Update All**.

The title appears below the table.

Location§	6am to 2pm§	2pm to 10pm§	10pm to 6am§	Weekend Hours§
Lobby 1§	Janet§	Pauly§	Samuel§	Tim§
Lab§	James§	John§	Carlos§	Tom§
Infirmary§	Jenny§	Craig§	Bill§	Gary§
Gate§	Jack§	Brad§	Torrey§	Larry§
Table 1: Staff Assignments§				

9. Change the Gap to **12 pt**.

10. Click **Update All**.

More space appears between the table and its title.

Location§	6am to 2pm§	2pm to 10pm§	10pm to 6am§	Weekend Hours§
Lobby 1§	Janet§	Pauly§	Samuel§	Tim§
Lab§	James§	John§	Carlos§	Tom§
Infirmary§	Jenny§	Craig§	Bill§	Gary§
Gate§	Jack§	Brad§	Torrey§	Larry§
Table 1: Staff Assignments§				

Default Cell Margins

The Default Cell Margins settings are used to specify the minimum amount of space that should appear between the text and the top, bottom, left, and right edges of all cells in the table.

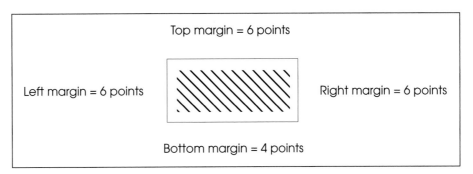

Exercise 4

Changing default cell margins

In the following steps, you'll increase the amount of space between the table text and the bottom of the table cells.

1. Make sure you have an insertion point in the table.

2. Change the Top default cell margin to **8.0 pt** and the Bottom default cell margin to **6.0 pt**.

3. Click **Update All**.

   More space appears between the top and bottom of the text and the edges of the cell.

Location§	6am to 2pm§	2pm to 10pm§	10pm to 6am§	Weekend Hours§
Lobby 1§	Janet§	Pauly§	Samuel§	Tim§
Lab§	James§	John§	Carlos§	Tom§
Infirmary§	Jenny§	Craig§	Bill§	Gary§
Gate§	Jack§	Brad§	Torrey§	Larry§

Table 1: Staff Assignments§

Exercise 5

Setting Ruling properties

In this exercise, you'll set various Ruling properties for the table.

1. From the View menu, turn off **Borders** so you can see the changes to the ruling more clearly.

2. Make sure you have an insertion point in the table.

3. In the Table Designer, from the Properties pop-up menu, choose **Ruling**.

The Table Designer displays the Ruling properties for the Staff table format.

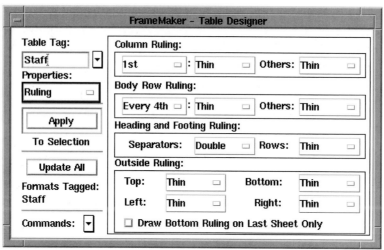

4. Set **Column Ruling** to **None**.

5. Set **Body Row Ruling** to display **Every 2nd** row with a **Very Thin** rule, and **Others** with **None**.

6. Make sure the Heading and Footing Ruling **Separators** are set to **Double** and **Rows** are set to **Thin**.

7. Set Outside Ruling to **Thick** on the **Top** and **Bottom** and to **None** on the **Left** and **Right**.

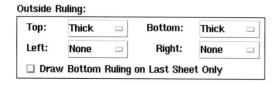

8. Click **Update All**.

The table looks as follows.

Location§	6am to 2pm§	2pm to 10pm§	10pm to 6am§	Weekend Hours§
Lobby 1§	Janet§	Pauly§	Samuel§	Tim§
Lab§	James§	John§	Carlos§	Tom§
Infirmary§	Jenny§	Craig§	Bill§	Gary§
Gate§	Jack§	Brad§	Torrey§	Larry§

Table 1: Staff Assignments§

Exercise 6

Project

Adding body shading

In this exercise, you'll set shading properties for the rows, as well as make the heading row 100% black with white text in the heading row cells.

1. Make sure you have an insertion point in the table.

2. In the Table Designer, from the Properties pop-up menu, choose **Shading**.

    The Table Designer displays Shading properties for the Staff table format.

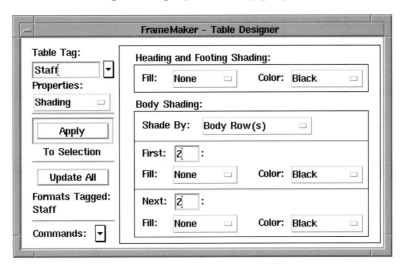

3. In the Heading and Footing Shading area, from the Fill pop-up menu, choose **100%**, and make sure the corresponding Color setting is **Black**.

4. Click **Update All**.

The heading row is shaded with solid black.

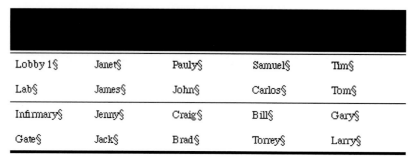

Lobby 1§	Janet§	Pauly§	Samuel§	Tim§
Lab§	James§	John§	Carlos§	Tom§
Infirmary§	Jenny§	Craig§	Bill§	Gary§
Gate§	Jack§	Brad§	Torrey§	Larry§

Table 1: Staff Assignments§

Later, you'll change the CellHeading paragraph format to a color of white for white text on a black background.

5. Set **Body Shading** to shade every other row with a Fill of **10% Black**:

   a. In the Body Shading area, make sure that **Body Row(s)** is the setting shown in the Shade By pop-up menu.

   b. Change the First setting to **1**.

   c. From the First Fill pop-up menu, choose **10%**, and make sure the corresponding Color setting is **Black**.

   d. Change the Next setting to **1**.

   e. Make sure the setting shown in the Next Fill pop-up menu is **None**. The corresponding color does not matter when the Fill setting is None.

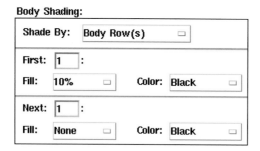

6. Click **Update All**.

Every other row is filled with 10% black.

Lobby 1§	Jane§	Pauly§	Samuel§	Tim§
Lab§	James§	John§	Carlos§	Tom§
Infirmary§	Jenny§	Craig§	Bill§	Gary§
Gate§	Jack§	Brad§	Torrey§	Larry§

Table 1: Staff Assignments§

7. Turn on Borders before continuing.

Using the Paragraph Designer with Tables

A table format includes four standard paragraph tags: CellHeading, CellBody, CellFooting, and TableTitle. These are modified in the Paragraph Designer. In the next three exercises, you'll modify these paragraph formats.

Exercise 7

Project

Modifying the CellHeading paragraph format

In this exercise, you'll modify the CellHeading paragraph format.

1. Put the insertion point in the heading row of the table.

Notice that the paragraph format for the cells in the heading row is CellHeading.

2. Change the default font for CellHeading to **White** and **Bold**:

   a. From the Format menu, choose **Paragraphs>Designer**.

   The Paragraph Designer appears.

   b. From the Properties pop-up menu, choose **Default Font**.

   The Paragraph Designer displays the Default Font properties for the CellHeading paragraph format.

   c. From the Weight pop-up menu, choose **Bold**.

   d. From the Color pop-up menu, choose **White**.

   e. Click **Update All**.

The text in the heading row appears white.

Location§	6am to 2pm§	2pm to 10pm§	10pm to 6am§	Weekend Hours§
Lobby 1§	Jane§	Pauly§	Samuel§	Tim§
Lab§	James§	John§	Carlos§	Tom§
Infirmary§	Jenny§	Craig§	Bill§	Gary§
Gate§	Jack§	Brad§	Torrey§	Larry§

Table 1: Staff Assignments§

3. Change the **Cell Vertical Alignment** to **Bottom**:

   a. From the Properties pop-up menu, choose **Table Cell**.

   The Paragraph Designer displays the Table Cell properties for the CellHeading paragraph format.

   b. From the **Cell Vertical Alignment** pop-up menu in the upper-right corner, choose **Bottom**.

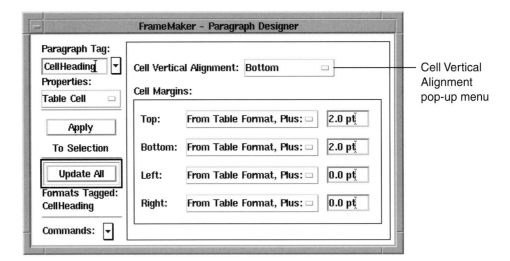

Cell Vertical Alignment pop-up menu

   c. Click **Update All**.

   The heading text appears aligned against the bottom of the cells.

Location§	6am to 2pm§	2pm to 10pm§	10pm to 6am§	Weekend Hours§
Lobby 1§	Jane§	Pauly§	Samuel§	Tim§
Lab§	James§	John§	Carlos§	Tom§
Infirmary§	Jenny§	Craig§	Bill§	Gary§
Gate§	Jack§	Brad§	Torrey§	Larry§

Table 1: Staff Assignments§

Exercise 8

Project

Modifying the CellBody paragraph format

In this exercise, you'll modify the CellBody paragraph format.

1. Put the insertion point in any body row of the table.

   Notice that the paragraph format for the cells in the body rows is CellBody.

2. Change the Alignment for CellBody to **Center**:

   a. In the Paragraph Designer, from the Properties pop-up menu, choose **Basic**.

   The Paragraph Designer displays the Basic properties for the CellBody paragraph format.

   b. From the Alignment pop-up menu, choose **Center**.

   c. Click **Update All**.

   The body rows appear centered.

Location§	6am to 2pm§	2pm to 10pm§	10pm to 6am§	Weekend Hours§
Lobby 1§	Jane§	Pauly§	Samuel§	Tim§
Lab§	James§	John§	Carlos§	Tom§
Infirmary§	Jenny§	Craig§	Bill§	Gary§
Gate§	Jack§	Brad§	Torrey§	Larry§

Table 1: Staff Assignments§

Exercise 9

Guided Tour

Modifying the TableTitle paragraph format

In this exercise, you'll modify the TableTitle paragraph format.

1. Put the insertion point in the table title text below the table.

   Notice that the paragraph format for the table title is TableTitle. The TableTitle paragraph format has the "Table 1:" autonumber.

2. Remove the autonumber for the TableTitle paragraph format:

   a. In the Paragraph Designer, from the Properties pop-up menu, choose **Numbering**.

   The Paragraph Designer displays the Numbering properties for the TableTitle paragraph format.

   b. Turn off the Autonumber Format checkbox above the text box.

   You have to click twice to turn it off (once for As Is, a second time for Off).

   ☐ Autonumber Format:

   T:Table <n+>:

c. Click **Update All**.

The TableTitle paragraph appears without the autonumber "Table 1:".

Location§	6am to 2pm§	2pm to 10pm§	10pm to 6am§	Weekend Hours§
Lobby 1§	Jane§	Pauly§	Samuel§	Tim§
Lab§	James§	John§	Carlos§	Tom§
Infirmary§	Jenny§	Craig§	Bill§	Gary§
Gate§	Jack§	Brad§	Torrey§	Larry§

Staff Assignments§

Exercise 10   Importing Table Formats

Guided Tour

A table format that you create initially exists only in the document in which it was created. To use a table format in a different document, you must import the format. In this exercise, you'll import the Staff table format you created earlier into a new document.

1. Leave the document containing the Staff table open, and create a new **Portrait** document.

2. From the Table menu, choose **Insert Table**.

   Notice that the Staff format does not appear in the Table Format scroll list.

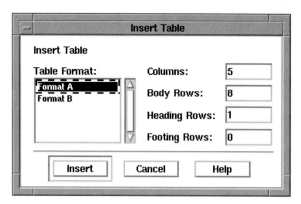

3. Click **Cancel**.

4. From the File menu, choose **Import>Formats**.

5. From the Import from Document pop-up menu, choose **assign**.

6. Turn off everything *except* **Table Formats**.

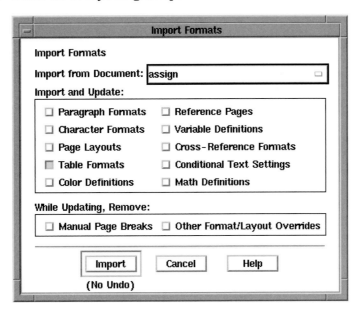

7. Click **Import**.

8. From the Table menu, choose **Insert Table**.

   The Staff format now appears in the Table Format scroll list.

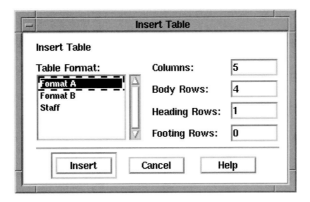

9. Make sure the Staff format is selected, and click **Insert**.

Notice that the new empty Staff table that is inserted has the same table formatting as the original Staff table.

> **Note:** In addition to importing the table formatting, the table cells of an imported format contain the same paragraph formatting as the original Staff table. However, the imported formats are overrides and therefore are not stored in the Paragraph Catalog.

10. Close the document without saving the changes. Save the `assign` file, and keep the document open if you intend to complete the optional exercises in this module. Otherwise, close the document.

Optional Exercises

The following exercise enables you to enhance your FrameMaker skills and to explore additional FrameMaker features. Some steps are intentionally brief so that they require more independent thought on your part.

Exercise 11

Optional

Creating a single-cell table format

In this optional exercise, you'll create a table format similar to the following Elaboration box.

> **Elaboration:** A single cell is not generally thought of as a table. The advantage to a table such as this is its flexibility to expand and contract with the amount of text inside. This table has one row, one column, shading, and no ruling.

1. Create a new **Portrait** document.

2. Use the Save As dialog box to save the document in the `Class` directory or folder with the new filename `box`.

3. Insert into the document a Format A table that has only one body row and one column:

   a. From the Table menu, choose **Insert Table**.

   b. Change Columns to **1**, Body Rows to **1**, and Heading Rows to **0**.

   c. Click **Insert**.

4. In the Table Designer, create a new table format called **Box**.

5. In the Basic properties, change the Title Position to **No Title**, and **Update All**.

6. In the Ruling properties, set all properties in the Outside Ruling area to **None**, and **Update All**.

7. In the Shading properties, in the Body Shading area, change the First Fill setting to **10%** and **Update All**.

8. **Control-click** (on the Macintosh, **Option-click**) to select the cell, and make it as wide as the column.

9. In the table, type: `This single-cell table appears in your document as a shaded paragraph.`

10. Save the file, and close the document.

Review

Test your understanding of the concepts and procedures covered in this module by answering the following review questions. You can check your answers with those listed after the questions.

Question 1: Unlike the Paragraph Catalog and Character Catalog, the Table Catalog is found in only one place in FrameMaker. Where?

Question 2: How do you create a new table format?

Question 3: Where do you go to change the alignment of text in table cells? To change the alignment of an entire table?

Question 4: How do you remove the autonumber "Table 1:" from a table?

Question 5: How do you make a table format created in one document available to another document?

Answer 1: In the Table Designer.

Answer 2: Use the New Format command in the Table Designer.

Answer 3: Text alignment is changed by using the Basic properties or the Table Cell properties in the Paragraph Designer. The Table Designer is used to change the alignment of the table itself.

Answer 4: In the Paragraph Designer, turn off autonumbering for the TableTitle format.

Answer 5: Open both documents, and import the table format from one document into the other.

For more information

For more information about table formats, see:

Chapter 7 of *Using FrameMaker*

Footnotes

Approximate time to complete: 30 minutes

Introduction

In this module, you'll become familiar with FrameMaker footnotes. Footnotes are used in the main document text and in tables to reference, explain, or comment on information in these areas.

Module Objectives

In this module, you'll learn how to

- Insert, move, and delete footnotes
- Modify the properties of footnotes
- Insert and modify table footnotes
- Number footnotes sequentially
- Locate footnotes in a document

FrameMaker Model

Footnotes are text-anchored *objects* whose anchors are footnote symbols.

Using Document Footnotes

When you create a footnote in the main flow of text in the document (not in a table), FrameMaker places the footnote reference at the insertion point and places the footnote at the bottom of the current text column.

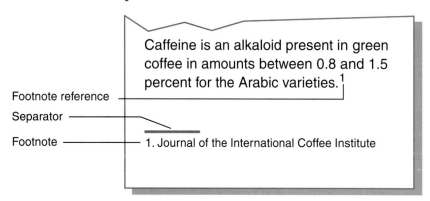

Footnote reference

Separator

Footnote

Caffeine is an alkaloid present in green coffee in amounts between 0.8 and 1.5 percent for the Arabic varieties.[1]

1. Journal of the International Coffee Institute

When you insert or delete a footnote, the rest of the footnotes are renumbered automatically.

Exercise 1

Guided Tour

Inserting a footnote into a document

In this exercise, you will become familiar with inserting document footnotes into the main flow of text in your document.

1. From the FrameMaker list of sample documents, open the book chapter **resource.doc**:

   a. Display the FrameMaker list of sample documents.

   Macintosh   From the [?] menu, choose **Samples & Clip Art**.

   Windows   From the Help menu, choose **Samples & Clip Art**.

   UNIX   From a document Help menu, choose **Samples & Clip Art**.
   (If there are no open documents, click **NEW**, then **Portrait**, first.)

   b. In the FrameMaker samples window, click **Book**.

   c. Double-click **resource.doc**.

2. Use the Save As dialog box to save the document in the `Class` directory or folder with the new filename `ftnote`.

3. From the View menu, turn on **Borders**.

4. Go to **page 7** of the document.

Notice the footnote at the bottom of the right column. The footnote reference appears approximately 12 lines above the footnote.

Footnote reference ———

For over two years the scientists on this Committee have continued to debate the rationale of the baseline study approach with seemingly little agreement.[1] An evaluation of baseline data being collected on the prototype oil shale leases has pointed to the need for more

5. Put the insertion point after the word "ecologists," six lines from the top of the right column.

interdisciplinary approaches which can add to our fund of information and understanding. Thus, at a time when usual federal sources of research support are relatively limited, these study efforts are of added importance to ecologists|

6. From the Special menu, choose **Footnote**.

FrameMaker inserts the footnote reference at the insertion point, displays the footnote number at the bottom of the column, and places the insertion point after the footnote number, renumbering any footnotes that follow.

conducted for evaluation of power plant impact in such coastal systems as Chesapeake Bay and

1. |
2. Many of these discussions are documented in the minutes of the Department of the Interior's OSC Environmental

Elaboration: A footnote is numbered according to its position relative to other footnotes in the text. If you move the footnote reference before or after an existing reference, the reference sequence will update automatically.

7. Type: The Federal Studies List is normally available in local libraries.

The text of the footnote appears at the bottom of the text column.

Exercise 2

Guided Tour

Cutting, pasting, and deleting a footnote

There may be times when you need to move your footnote reference within the document or delete the footnote entirely. In this exercise, you will cut and paste the footnote reference number, moving the footnote with it. You will also see how to delete a footnote and its reference number from your document.

1. Select the footnote reference "1" after the word "ecologists" in the document (*not* the actual footnote at the bottom of the page).

    > **Note:** Sometimes it's helpful to increase the zoom setting so you can see the footnote reference more easily.

    When you select the footnote reference, the entire footnote at the bottom of the column is selected automatically.

2. From the Edit menu, choose **Cut**.

    The footnote reference and its corresponding footnote are placed on the Clipboard.

3. In the first sentence of the second paragraph of the left column, put the insertion point after the word "study."

    > environmental disturbance than the projected coal mining.
    >
    > In short, the environmental baseline study has assumed major importance. Heavy reliance is being placed upon baseline studies to help

4. From the Edit menu, choose **Paste**.

    The footnote reference is pasted at the insertion point, and its corresponding footnote appears at the bottom of the left column.

5. Select the same footnote reference you just moved (the "1" after the word "study").

6. Press the **Delete** or **Backspace** key on the keyboard.

    The footnote reference and its corresponding footnote are deleted.

    > **Elaboration:** If you press Delete or Backspace without first selecting the footnote, the insertion point will pass over the footnote and delete adjacent text.

Footnote Properties

You can create a footnote straddle by changing the Pagination properties in the Paragraph Designer, just like a regular paragraph. A footnote straddle differs from a regular paragraph straddle in that it will always appear at the bottom of the text frame, even if the footnote reference is above another straddle, as shown in the example below.

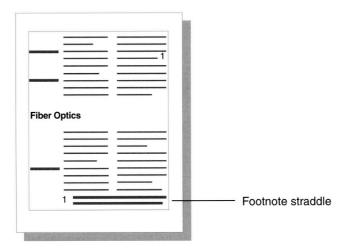

Footnote straddle

You can change the footnote numbering format from consecutive numbers to consecutive uppercase or lowercase letters, or to asterisks and daggers (*†‡), by changing the Footnote properties.

Exercise 3

Guided Tour

Setting footnote straddles in Paragraph Designer

In the following exercise, you will create a footnote that straddles two columns.

1. Put the insertion point in the footnote text at the bottom of the right column. Notice that the footnote uses the Footnote paragraph format.

2. In the Paragraph Designer, change the Pagination properties for the footnote to a format of Across All Columns:

   a. From the Format menu, choose **Paragraphs>Designer**.

   b. From the Properties pop-up menu, choose **Pagination**.

   c. In the Format area, turn on **Across All Columns**.

   d. Click **Update All**.

   e. If you need to refresh the screen to see the footnote, press **Control-l** (lowercase L).

Look at the footnote area at the bottom of the page, and notice that the footnote now spans both columns of the document.

3. Remove the paragraph straddle:

   a. In the Format area in the Paragraph Designer, turn on **In Column**.

   b. Click **Update All**.

   The straddle is removed, and the footnote is again in one column.

Exercise 4

Guided Tour

Changing the footnote numbering format

In this exercise, you will change the footnote numbering format to an asterisk and dagger symbols.

1. From the Format menu, choose **Document>Footnote Properties**.

   The Footnote Properties dialog box appears.

2. In the Numbering Style area, turn on **Custom**.

3. In the In Footnote area, in the Suffix text box, delete the period (.), but leave the tab character (\t).

4. Click **Set**.

5. The footnote reference and the corresponding number of the footnote at the bottom of the column have changed to asterisks.

   Elaboration: When Custom is turned on, the first footnote uses an asterisk, the second a dagger, the third a double dagger, the fourth two asterisks, the fifth two daggers, the sixth two double daggers, and so on. Because you deleted the period in the Suffix text box, these special characters appear without periods following them.

6. Put the insertion point after the word "ecologists," six lines from the top of the right column.

7. From the Special menu, choose **Footnote**.

8. The footnote reference and number of the new footnote are asterisks. The footnote reference and number of the second footnote have changed to daggers.

9. Select the asterisk footnote reference, and delete it.

Using Table Footnotes

In the next few exercises you'll see that table footnotes function similarly to document footnotes. They differ only in their placement and the way they are numbered. Instead of placing table footnotes at the bottom of the page, FrameMaker places them at the end of a table. And rather than consecutive numbering, table footnotes are numbered using lowercase letters.

Exercise 5

Adding a footnote to a table

Project

In this exercise, you will create a table and insert a footnote into the table.

1. Go to **page 6** of the document.

2. Put the insertion point after the word "ecosystem" near the bottom of the left column.

> remain as agricultural grasslands still under
> some tidal influence, while others have been
> filled to become uplands. All are partially or even
> wholly removed form directly interacting as
> a part of the estuarine ecosystem.

3. Insert a table using Format A, consisting of three columns and three body rows, into the document:

   a. From the Table menu, choose **Insert Table**.

   The Insert Table dialog box appears.

   b. In the Table Format scroll list, click **Format A**.

   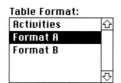

   Table Format:
   - Activities
   - **Format A**
   - Format B

   c. Set Columns to **3** and Body Rows to **3**.

   d. Click **Insert**.

   A table appears.

4. Add the title and text to each cell, as follows.

Ecosystems

Type		
Wetlands		
Grasslands		
Desert		

5. Add a footnote to the cell containing the word "Wetlands:"

a. Put the insertion point after the word "Wetlands."

b. From the Special menu, choose **Footnote**.

FrameMaker inserts the footnote reference (a superscript "a") at the insertion point, displays the footnote letter at the end of the table, and places the insertion point after the footnote letter.

c. Type: Including Bastinado River delta.

The text of the footnote appears at the end of the table.

Ecosystems

Type		
Wetlands[a]		
Grasslands		
Desert		

a. Including Bastinado River delta.

Note: You can cut, paste, and delete table footnotes the same way as you can regular footnotes.

Exercise 6

Guided Tour

Changing table footnote properties

To change table footnote properties, the insertion point must be in a table (in a title, cell, or table footnote) when you choose the Document>Footnote Properties command from the Format menu. If the insertion point is not in a table, the Footnote Properties dialog box that appears will show properties of *document* footnotes, not *table* footnotes.

In this exercise, you will change the footnote numbering format to Numeric.

1. Change the numbering style to **Numeric** for a footnote:

   a. With the insertion point anywhere in the table, from the Format menu, choose **Document>Footnote Properties**.

   The Table Footnote Properties dialog box appears.

   b. In the Numbering Style area, from the pop-up menu, choose **Numeric (4)**.

   c. Click **Set**.

   Notice that the table footnote reference and its corresponding footnote display the number 1.

2. Save the file, and keep the document open if you intend to complete the optional exercises in this module. Otherwise, close the document.

Optional Exercises

The following exercises enable you to enhance your FrameMaker skills and to explore additional FrameMaker features. Some steps are intentionally brief so that they require more independent thought on your part.

Exercise 7

Optional

Numbering footnotes sequentially

For footnotes you've inserted into this document, numbering restarts on each page. In this optional exercise, you will learn how to number footnotes sequentially throughout a document.

1. Go to **page 14** in the document, and put the insertion point anywhere in the first paragraph.

2. Change the footnote numbering properties of the regular footnotes back to Numeric:

   a. From the Format menu, choose **Document>Footnote Properties**.

   b. In the Footnote Properties dialog box, in the Numbering Style area, turn on **Numeric**.

   c. Click **Set**.

   The footnote on this page is numbered 1 even though it is the second regular footnote in the document.

3. Change the numbering style to **Sequentially From**:

   a. From the Format menu, choose **Document>Footnote Properties**.

   b. In the Footnote Properties dialog box, in the Numbering Style area, turn on **Sequentially From**.

   c. Click **Set**.

   Notice that the footnote is now numbered 2.

4. Go to the next page, and insert a footnote anywhere on the page.

   Notice that because numbering for footnotes is sequential, the footnote is numbered 3.

5. Save the file, and keep the document open.

Exercise 8   **Finding footnotes**

Optional

In this optional exercise, you'll use the Find/Change window to find footnotes.

1. From the Edit menu, choose **Find/Change**.

2. From the Find pop-up menu in the Find/Change window, choose **Footnote**.

3. Click **Find** to search through the document, and select the various footnote references.

4. Close the document.

Review Test your understanding of the concepts and procedures covered in this module by answering the following review questions. You can check your answers with those listed after the questions.

Question 1: How do you move a footnote and its reference to a different location in the document?

Question 2: How do you delete a footnote?

Question 3: How do you change the numbering style of a footnote so the footnote references are asterisks and daggers?

Question 4: To change the footnote properties of table footnotes, where must the insertion point be when you choose Document>Footnote Properties from the Format menu?

Question 5: How do you create sequentially numbered footnotes instead of footnotes that restart numbering on each page?

Answer 1: Select the footnote reference, and cut it; then paste the reference into a new location. The footnote accompanies the pasted reference.

Answer 2: Select the footnote reference, and press Backspace or Delete.

Answer 3: From the Format menu, choose Document>Footnote Properties, and in the Numbering Style area, turn on Custom. Then in the In Footnote area, delete the period from the Suffix text box.

Answer 4: In a table title, table cell, or table footnote.

Answer 5: In the Footnote Properties dialog box, turn on Sequentially From.

For more information

For more information about footnotes, see:

Chapter 11 of *Using FrameMaker*

Variables

Approximate time to complete: 1 hour

Introduction

In this module, you'll use system variables to add the date and running headers and footers to documents. You will change a variable by editing the definition and then create a user variable and update the definition.

Module Objectives

In this module you'll learn how to

- Use system variables
- Edit system variables
- Create user variables
- Use and edit table system variables

FrameMaker Model

A variable is *text* that is defined once but that can be used several times.

Working with Variables

There are two types of FrameMaker variables: user variables and system variables. A *user variable* is a variable you can define to use in place of text that appears repeatedly—for example, a product name. A *system variable* is a built-in variable used mainly in headers and footers—for example, to display the current date, chapter name, current page number, and total number of pages. FrameMaker automatically updates the values of system variables and displays them on body pages. You can delete, cut, copy, and paste variables the same way you do text.

Using System Variables

FrameMaker provides a set of system variables for each document. You can't add, delete, or rename a system variable, but you can change its definition. FrameMaker automatically updates the value of system variables inserted on master pages. Common system variables include the current date, page number, page count, and running headers and footers.

System variables are most commonly found in background text frames on master pages, as shown in the following example.

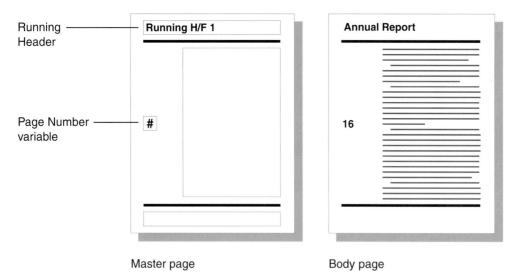

Running Header

Page Number variable

Running H/F 1

\#

Annual Report

16

Master page

Body page

Although most system variables can be inserted into any text frame on a body, reference, or master page, the Current Page # and the four Running H/F variables can be inserted only in a background text frame on a master page.

A partial list of FrameMaker system variables follows.

System Variable	Default Definition
Current Page #	<$curpagenum>
Page Count	<$lastpagenum>
Current Date (Long)	<$monthname> <$daynum>, <$year>
Modification Date (Long)	<$monthname> <$daynum>, <$year>, <$hour>:<$minute00> <$ampm>
Creation Date (Long)	<$monthname> <$daynum>, <$year>
Running H/F 1	<$paratext[Title]>
Running H/F 2	<$paratext[Heading1]>

Exercise 1

Project

Modifying system variables

In this exercise, you'll modify system variables in a sample report.

1. From the FrameMaker list of standard templates, open a copy of the **ReportNumeric** template with sample text:

   a. Open the New dialog box.

Macintosh	From the File menu, choose **New**.
Windows	From the File menu, choose **New**.
UNIX	In the main FrameMaker window, click **NEW**.

   b. At the bottom of the dialog box, click **Explore Standard Templates**.

   c. In the list of templates, click **Report, Numeric**.

   d. Click **Show Sample**.

2. Use the Save As dialog box to save the document in the `Class` directory or folder with the new filename `sysvar`.

3. Put the insertion point in the title, "Report on the San Francisco Earthquake of 1906."

   In the status bar, notice that the paragraph tag is ReportTitle.

   | Flow: A ¶: ReportTitle |

4. Go to **page 2**.

   Notice that the title of the report is in the footer, after the page number. This running footer is displayed by using a system variable.

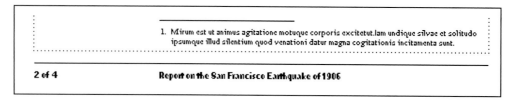

5. Go back to **page 1**, and in the title of the document, change "San Francisco" to "Loma Prieta," and "1906" to "1989."

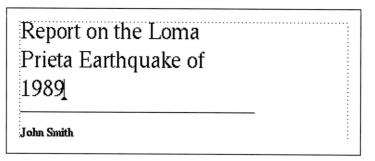

6. Go to **page 2**.

   Notice that the footer has the new text of the title.

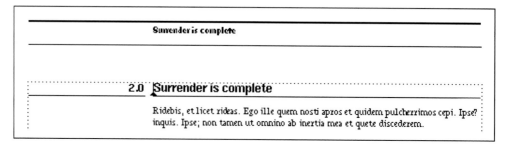

7. On **page 2**, click the first heading on the page, "2.0 Surrender is complete."

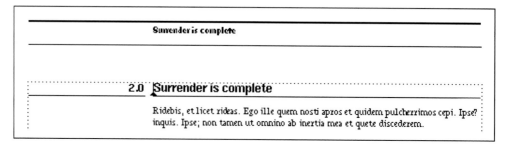

   Look in the status bar, and notice that this is a Heading1 paragraph. Also, notice that the header on the page displays the text of the Heading1 paragraph.

8. Put your insertion point in the paragraph, "2.1 The first day."

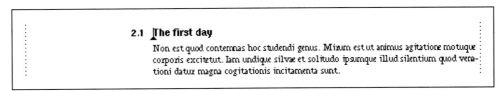

Notice that this is a Heading2 paragraph.

9. Go to the **Left** master page.

10. In the header text column, double-click the **Running H/F2** variable.

   The Variable dialog box appears.

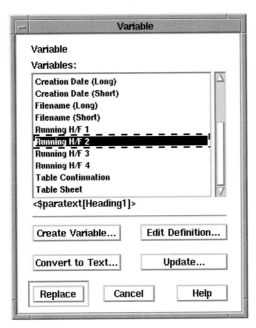

11. Click **Edit Definition**.

   The Edit System Variable dialog box appears.

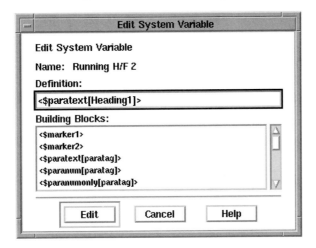

12. In the Definition text box, change "Heading1" to "Heading2."

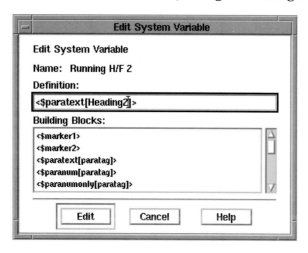

13. Click **Edit**.

    The Variable dialog box appears.

14. Click **Replace**.

15. Go to body **page 2**.

    Notice that the running header now displays the text of the Heading2 paragraph.

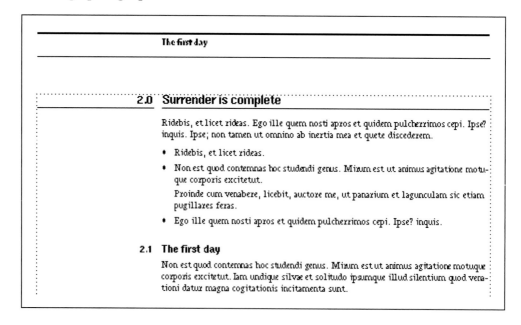

Running Header/Footer Variables

When you want the text of a title or heading to appear in a document's header or footer, you use a running header/footer system variable. FrameMaker provides four running header/footer variables. You can use the variables as is or edit them by using a combination of text you type in and building blocks you select.

For example, assume the second chapter of your document is titled "Changing a Filter" and that this text has been tagged with a paragraph format named "Chapter." The paragraph format has an autonumber format of Chapter <n+>\t so that the chapter title appears as follows:

Chapter 2	**Changing a Filter**

The following running headers or footers would appear, given the indicated variable definitions:

Variable Definition	Appearance of Variable on Body Pages
<$paratext[Chapter]	Changing a Filter
<$paranum[Chapter]>	Chapter 2
<$paranumonly[Chapter]>	2
<$paranum[Chapter]>: <$paratext[Chapter]>	Chapter 2: Changing a Filter

Exercise 2

Project

Inserting a new running header/footer system variable

In this exercise, you will insert a new running header/footer system variable that will display the autonumber of the Heading1 paragraph.

1. Go to the **Left** master page.

2. From the View menu, turn on **Text Symbols**.

3. Click the header text frame, and create a right-aligned tab at 7.5 inches on the ruler.

```
  |1|      |2|    ▼  |3|      |4|      |5|      |6|      |7|  ▼
_____↑




_____
Running H/F 2§
```

4. Click in front of the Running H/F 2 variable, and then press **Tab**.

5. Put your insertion point in front of the tab character.

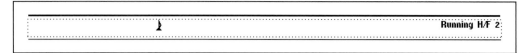

6. Type: `Section`

7. Type a space.

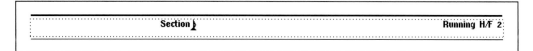

8. From the Special menu, choose **Variable**.

   The Variable dialog box appears.

9. In the Variables scroll list, click **Running H/F 3**.

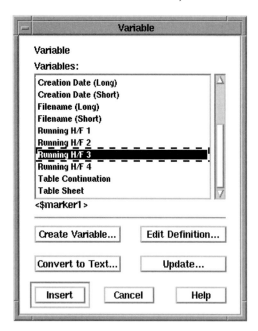

10. Click **Edit Definition**.

    The Edit System Variable dialog box appears.

11. Delete the contents of the Definition text box, and in the Building Blocks scroll list, click **<$paranum[paratag]>**.

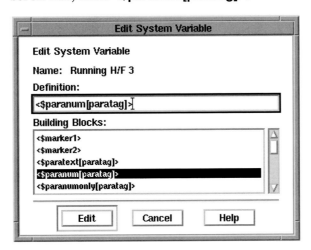

12. Change "paratag" to **Heading1**.

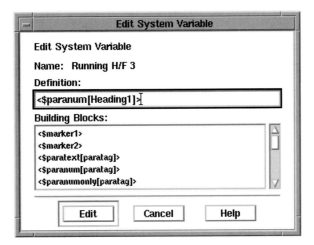

13. Click **Edit**, and in the Variable dialog box, click **Insert**.

The Running H/F 3 variable appears after the word "Section" in the header.

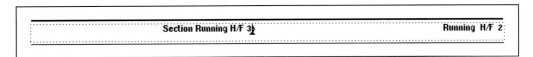

14. Go to body **page 2**.

Notice that the header now has the section number in it.

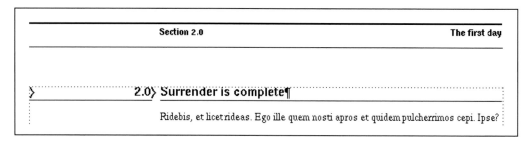

15. Go to the **Left** master page, and **Control**-click (on the Macintosh, **Option**-click) to select the header text frame.

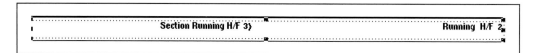

16. From the Edit menu, choose **Copy**.

17. Go to the **Right** master page, and delete the header text frame.

18. From the Edit menu, choose **Paste**.

The Add New Text Frame dialog box appears. Make sure Background Text is turned on.

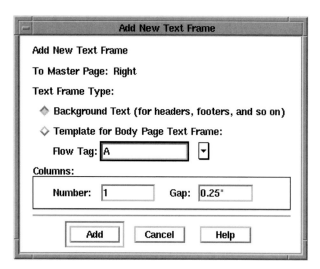

19. Click **Add**.

The header is pasted between the lines.

20. Align the right edge of the header text frame, with the right edge of the line above the text frame.

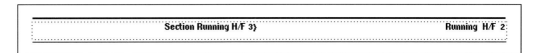

21. Go to body **page 3**.

    Notice that the running header text to the left is "Section 2.0" and that the text on the right is still "The first day."

22. Click at the end of the first body paragraph.

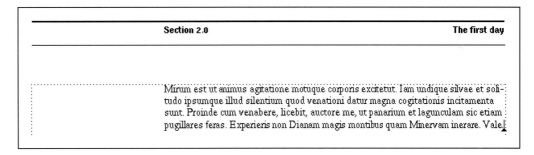

23. Press **Return**, tag the new paragraph **Heading1**, and type: The weeks that followed

24. Press **Control-l** (lowercase L) to refresh display of the document.

    Notice that the header now displays "Section 3.0."

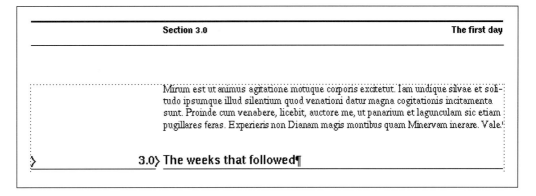

25. Press **Return**, tag the new paragraph **Heading2**, and type:
    The cleanup began

26. Press **Control-l** (lowercase L).

Notice that the header now displays the text, "The cleanup began."

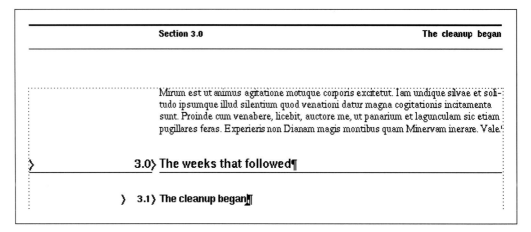

Exercise 3 — Changing the definition of a system variable

You cannot change the name of a system variable or create new system variables, but you can change the appearance of a system variable by editing its definition.

In this exercise you will change the format of the Modification Date variable.

1. Go to the **First** master page.

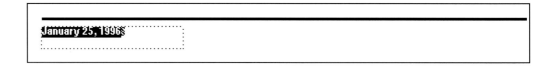

2. Select the Date variable.

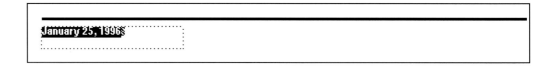

3. From the Special menu, choose **Variable**.

The Variable dialog box appears.

4. Click **Edit Definition**.

5. Delete the <$daynum> building block and the space, and insert a new <$daynum> building block at the beginning of the Definition text box.

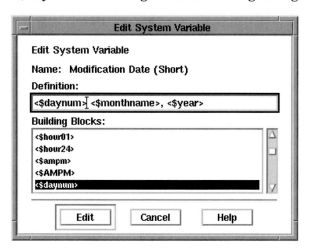

6. Click **Edit**, and in the Variable dialog box, click **Replace**.

7. Go to body **page 1**.

   Notice that the format of the date has changed.

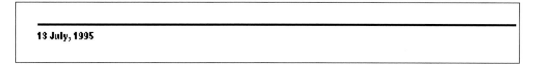

8. Save the file, and close the document.

Adding User Variables

When you create a user variable, you give it a name and then you define it. The definition includes the text of the variable and any character formatting it requires. When you insert the variable, FrameMaker displays its value—the text in the character format you specified. If you insert the variable in several places in the document, the same text in the same format appears at each place.

The advantage to using user variables is that you can change their definitions. For example, if you're using a variable to represent the name of a product that will change later in the development cycle, you can change the definition of the variable when the final name is determined. If you change the definition, FrameMaker updates all occurrences of the variable in your document to use the new definition.

You can't edit particular occurrences of a variable directly in a document. To change an occurrence of a variable, you convert it to text and then edit the text. FrameMaker no longer treats the text as a variable.

Exercise 4   Creating a user variable

Project

In this exercise, you'll create a user variable for the code name of a project. After inserting the variable into several places, you will change its definition and update all occurrences of it.

1. From the FrameMaker list of sample documents, open the book chapter **response.doc**:

   a. Display the FrameMaker list of sample documents.

Macintosh	From the [?] menu, choose **Samples & Clip Art**.
Windows	From the Help menu, choose **Samples & Clip Art**.
UNIX	From a document Help menu, choose **Samples & Clip Art**. (If there are no open documents, click **NEW**, then **Portrait**, first.)

      A list of FrameMaker samples appears.

   b. Click **Book**.

   c. Double-click **response.doc**.

2. Use the Save As dialog box to save the document in the `Class` directory or folder with the new filename `uservar`

3. On page 1, click after the first paragraph and type: `Our attempt to keep the Earth clean is through the`

   forms of life on earth originated in the sea. We have only recently begun to fathom our need to protect the oceans as a way to keep the planet alive and healthy. Our attempt to keep the earth clean is through the|

   3.1   **Water Pollution**

4. From the Special menu, choose **Variable**.

   The Variable dialog box appears.

5. Click **Create Variable**.

   The Edit User Variable dialog box appears.

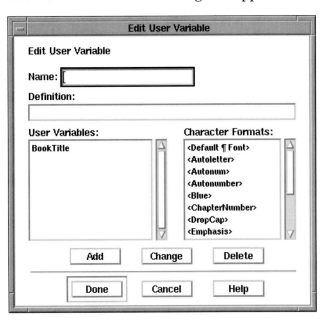

6. In the Name text box, type: `ProjectName`

7. In the Definition text box type: `Corporate Cleanup Campaign`

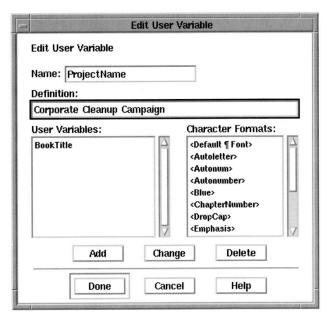

8. Click **Add**, and then click **Done**.

   The Variable dialog box reappears.

9. Click **Insert**.

   The user variable you created is added to the document.

10. In the document, type a **period** after the variable.

   > have only recently begun to fathom our need to
   > protect the oceans as a way to keep the planet
   > alive and healthy. Our attempt to keep the earth
   > clean is through the Corporate Cleanup
   > Campaign
   >
   > **3.1   Water Pollution**

11. Go to the next page, and in the first line below the heading, "3.4 Impact Assessment Study focus," delete the words "this process."

   > **3.4   Impact Assessment Study focus**
   > The importance and value of this process, as well
   > as its points of weakness, are well-known to the
   > nation's ecologists—a sizable number of whom
   > have participated in it. The symposium permitted
   > ecologists to voice their views on improving the
   > process.

12. Type the word the followed by a space.

13. From the Special menu, choose **Variable**.

14. In the Variables scroll list, click **ProjectName**.

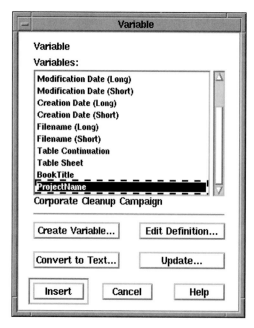

15. Click **Insert**.

The ProjectName variable is inserted.

3.4   Impact Assessment Study focus

The importance and value of the Corporate Cleanup Campaign as well as its points of weakness, are well-known to the nation's ecologists—a sizable number of whom have participated in it. The symposium permitted ecologists to voice their views on improving the process.

16. Go to **page 1** and double-click the **ProjectName** user variable (the words "Corporate Cleanup Campaign").

    The Variable dialog box appears.

17. Click **Edit Definition**.

18. In the Definition text box, delete "Corporate" and type: Star Company

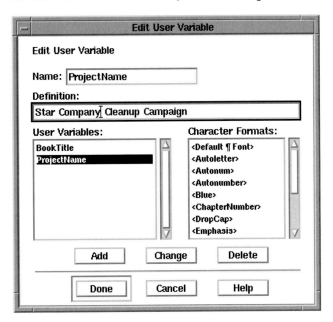

19. Click **Change**, and then click **Done**.

    The Variable dialog box reappears.

20. Click **Replace**.

21. Go to **page 2**, and notice that the user variable has changed.

22. Save the file, and close the document.

Using Table Variables

There are two table system variables you can use to add special text to multipage tables:

- Table Continuation

- Table Sheet

In the example below, the Table Continuation variable is inserted into the title on the first page of the table. On the first page, FrameMaker inserts a nonbreaking space symbol (⊔), which does not print but indicates the presence of the variable. The current definition of the variable appears on all pages after the first.

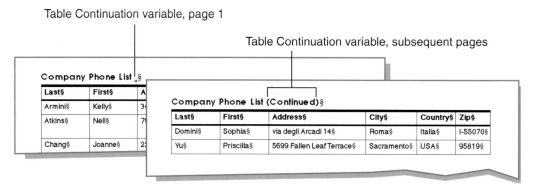

Table Continuation variable, page 1

Table Continuation variable, subsequent pages

In multipage tables, the Table Sheet variable displays the current page and the total number of pages that the table spans. If the table doesn't break across pages, it displays a nonbreaking space, which does not appear in print.

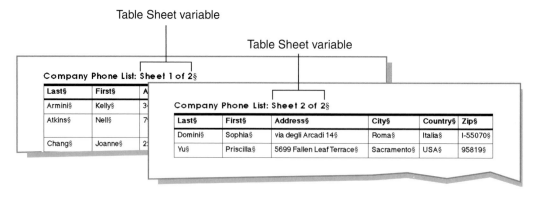

Table Sheet variable

Table Sheet variable

Exercise 5

Project

Inserting a Table Continuation variable

In this exercise, you will create a table that has several pages. You will then insert two table variables and edit one of them.

1. Create a new **Portrait** document:

   a. Open the New dialog box.

Macintosh	From the File menu, choose **New**.
Windows	From the File menu, choose **New**.
UNIX	In the main FrameMaker window, click **NEW**.

   b. Click **Portrait**.

2. Use the Save As dialog box to save the document in the `Class` directory or folder with the new filename `tablevar`.

3. Make sure the insertion point is in the top of the document.

4. From the Table menu, choose **Insert Table**.

   The Insert Table dialog box appears.

5. Make sure **Format A** is selected, and change Body Rows to **80** and Footing Rows to **1**.

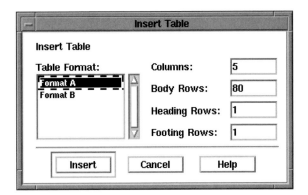

6. Click **Insert**.

   The table is inserted into the document. Notice that the table spans four pages.

7. In the title area, after "Table 1:", type: Lakes of the World

8. Page through the document, and notice that the title is repeated on every page of the table.

9. Go back to page 1.

> **Note:** Table variables can be inserted and edited only on the first page of a table.

10. Put your insertion point after the title, "Lakes of the World."

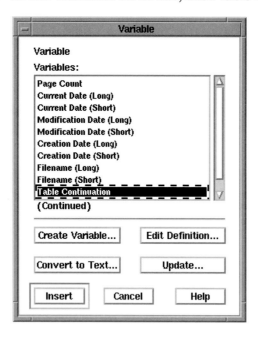

11. From the Special menu, choose **Variable**.

The Variable dialog box appears.

12. In the Variables scroll list, click **Table Continuation**.

13. Click **Insert**.

A nonbreaking space appears after the title.

14. Go to page 2.

Notice that the text "(Continued)" appears after the title.

Table 1: Lakes of the World (Continued)§				
§	§	§	§	§
§	§	§	§	§

15. Go back to page 1.

16. Double-click the nonbreaking space in the title.

The Variable dialog box appears with the Table Continuation variable highlighted.

> **Tip:** If the Variable dialog box does not appear when you double-click the nonbreaking space, make that symbol larger by increasing the magnification of the page and then double-click again.

17. Click **Edit Definition**.

The Edit System Variable dialog box appears.

18. Put the insertion point before "(Continued)" in the Definition text box.

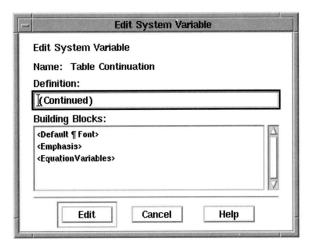

19. In the Building Blocks scroll list, click **<Emphasis>**.

20. Change "Continued" to "Cont'd."

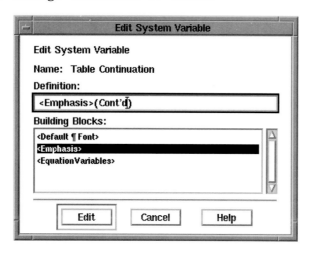

21. Click **Edit**, and in the Variable dialog box, click **Replace**.

22. Go to **page 2**, and look at the title.

The variable text after the title has an Emphasis (italic) character format and is abbreviated.

Exercise 6

Project

Inserting a table sheet variable

In the next exercise, you will insert the Table Sheet variable into the footer of the table.

1. Go to page 1.

2. **Straddle** the footer cells, and change the alignment of the CellFooting paragraph to **Left**:

   a. Select the footer row.

   b. From the table menu, choose **Straddle**.

   c. In the formatting bar at the top of the document, from the Alignment pop-up menu, choose **Left**.

3. Put the insertion point in the footer.

4. From the Special menu, choose **Variable**.

   The Variable dialog box appears.

5. Scroll down the Variables scroll list, and click **Table Sheet**.

   The current definition of Table Sheet appears under the scroll list.

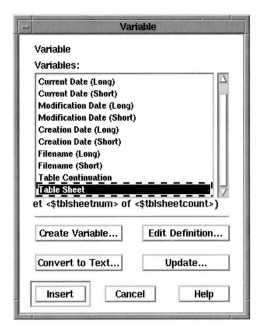

6. Click **Insert**.

   The Table Sheet variable is inserted.

§	§	§	§	§
(Sheet 1 of 4)§				

7. Page through the document, noticing the Table Sheet variable in the footer.

8. Save the document, and keep it open if you intend to complete the optional exercise. Otherwise, close the document.

Optional Exercise

The following exercise enables you to enhance your FrameMaker skills and to explore additional FrameMaker features. Some steps are intentionally brief, so they require more independent thought on your part.

Exercise 7 **Editing the Table Sheet variable**

Optional

In this optional exercise, you'll change the word "Sheet" in the definition of the Table Sheet variable to "Page."

1. On the first page of the document, double-click the Table Sheet variable to display the Variable dialog box.

2. Click **Edit Definition**.

3. Change the text of the variable from "Sheet" to "Page" by editing the variable.

4. Page through the document to see the change.

5. Save the file, and close the document.

Review   Test your understanding of the concepts and procedures covered in this module by answering the following review questions. You can check your answers with those listed after the questions.

Question 1:   What are two types of FrameMaker variables?

Question 2:   In a variable, what does the <$paratext> building block do?

Question 3:   If you add new text that will be displayed with a variable (such as a heading displayed with a RunningH/F variable), when will the value of the variable be updated?

Question 4:   How do you change the font of a variable?

Question 5:   What are the two table system variables? In what kind of table do you normally use these variables?

Answer 1:   User variables and system variables.

Answer 2:   The <$paratext> building block displays the text of a paragraph you specify.

Answer 3:   When the page is redisplayed. You can press Control-l (lowercase L) or turn the page.

Answer 4:   In the Edit System Variable dialog box, put a building block for the character tag you want to apply before the text you want to reformat.

Answer 5:   Table Continuation and Table Sheet. You use these variables in multipage tables.

For more information

For more information about system and user variables, see:

Chapter 12 of *Using FrameMaker*

Conditional Text

Approximate time to complete: 1 hour

Introduction

In this module, you'll become familiar with using conditional text. With conditional text, several versions of a document can be produced from a single FrameMaker document.

Module Objectives

In this module, you'll learn how to

- View different versions of a conditional document

- Change the appearance of condition indicators

- Prepare separate versions of a document for distribution

- Make text conditional and unconditional

- Add text to conditional documents

- Create and apply condition tags

- Edit conditional documents

FrameMaker Model

A conditional text setting is a *format* that can be applied to both text and text-anchored objects such as tables or graphics.

Working in a Conditional Document

If you're preparing several versions of a document, each with minor differences, you can use one FrameMaker document for all versions. You create multiple versions of the same document by using *conditional* text. Text common to all versions of the same document is referred to as *unconditional*.

You can use conditional text to

- Produce documents for similar but not identical models of a product

- Include comments from one or more reviewers or editors—comments you can hide before you go into final production

- Produce a document to be distributed both in print and online

Any unit of text can be conditional: one character, a text block, or entire sections. Graphics, tables, cross-references, footnotes, markers, and table rows can be conditional.

You can view all versions of a document at the same time, or you can view selected versions of the document while hiding others. Whatever you display is what FrameMaker prints.

Exercise 1

Guided Tour

Viewing a conditional document

In this exercise, you'll examine a conditional document. The document is a flyer that contains information for two vehicle models: sedan and pickup truck.

1. From the FrameMaker list of sample documents, open the **Conditional text** sample document:

   a. Display the FrameMaker list of sample documents.

Macintosh	From the 🔲 menu, choose **Samples & Clip Art**.
Windows	From the Help menu, choose **Samples & Clip Art**.
UNIX	From a document Help menu, choose **Samples & Clip Art**. (If there are no open documents, click **NEW**, then **Portrait**, first.)

   b. In the list of FrameMaker samples, click **Conditional text**.

   The sample document appears on your screen.

2. Turn on **Borders**.

The sample document contains text describing both the DynaLoadster Sedan and the DynaLoadster Pickup Truck.

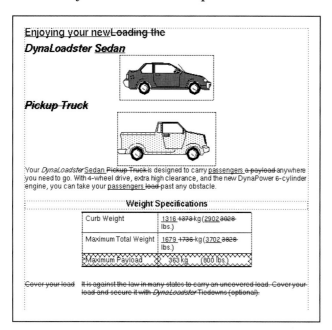

This single conditional document can be used to produce the two separate versions.

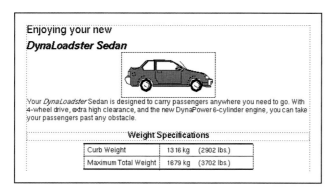

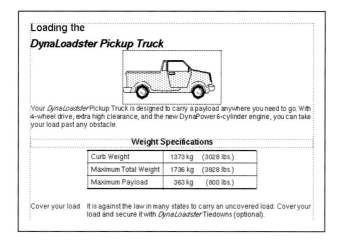

Exercise 2

Examining condition tags and condition indicators

In a conditional document, a separate condition tag exists for each version of the document. Text in a document is assigned a condition tag based on the version of the document in which the text will appear. In the sample file, there are two condition tags—Sedan and Pickup Truck.

A condition indicator changes the appearance of conditional text to identify which version of the document the text belongs to. Each condition tag has a corresponding condition indicator so that text with a particular condition tag can be easily identified. Condition indicators do not affect the text's paragraph or character format.

In this exercise, you'll identify the condition tags and condition indicators in the sample file.

1. Take a look at the document's first line of text.

    Enjoying your new~~Loading the~~

    Two different condition tags have been applied to the text in this line. The condition indicator of the first tag makes text appear red (if you have a color monitor) and underlined. The condition indicator of the second tag makes text appear with a green strikethrough font style.

2. Put the insertion point in any of the first three words.

    Enjoying your new~~Loading the~~

    The status bar in the lower-left corner of the document window indicates that the Sedan tag is assigned to this text.

    (Sedan) Flow: A ¶: Head1

    This condition tag identifies conditional text that will appear in the DynaLoadster Sedan version of the document.

3. Put the insertion point in either of the last two words.

    Enjoying your new~~Loading the~~

    The status bar indicates that the Pickup Truck tag is assigned to this text.

    (Pickup Truck) Flow: A ¶: Head1

This condition tag identifies conditional text that will appear in the Pickup Truck version of the document.

4. In the second line of text, put the insertion point in the word "DynaLoadster."

This text is unconditional, so it has no condition indicator, and no condition tag appears in the status bar.

5. Select the anchored frame that surrounds the Sedan picture.

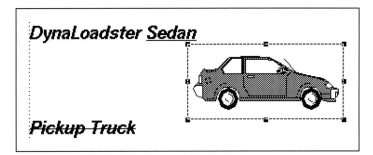

The status bar indicates that the Sedan condition tag is assigned to the anchored frame.

6. Drag to highlight the last row of the Weight Specifications table.

Weight Specifications	
Curb Weight	1316 ~~1373~~ kg (2902 ~~3028~~ lbs.)
Maximum Total Weight	1679 ~~1736~~ kg (3702 ~~3828~~ lbs.)
Maximum Payload	363 kg (800 lbs.)

The status bar indicates that the Pickup Truck condition tag is assigned to this row of the table.

> **Elaboration:** Graphics and table rows do not display condition indicators the same way text does. Conditional table rows display a colored crosshatch pattern. Conditional graphics look the same as unconditional graphics.

Exercise 3

Project

Modifying condition indicators

In this exercise, you'll edit the Sedan condition tag by changing its condition indicator.

1. In the third line of the paragraph below the pickup truck picture, put the insertion point in the word "passengers."

> *dster* Sedan ~~Pickup Truck~~ is des
> With 4-wheel drive, extra high
> an take your passengers ~~load~~ p

2. From the Special menu, choose **Conditional Text**.

The Conditional Text window appears.

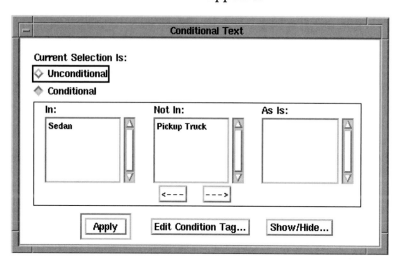

3. In the In scroll list, make sure **Sedan** is selected; then click **Edit Condition Tag**.

The Edit Condition Tag dialog box appears.

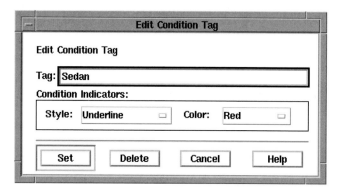

The selected condition tag appears in the Tag text box, and its condition indicators appear in the Condition Indicators area. The current condition indicators underline the text and color it red.

4. In the Condition Indicators area, from the Style pop-up menu, choose **Overline**.

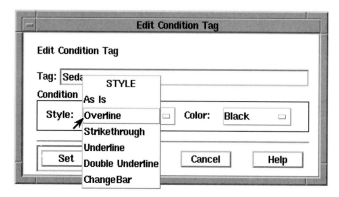

5. Click **Set**.

The condition indicator for the word "passenger" and the other words in the document assigned the Sedan tag now appear with an overline instead of an underline.

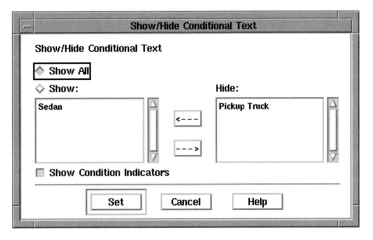

Note: Some of the words in larger type sizes may not display the overline.

6. Use the Save As dialog box to save the document in the `Class` directory or folder with the new filename `allcars`.

Exercise 4

Guided Tour

Viewing different versions of a document

The separate versions contained in a conditional document can be displayed on-screen individually.

In this exercise, you'll view the two versions contained in the `allcars` file.

1. In the Conditional Text window, click **Show/Hide**.

The Show/Hide Conditional Text dialog box appears.

2. Turn on **Show**.

3. Make sure **Sedan** is in the Show scroll list and **Pickup Truck** is in the Hide list.

4. Click **Set**.

Only the unconditional text and text assigned the Sedan condition tag (the red overline) are displayed.

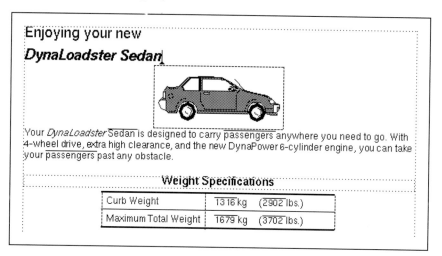

5. In the Conditional Text window, click **Show/Hide**.

6. Turn off **Show Condition Indicators**.

7. Click **Set**.

   The Sedan version now appears without condition indicators.

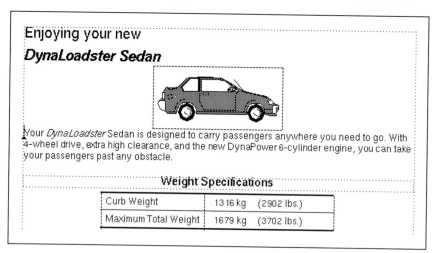

8. Turn off **Borders**.

   The document now appears on-screen the same way it would when printed.

9. Turn on **Borders**.

10. In the Conditional Text window, click **Show/Hide**.

11. Move **Sedan** into the Hide scroll list and **Pickup Truck** into the Show list:

    a. Select **Sedan** in the Show list.

    b. Click the **right arrow**.

    c. Select **Pickup Truck** in the Hide list.

    d. Click the **left arrow**.

12. Click **Set**.

    Only unconditional text and text assigned the Pickup Truck condition tag are displayed.

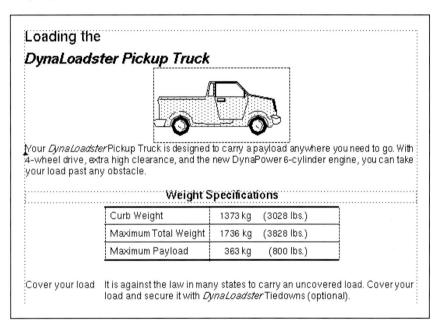

Exercise 5

Project

Preparing separate versions for distribution

Often you will need to distribute individual versions of a conditional document. For example, you may need to send a file to a commercial printer, or make it accessible on a network server. To minimize the size of the distributed files, you may want to remove unnecessary conditional text and conditional text tags, but keep the original conditional document on file and use it to update the different versions as necessary.

In this exercise, you'll save a copy of the sample file that displays only the Pickup Truck information and then remove the unnecessary conditional text and condition tags from the document.

1. Use the Save As dialog box to save the `allcars` document as `truck`.

2. Turn on Text Symbols.

    Conditional text markers (**T** symbols) indicate where hidden conditional text is present in the document.

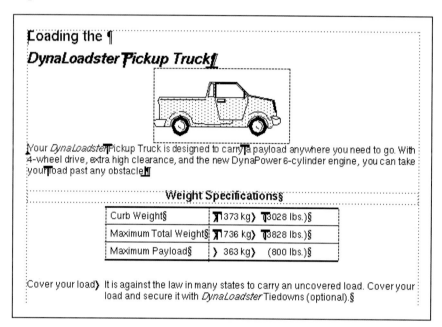

3. Put the insertion point at the beginning of the document, and in the Conditional Text window, select **Sedan**.

4. Click **Edit Condition Tag**.

5. In the Edit Condition Tag dialog box, click **Delete**.

The Delete Condition Tag dialog box appears.

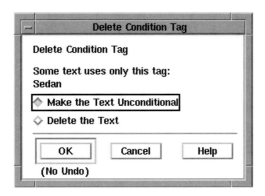

6. Turn on **Delete the Text**.

7. Click **OK**.

The Sedan text is deleted. As a result, the conditional text symbols disappear.

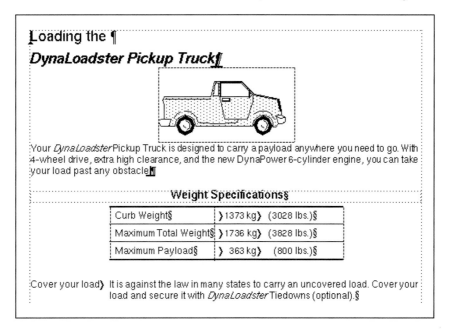

8. Look at the Conditional Text window, and notice that the Sedan condition tag is no longer displayed.

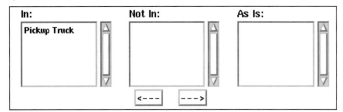

9. In the Conditional Text window, select **Pickup Truck**.

10. Click **Edit Condition Tag**.

11. In the Edit Condition Tag dialog box, click **Delete**.

12. In the alert box, turn on **Make the Text Unconditional**.

13. Click **OK**.

Notice that although the document appears unchanged, the Pickup Truck tag is no longer displayed in the Conditional Text window.

14. Save the file, and close the document.

Modifying a Conditional Document

When you create condition tags, you should create a tag for each version you intend to print, using condition indicators so you can distinguish text in one version from another. If available, use color indicators and a color monitor. Try to use meaningful names, beginning with a unique first letter for quick tagging from the keyboard.

Exercise 6 Creating a new condition tag

Project

In this exercise, you'll create a condition tag and condition indicator for a new product in the DynaLoadster line—a van.

1. Open the document named `allcars`, which you saved earlier.

2. In the Conditional Text window, click **Edit Condition Tag**.

The Edit Condition Tag dialog box appears.

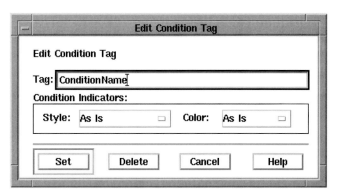

3. Delete the contents of the Tag text box, and type: Van

4. In the Condition Indicators area, from the Style pop-up menu, choose **Double Underline**.

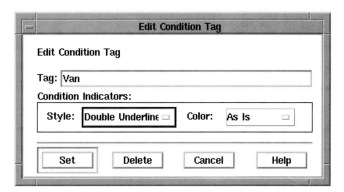

5. From the Color pop-up menu, choose **Blue**.

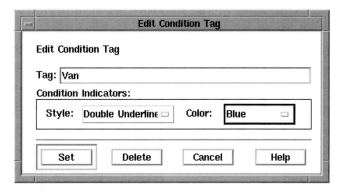

6. Click **Set**.

The new condition tag, Van, appears in the Not In scroll list in the Conditional Text window.

Exercise 7 **Applying a condition tag**

It's best to edit a conditional document with all condition tags visible so you can easily distinguish between the document's versions. Work with conditional text hidden only if you don't want global changes, such as spell checking, to affect text.

In this exercise, you'll add text and a graphic to the document, and you'll apply the Van condition tag you created in the previous exercise to the additional items.

1. In the second line at the top of the page, put the insertion point just after the word "DynaLoadster."

> *DynaLoadster⎸Sedan*

2. Press **Return**.

3. Put the insertion point after the word "DynaLoadster" again.

> *DynaLoadster⎸*
> *Sedan*

4. Add a space.

5. Type: VanMaster

> *DynaLoadster VanMaster⎸*
> *Sedan*

6. Copy and paste a graphic of the vehicle from the list of FrameMaker clip art:

   a. Display the FrameMaker list of sample documents.

Macintosh	From the [?] menu, choose **Samples & Clip Art**.
Windows	From the Help menu, choose **Samples & Clip Art**.
UNIX	From a document Help menu, choose **Samples & Clip Art**.

   The list of FrameMaker samples appears.

   b. Click **Clip art**.

   c. In the list of clip art, double-click **Transport**.

   The Transport clip art document appears.

7. Select the van.

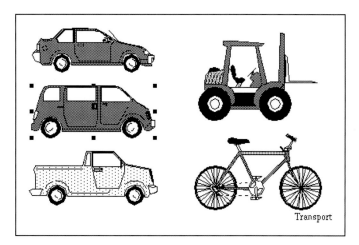

8. From the Edit menu, choose **Copy**.

9. In the document window, put the insertion point after the word "VanMaster," and from the Edit menu, choose **Paste**.

The graphic appears in an anchored frame.

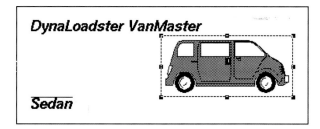

10. Select the word "VanMaster" and the anchored frame that follows it.

11. In the Conditional Text window, select the **Van** condition tag, and click the left arrow to move it into the In scroll list.

   Note: You can also double-click a tag in the Not In or As Is scroll list to move it to the In scroll list.

12. Click **Apply**.

   The Van condition tag is applied to the selected text and to the anchored frame. The double underlining and blue color appear as a result of the condition indicator you chose when you created the tag.

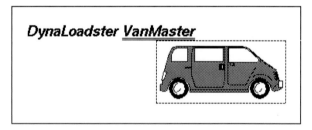

13. Select the first three words in the document.

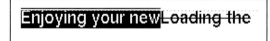

   Notice that the Sedan condition tag appears in the status bar.

14. In the Conditional Text window, move the **Van** condition tag into the In scroll list.

15. Click **Apply.**

Both overline and double-underline condition indicators now appear (and on color monitors, the text color is now magenta) to indicate that the selected text is assigned both the Sedan and Van condition tags.

> Enjoying your new~~Loading the~~

> **Note:** You may need to turn off **Borders** to see the overline indicator clearly.

The status bar also indicates that both the Sedan and Van tags have been applied.

> (Sedan+Van) Flow: A ¶: Head1

Exercise 8

Project

Applying a condition tag as you type

In this exercise, you'll use keyboard shortcuts to apply a condition tag as you type text in the document.

1. In the paragraph beneath the picture of the pickup truck, put the insertion point in front of the word "Sedan."

> Your *DynaLoadster*|Sedan Pie
> you need to go. With 4-wheel

> **Note:** It is suggested that you enter conditional text for different versions in the same order. In this document, the order is Van, Sedan, and Pickup Truck.

2. Type: VanMaster

> Your *DynaLoadster* VanMaster Sedan
> anywhere you need to go. With 4-wh

3. Add a space after the word "VanMaster."

4. Select the text you just typed, including the space.

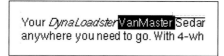

5. If the words are italicized, apply the **Default Font** character format.

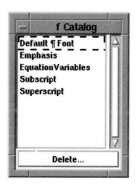

6. Press **Control-4**.

   In the status bar, a question mark followed by a colon appears. (In UNIX, the name of the first condition indicator appears to the right of the question mark.)

7. Type: V

   The word "Van" appears in the status bar.

8. Press **Return**.

   The text is now assigned the Van condition tag.

   Your *DynaLoadster* VanMaster Sedar
   anywhere you need to go. With 4-wh

   Elaboration: You need to type only enough letters to identify the tag. As with paragraph and character formats, you can also use the up arrow and down arrow keys to scroll through the condition tags.

9. In the Weight Specifications table, use the keyboard shortcut to apply the **Van** condition tag to all the text currently using the Pickup Truck condition tag (the strikethrough text).

Weight Specifications	
Curb Weight	1316 ~~1373~~ kg (2902 ~~3028~~ lbs.)
Maximum Total Weight	1679 ~~1736~~ kg (3702 ~~3828~~ lbs.)

Notice that both condition tags appear in the Status area.

(Pickup Truck+Van) Flow: A ¶: Ce

10. At the end of the document, add a short paragraph about the fall preview for DynaLoadster vehicles, as follows:

Additional paragraph

~~Cover your load~~   ~~It is against the law in many states to carry an uncovered load. Cover your load and secure it with *DynaLoadster* Tiedowns (optional).~~
To receive your invitation to the fall preview, call (408) 333-1212.5656.8484.

a. Type the following unconditional text in the document:

```
To receive your invitation to the fall preview,
call (408)333-1212.5656.8484.
```

b. Apply the appropriate condition tag settings from the keyboard.

Exercise 9

Project

Assigning a condition tag before typing

In this exercise, you'll assign a condition tag before you begin typing.

1. In the first line of the paragraph below the pickup truck graphic, put the insertion point before the word "passengers."

carry passengers ~~a payload~~
ce, and the new DynaPower

2. Press **Control-4**.

3. Type V, and press **Return**.

4. Type: family, friends, and cargo

5. Add a space after the word "cargo."

The text you type is assigned the Van condition tag.

Your *DynaLoadster* VanMaster Sedan ~~Pickup Truck~~ is designed to carry family, friends, and cargo ~~passengers a payload~~ anywhere you need to go. With 4-wheel drive, extra high clearance, and the new DynaPower 6-cylinder engine, you can take your passengers ~~load~~ past any obstacle.

Exercise 10 Making text unconditional

In this exercise, you'll revise the document to show just one phone number for all three DynaLoadster vehicle models. You'll delete two of the conditional phone numbers you added in a previous exercise, and you'll remove a condition tag from the remaining number.

1. Select the last two phone numbers in the last paragraph.

   > To receive your invitation to the fall preview, call (408)333- 1212. 5656.8484.

2. Press **Delete**.

3. Select the remaining phone number and the period that follows it.

   > To receive your invitation to the fall preview, call (408)333-1212.

4. In the Conditional Text window, in the Current Selection Is area, turn on **Unconditional**.

5. Click **Apply**.

   The text is now unconditional and therefore displays no condition indicator, and no condition tag appears in the status bar.

6. Save the file, and keep the document open if you intend to complete the optional exercises. Otherwise, close the document and any other open windows.

Optional Exercises

The following exercises enable you to enhance your FrameMaker skills and to explore additional FrameMaker features. Some steps are intentionally brief so that they require more independent thought on your part.

Exercise 11

Optional

Using additional keyboard shortcuts

Several additional keyboard shortcuts are available to help you work with conditional text. In this optional exercise, you'll see how to use some of those keyboard shortcuts.

1. Open the `allcars` document.

2. Use a keyboard shortcut to select conditional text that is contiguous with, and has the same condition tag as, the text at the insertion point:

   a. Put the insertion point in any word in the phrase, "family, friends, and cargo."

   > Your *DynaLoadster* VanMaster Sedan Pickup Truck is designed to carry family, friends, and cargo passengers a payload anywhere you need to go. With 4-wheel drive, extra high clear-

   b. Press **Esc h C**.

   > **Note:** Be sure to type a *lowercase* h and an *uppercase* C.

   The words "family, friends, and cargo" are now highlighted.

   > Your *DynaLoadster* VanMaster Sedan Pickup Truck is designed to carry family, friends, and cargo passengers a payload anywhere you need to go. With 4-wheel drive, extra high clear-

   Next, you'll use a keyboard shortcut to remove all condition indicators from selected text.

3. With "family, friends, and cargo" still highlighted, press **Control-6**.

   The Van condition indicator no longer appears, and the Van tag is no longer displayed in the status bar.

4. Remove a single condition tag from text that is assigned multiple condition tags:

a. In the first row of the Weight Specifications table, select the number **1373**.

Notice that the text displays both the Pickup Truck condition indicator (strikethrough text) and the Van condition indicator, and that the status bar indicates that this text is assigned both the Pickup Truck and Van condition tags.

Weight Specifications	
Curb Weight	1316 ~~1373~~ kg (2902 ~~3028~~ lbs.)

b. Press **Control-5**, type **P**, and press **Return**.

The text no longer displays the Pickup Truck condition indicator, and the Pickup Truck tag no longer appears in the status bar.

Exercise 12   **Finding conditional text**

Optional

You can use the Find/Change dialog box to search for text belonging to any visible condition tag. Although in this one-page example, it is easy to find conditional text by simply scanning the page, when conditional text is distributed throughout a long document, the Find command is much quicker than a visual search.

FrameMaker will find conditional text in text frames, graphic frames, and table cells, but it will not find conditional table rows. FrameMaker doesn't search through hidden conditional text.

In this optional exercise, you'll see how to use the Find/Change dialog box to find conditional text.

1. In the Find/Change dialog box, choose **Conditional Text** from the Find pop-up menu.

2. In the Find Conditional Text dialog box, select the conditions you want to find, and click **Set**.

3. In the Find/Change window, click **Find**.

Review   Test your understanding of the concepts and procedures covered in this module by answering the following review questions. You can check your answers with those listed after the questions.

Question 1: What is a conditional document? What do you call the text that appears in all versions?

Question 2: What is a quick way of determining what condition tag has been applied to text?

Question 3: Why are condition indicators used, and where do you turn them on or off?

Question 4: How do you make text in a document appear in multiple versions of a document, but not in all versions?

Question 5: How do you view a single version of a conditional document that is suitable for printing?

Answer 1: A conditional document contains text for multiple versions of a document. Unconditional text appears in all versions of a conditional document.

Answer 2: Put the insertion point in the text, and look at the status bar. It displays the condition tag or tags of text at the insertion point.

Answer 3: Condition indicators are used to change the appearance of conditional text to make it easier to locate. To turn condition indicators on or off, in the Conditional Text window, click Show/Hide, and then turn Show Conditional Indicators on or off in the Show/Hide dialog box.

Answer 4: Apply multiple condition tags to the text.

Answer 5: Make sure that only the condition tag of the version you want to print is showing, and turn off condition indicators.

For more information

For more information about conditional documents and conditional text, see:

Chapter 26 of *Using FrameMaker*

Creating a Directory

Introduction

In this appendix, you'll create a directory (called a *folder* on the Macintosh) for storing all files created in this course. Follow only the instructions that are appropriate for your computer:

Macintosh	Exercise 1
Windows 3.1	Exercise 2
Windows 95	Exercise 3
UNIX	Exercise 4

Be sure to remember the location within your file system where you create the directory so that you can come back to it in later exercises.

Exercise 1

Guided Tour

Creating a folder on the Macintosh

In this exercise, you'll create a folder named `Class`, in which all files created in this course will be saved.

1. In the Finder, from the File menu, choose **New Folder**.

2. Press **Delete** to delete the default name of Untitled, and then type `Class` as the new name for the folder.

3. Place the folder in the location where you would like to store your course files.

4. Return to "Before You Begin" on page xiv of "Getting Started."

Exercise 2

Guided Tour

Creating a directory in Windows 3.1

In this exercise, you'll create a directory named Class, in which all files created in this course will be saved.

1. In the Program Manager, double-click the **File Manager** icon.

   The File Manager window appears.

2. Click the icon on the drive bar where you would like to create your directory.

   Typically, this would be on your hard disk, drive C.

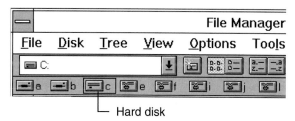

Hard disk

3. Click the **Directory Folder** under which you would like to make the Class directory. (The root directory folder is shown selected below.)

Root directory ⎯⎯

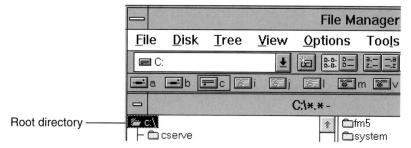

4. From the File menu, choose **Create Directory**.

   The Create Directory dialog box appears.

   Notice that it confirms the path you have chosen.

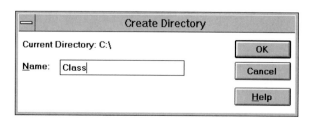

5. In the text box, type: Class

6. Click **OK**.

7. Return to "Before You Begin" on page xiv of "Getting Started."

Exercise 3

Guided Tour

Creating a directory in Windows 95

In this exercise, you'll create a directory named `Class`, in which all files created in this course will be saved.

1. On the Windows desktop, double-click the **My Computer** icon.

My Computer

The My Computer window appears.

> **Note:** The appearance of your window depends on what peripheral devices are attached to your computer, so it will probably differ from the picture above.

2. Double-click the icon of the drive where you would like to create your directory. Typically, this would be on your hard disk, drive C.

Your hard disk window appears.

3. In your hard disk window, from the File menu, choose **New>Folder**.

A folder named "New Folder" appears in your hard disk window.

4. Press **Delete** to delete the default name of New Folder, and then type Class as the new name for the folder.

5. Close your hard disk window and the My Computer window.

6. Return to "Before You Begin" on page xiv of "Getting Started."

Exercise 4

Guided Tour

Creating a directory in UNIX

In this exercise, you'll create a directory named `Class`, in which all files created in this course will be saved.

1. Open a shell window:

   a. Press the left mouse button anywhere on the desktop to display the pop-up menu.

   b. Choose **Shell Tool** (or Command Tool, or Xterm).

   A shell window appears.

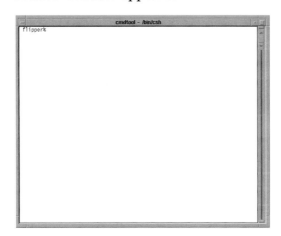

2. Create a directory named `Class`.

   a. Put the insertion point in the shell window.

   b. Type: `cd`

   c. Press **Return**.

   d. Type the "make directory" command, a space, and the name of the directory as follows: `mkdir Class`

   e. Press **Return**.

3. To confirm that the directory was created, type `ls` and press **Return**.

   A list of the files and directories in your Home directory appears. The Class directory should appear in the list.

4. Return to "Before You Begin" on page xiv of "Getting Started."

Starting FrameMaker

Introduction

In this appendix, you'll start the FrameMaker application. Choose Exercise 1, 2, 3, or 4, depending on the computer you are using.

Macintosh	Exercise 1 below
Windows 3.1	Exercise 2 on page B-1
Windows 95	Exercise 3 on page B-2
UNIX	Exercise 4 on page B-3

Exercise 1

Guided Tour

Getting started on the Macintosh

In this exercise, you'll start the FrameMaker application.

1. Double-click the FrameMaker icon located in the folder where FrameMaker was installed.

FrameMaker is now active.

The FrameMaker application appears and replaces the Finder menu choices at the top of the screen.

2. Return to "Before You Begin" on page xiv of "Getting Started."

Exercise 2

Getting started in Windows 3.1

In this exercise, you'll start the FrameMaker application.

1. In the Program Manager, double-click the FrameMaker icon.

The FrameMaker document window appears.

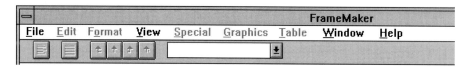

2. Return to "Before You Begin" on page xiv of "Getting Started."

Exercise 3

Getting started in Windows 95

In this exercise, you'll start FrameMaker.

1. From the Start Button menu, choose **Programs>Frame Products>FrameMaker 5**.

The FrameMaker document window appears.

2. Return to "Before You Begin" on page xiv of "Getting Started."

Exercise 4   **Getting started in UNIX**

Guided Tour

In this exercise, you'll start the FrameMaker application.

1. If it is not already open, open a shell window (a window for typing UNIX commands).

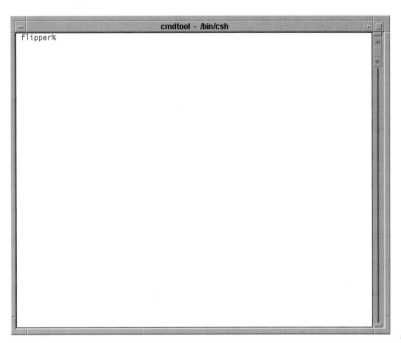

> **Note:** Since the procedure for opening a shell window varies from one UNIX windowing system to another, your system administrator should supply the steps for opening a shell window on your computer.

2. Change to your home directory:

    a. Put the insertion point into the shell window.

    b. Type: `cd`

    c. Press **Return**.

3. In the shell window, type the command to start FrameMaker: `maker`

4. Press **Return**.

    After a few moments, the main FrameMaker window appears.

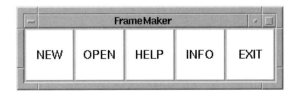

5. Move the main FrameMaker window to the upper-right corner of the screen:

a. Move the mouse to place the pointer on the title bar, at the top of the main FrameMaker window.

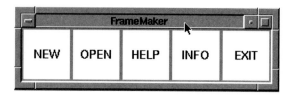

An outline of the FrameMaker window appears as you move the window.

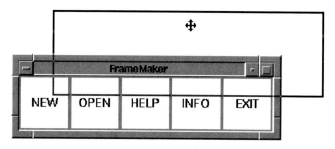

b. Release the mouse button.

Note: All FrameMaker windows and dialog boxes can be moved anywhere on your screen.

6. Return to "Before You Begin" on page xiv of "Getting Started."

Index

Colophon

Writing: Peter Olguin, Carol Scharlau, John Lewis, Andrea Dodd, Nancy Schroer, Christine Franco

Project Manager: Peter Olguin

Editing: Mary Lou Carlson, Jack Farrell, Adrienne Juliano, John Taylor

Instructional Design: Peter Olguin, Carol Scharlau, John Lewis

Learning Resources Manager: Kisa Harris

Cover Design: Sharon Anderson

Book Production: Lauren Buchholz, Dayna Musto

Adobe Press: Patrick Ames

Technical Advisor: Carol Scharlau

Pilot Test Participants: John Beckwith, Patricia Bozzoli, Gigi Bugarin, David Butler, Louise Cate, Jo Davies, Jeff Doust, Victoria Gilbert, Tim Girard, Carlos Hueso, Paul Maccan, Dan Monda, Noelle McReynolds, Michell Qi, Lisa Schneider, John Tafe, Jim Thompson, Karen Winguth, Warren You

Special Thanks to: Jeff Vasek, Barrie Barrett

Production Notes

This book was created electronically using Adobe FrameMaker on a Power Macintosh and a Sun SPARCstation. Art was produced using FrameMaker, Adobe Photoshop, FlashIt, and XV. Working film was produced with the PostScript language on an Agfa 5000 Imagesetter. The Avant Garde and New Century Schoolbook typefaces are used throughout this book.